The International Behavioural and Social Sciences Library

PRODUCTIVITY AND SOCIAL ORGANIZATION

TAVISTOCK

The International Behavioural and Social Sciences Library

ORGANIZATIONAL BEHAVIOUR
In 10 Volumes

I	The Ideology of Work *P D Anthony*
II	Communication or Conflict *Edited by Mary Capes*
III	Creativity and Performance in Industrial Organization *Andrew Crosby*
IV	Organizational Paradoxes *Manfred F R Kets de Vries*
V	Systems of Organization *E J Miller and A K Rice*
VI	The Politics of Organizational Decision-Making *Andrew M Pettigrew*
VII	Productivity and Social Organization *A K Rice*
VIII	Learning for Leadership *A K Rice*
IX	The Organization from Within *Cyril Sofer*
X	Critical Path Analysis in Practice *Edited by Gail Thornley*

PRODUCTIVITY AND SOCIAL ORGANIZATION

The Ahmedabad Experiment: Technical Innovation, Work Organization and Management

A K RICE

Routledge
Taylor & Francis Group
LONDON AND NEW YORK

First published in 1958 by
Tavistock Publications Limited

Published in 2001 by
Routledge
2 Park Square, Milton Park, Abingdon, Oxfordshire OX14 4RN
711 Third Avenue, New York, NY 10017

First issued in paperback 2014

Routledge is an imprint of the Taylor and Francis Group, an informa business

British Library Cataloguing in Publication Data
A CIP catalogue record for this book
is available from the British Library

Productivity and Social Organization
ISBN 0-415-26469-3
Organizational Behaviour: 10 Volumes
ISBN 0-415-26513-4
The International Behavioural and Social Sciences Library
112 Volumes
ISBN 0-415-25670-4

ISBN 13: 978-1-138-87930-0 (pbk)
ISBN 13: 978-0-415-26469-3 (hbk)

A. K. RICE

Productivity and Social Organization The Ahmedabad Experiment

TECHNICAL INNOVATION, WORK ORGANIZATION AND MANAGEMENT

TAVISTOCK PUBLICATIONS LTD

First published in 1958
by Tavistock Publications Limited
2 Park Square, Milton Park,
Abingdon, Oxon, OX14 4RN

in 12 pt. Bembo by
Simson Shand Ltd
London, Hertford and Harlow

CONTENTS

FIGURES

ACKNOWLEDGMENTS

My very grateful thanks are due to the members of the Ahmedabad Manufacturing and Calico Printing Company Ltd., in whose Mills the work described in this book was carried out, and to my colleagues, both past and present, on the staff of the Tavistock Institute of Human Relations.

The thanks of a consultant to his client for the opportunity to practise his profession must always be implied in any consultant-client relationship. My thanks are due for far more: for the opportunity to carry out experiments in new fields of work; for the deep interest shown by those with whom I have worked and with whom I have waited, often anxiously, for the results of experiments, and for permission to publish the results of our collaborative efforts. So many managers and workers have been involved, either directly or indirectly, in the project that it is not possible to thank them all by name, and I hope that they will accept this acknowledgment of my debt to them.

I must make more personal acknowledgment to some who have been very directly concerned. First and foremost I must acknowledge a deep debt of gratitude to Gautam Sarabhai, the Chairman of the Company, who has gone so much further than a client in his interest in our joint work. I only hope that he has found our many discussions as fruitful and constructive as I have. I am also deeply grateful to his sister, Gira Sarabhai, for her help and encouragement, and I hope that she will be able to forgive me my share in turning her from a sister into an executive subordinate. Ambalal Sarabhai, the former Chairman of the Company and father of the present Chairman, told me many stories of the early days of the Company and of the textile industry in Ahmedabad, stories which I feel deserve a volume to themselves. I am grateful for his interest and help, and for that of his sister, Anasuyaben Sarabhai, the President of the Textile Labour Association, and of her colleague Shankarlal Banker. All of them were very kind and considerate to a stranger to India and to Indian industry.

J. A. Gandhi, former Manager and present General Manager, and Jethalal Thaker, former Works Manager and now Divisional Manager (Manufacturing), carried the main burden of all the early changes; their ordinary work has been interrupted so much that they have frequently had to put in extremely long hours and to postpone or cancel holidays. They have borne it all with remarkable patience and, even though we have frequently disagreed at the beginning of some new venture, we have always found it possible to work together and to allow our disagreements to make a constructive contribution to the outcome of the experiments. W. F. Titchener, the Financial Controller, and B. V. Bhatt, the Acting Purchasing Manager and now Sales Manager, were appointed later, but apart from the reorganizations they have themselves been involved in, they have also been affected by the reorganizations in other parts of the mill and in particular in the management reorganizations. Their help and especially their friendly and effective collaboration and their willingness to consider ideas, however strange, are gratefully acknowledged.

The Mill Managers, W. H. Date, C. J. Patel, and B. Mitra; the members of the newly-created Development and Research Division, S. K. Dutta, H. V. Bhavnani, B. Sarkar, and members of their staffs; the heads of departments, L. C. Patel, P. S. Trivedi, Spinning and Weaving Masters of the Calico Mills; V. C. Joshi, D. Bhattacharyya, P. M. Desai, and C. P. Caprihan, Spinning Master, Preparation Master-elect, Weaving Master, and Weaving Master-elect of the Jubilee Mills; A. M. Mehta of the Processing Mill; Ramanlal Shah, Company Secretary; S. A. Kher, former Manager, now General Manager, Chemical Operations; and K. S. Dave, Labour Officer, now Joint Company Secretary: all have been involved in varying degrees in the discussions that have taken place and have experienced changes as a result of the work that has been done.

My especial thanks are due to those who took part in the experimental reorganizations of automatic and non-automatic weaving, in particular to C. P. Caprihan who took charge of both sheds during the experimental periods. His technical help, and above all his willingness to try new kinds of organization, were especially valuable. Under the direction of Jethalal Thaker, he was responsible for the erection of the looms, for the selection of supervisors and workers, and not only carried the major technological burdens throughout the experimental periods, but was responsible for the implementation of decisions about social reorganization. The shift supervisors of the automatic loom shed during the period were B. B. Dave, who became Top Supervisor when C. P. Caprihan went to non-automatic weaving, M. M. Bhatt who is now in charge of one of the non-automatic loom sheds, and S. R. Rajguru. The supervisors of the experimental non-automatic shed were V. D. Chiplunkar, who is now in charge of the shed since C. P. Caprihan has been appointed Weaving Master of the Jubilee Mills, G. B. Vyas, and J. P. Patel. I acknowledge their help with gratitude and that of all the group leaders and workers of both sheds who in spite of their frequent misgivings were always willing to state their views and to try new kinds of organization.

My debt to my colleagues is of a different kind. When one works as a member of a group for a long time it is difficult to know where ideas, concepts, or methods of tackling various problems first originate. Ideas that I have now adopted as my own originated in conversations and discussions with my colleagues about my own work and about theirs. I was a member of the team that took part in the Glacier project, and although I have, at various places throughout this book, made reference to Elliott Jaques's account of that project[1] its general influence on the present work will be plain to all who have read it. The particular concepts and assumptions upon which the work described in this book is based have frequently been discussed in the Institute, not necessarily in relation to the work in India, but in relation to other Institute projects as well. I am grateful to my colleagues for the help they have given me in recent years. To Eric Trist in particular, however, I would like to pay a more personal tribute. The original concept of socio-technical systems was his, and it is to him that I have turned very frequently for help and assistance not only with the work, but in the preparation of the papers which preceded the book and in the writing of the book itself. He always gives unstintingly of his ideas, his time, his knowledge, and his experience.

Leon Festinger of the University of Stanford, and W. R. Hawthorne of Cambridge University, read previous drafts; their highly constructive criticisms were most helpful in its redrafting.

The writing of the book was made possible by a grant to the Tavistock Institute from the Old Dominion Trust of America.

I would like to thank Shirin Vakil for her help as interpreter in discussions with workers, and I am especially grateful to K. P. V. Malai of the Calico Mills, for his recording of so much of the data, and to him and to members of the Institute staff for their secretarial assistance. I also wish to thank David Owen for his work on the diagrams.

A. K. R.

2 Beaumont Street
London, W.1

October 1956

[1] Jaques, Elliott, *The Changing Culture of a Factory*. London, Tavistock Publications, 1951.

PART I

The Project and its Background

CHAPTER 1

Introduction

PRODUCTIVITY AND SOCIAL ORGANIZATION

This book is an account of the work undertaken by the Tavistock Institute of Human Relations in collaboration with the Ahmedabad Manufacturing and Calico Printing Company Ltd. in India. The work, which falls within the field of 'operational' or 'action' research, has been concerned with the interaction of social and technological change in a textile mill employing over eight thousand workers. Experiments which achieved both social and technological changes were carried out over a period of some three years. Measurements of their effects on each other and on productivity were made.

In 1951 Trist, in a study he made with Bamforth of the longwall method of coal-getting in Great Britain, introduced the concept of a production system as a *socio-technical system*. This concept was later extended to designate a general field of study concerned with the interrelations of the technical and socio-psychological organizations of industrial production systems.[1] Trist and Bamforth showed that the introduction of the three-shift longwall cycle into British coal-mining resulted in the breakdown of an established social system at the coal face.

A new social system came into being, characterized by maladaptive mechanisms, as a defence against the social and psychological consequences of the new technology. The close tie between technological process and sociological and psychological phenomena has also been demonstrated by other workers in both Europe and America. Wilson, speaking at the International Congress of Psychology in Montreal in 1954, said: 'Perhaps the most striking fact about recent work is its independent appearance in

[1] Trist, E. L., and Bamforth, K. W., 'Some Social and Psychological Consequences of the Longwall Method of Coal-Getting', *Human Relations*, 1951, Vol. IV, No. 1.

various countries and centres, and the emergence of similar findings in such studies as are comparable.'[1]

The concept of a socio-technical system arose from the consideration that any production system requires both a technological organization—equipment and process layout—and a work organization relating to each other those who carry out the necessary tasks. The technological demands place limits upon the type of work organization possible, but a work organization has social and psychological properties of its own that are independent of technology. While industrial production systems are, of necessity, designed in accordance with technological demand, there has been a tendency to project the technological into the associated work organization. The assumption is then made that there is only one work organization that will satisfy the conditions of task performance. This has meant treating groups and individuals as though they were machines and has led to what has aptly been called the 'machine theory of organization'.[2] Where, as has frequently happened, the resulting work organization has failed to satisfy the social and psychological needs of its members, their attitudes to task performance have inhibited the full realization of technological potential and lowered productivity.

A socio-technical system must also satisfy the financial conditions of the industry of which it is a part. It must have economic validity. It has, in fact, social, technological and economic dimensions, all of which are interdependent, but all of which have independent values of their own. These need to be taken into account in any reorganization due to change in any one dimension.

In the experiments described in this book attempts were made to take into account both the independent and interdependent properties of the social, technological, and economic dimensions of existing socio-technical systems, and to establish new systems in which all dimensions were more adequately interrelated than they had previously been.

The work with the Ahmedabad Manufacturing and Calico Printing Company Ltd. was carried out in the cultural setting of an old and eastern civilization into which western technology has been introduced only re-

[1] Wilson, A. T. M., 'Some Contrasting Socio-Technical Production Systems in Industry'. A paper given in a symposium on 'The Interaction of Technological and Social Factors in Industrial Production Systems' at the 14th International Congress of Psychology, Montreal, June 1954. The other contributors were John Hemphill, Rensis Likert, and Gunnar Westerlund.

[2] Katz, Daniel, and Kahn, Robert L., 'Human Organization and Worker Motivation', *Industrial Productivity*, L. R. Tripp (Ed.), 1951, Industrial Relations Research Association.

cently, and with only limited impact. Ruth Benedict has said that 'every culture, every era, exploits a few out of a great number of possibilities'.[1] The generality of the findings of the work described in this book is based upon the belief that, in our era, the majority of cultures are endeavouring to exploit the same possibility—the increased productivity arising from the application of technological advance to human effort. While it would be an over-simplification to suggest that the findings of experiments in the interaction of social, technological, and economic change in an Indian textile mill could have unqualified application elsewhere, nevertheless, the limits imposed on productive organization by technological demand and the universal endeavour to exploit the same kind of technology do suggest that the findings may have more than local significance.

THE PROJECT

The Ahmedabad Manufacturing and Calico Printing Company Ltd., more familiarly known as the 'Calico Mills', manufactures finished cloth from raw cotton in two mills, the Calico Mills and the Jubilee Mills, both situated in Ahmedabad. There is also a chemical division manufacturing bulk chemicals such as caustic soda, chlorine, and chlorine products. One chemical plant is in Ahmedabad on the same site as the Calico Mills. Another, now in the course of erection, is in Bombay, some three hundred miles south of Ahmedabad. Throughout the book the Calico and Jubilee Mills will usually be referred to by their more familiar collective title of the 'Calico Mills'. Where reference is made to the Calico Mills, as distinct from the Jubilee Mills, the context will, I hope, make the distinction clear.

Towards the end of 1952, the Chairman of the Company visited the Tavistock Institute in London. He described the immediate problem facing his Company as one in which the introduction of modern machinery and modern working methods was creating social and psychological problems for management and workers, both in their relations with each other and with the trade unions.

His problem was a part of a more general problem arising from the rapid industrial development in India since independence. In Britain, the first country to develop industrially, over ninety per cent of the working population is engaged in industry and commerce and lives in cities and towns. In America the rural population has decreased from fifty to twenty

[1] Benedict, R., *Patterns of Culture*. London, Routledge and Kegan Paul, 1949.

per cent in the past few decades. The industrialization of India is relatively recent. Even today, probably only about one per cent of the population is engaged in modern mechanized industry. Though in such centres as Bombay, Ahmedabad, and Kanpur a textile industry has been established for nearly a hundred years, attitudes towards mechanization and modernization are still affected by the more conservative majority engaged in agriculture and village crafts. The tropical climate, physical conditions, and standards of nutrition all contribute to a belief, widely held in India, that whatever mechanization or modernization of working methods may be introduced, norms of output will always remain lower than in the more highly industrialized countries situated in more temperate climates. While wages are still far below those in Europe and America they have increased considerably since independence. As elsewhere in the world there is strong and continuous pressure from industrial workers for improved standards of living. There has not, however, been any corresponding increase in productivity.

The Chairman of the Calico Mills recognized that changes in working methods and in attitudes towards mechanization would be unlikely to be successful without corresponding changes in the methods and organization of management, and that a study of management structure and behaviour would be a necessary corollary to any study of the workers and work organization. As a result of discussions with the Chairman of the Company I went to India early in 1953 for a short visit to explore the possibility of establishing a collaborative relationship between the Company and the Institute and to allow the members of the Company and myself to have some experience of working together. So far I have visited the mills four times for periods varying between three and nine months. On one visit I was accompanied by a second staff member for six months. Terms of reference have been very broad—to collaborate with management and workers in attempts to solve the social and psychological problems which faced them through changes in methods of work or of management. In practice, this has meant discussion of whatever problem has been urgently confronting the Chairman, other members of management or the workers, and working with them in trying to find some kind of solution. Starting points have been technological, economic, social or psychological—the terms of reference have set no limit either for the Company or for myself.

During the first visit my terms of reference were discussed with the

Chairman and then with other senior managers. It was agreed that I should be responsible directly and only to the Chairman and that, except in any selection procedures in which I might be involved, I would not report on individuals working in the Company. It was also agreed that any managers or workers within the Company could, if they wished, discuss with me, as individuals or as groups, their work, their roles, and their relationships, and that such discussions would be private; that is, nothing would be reported except with their permission. A meeting was held of all ranks of management of the Calico Mills at which the kind of work projected, the methods, and the terms of reference were explained and discussed. The President and leading members of the Textile Labour Association (the recognized trade union) and some technical members of the Ahmedabad Textile Industry Research Association also attended the meeting.

The account to be presented in this book is an interim report of work not completed, and still continuing. Because of the technological, social, and economic changes that will continue to take place in India, as elsewhere, changes will continue in the Calico Mills. In this sense the work will never be completed, and no final report will be possible.

The project was carried out within a consultant-client relationship, in which my primary professional responsibility was to give such assistance as I could to the solution of problems causing concern to the client. For this reason almost the only quantitative data available are the data of normal industrial practice and the qualitative data are such records of events as I was able to make either directly or through the collaboration of members of the Company. Although the work was directed towards specific problems, and specific steps were taken to deal with them, at no time could any of the resultant processes be kept isolated from other contemporary processes. Nor, because of the urgency of the problems, was it ever possible to consider long-term experiments, even had control been theoretically possible. The data available, therefore, are a collection of industrial data and a record of observed events arising from a complex variety of simultaneous processes. The problem has been to relate the changes and the events to each other; the danger that, in the analysis of any one process, the effects of other events and other processes would be ignored.

In subsequent chapters three changes are described, two in different kinds of weaving and one in management. In the first, changes were initiated in the social organization of a production system which had recently undergone violent disturbance by the introduction of a new technology—automatic weaving. The changes introduced into the social organization enabled the production system to settle down by making possible the acceptance of the changes in the technological organization. The changes were implemented as soon as they were suggested. In the second, in weaving with Lancashire looms ('non-automatic' looms in which the traditional method of weaving was practised), technological and social changes were initiated simultaneously and took far longer to be accepted and become effective. In the third, in management, disturbance had already occurred as a result of changes in the social and economic conditions of the society in which the Company existed, and as a result of the changes introduced into the weaving and other production systems. The changes introduced into management took into account the resultant changes in all parts of the Company and provided the opportunity for the whole system to settle down at a more effective level of performance.

ANALYSIS OF THE CHANGES

Changes occasionally occur with dramatic suddenness. More frequently they are slow, difficult to observe and still more difficult to analyse. It is often only possible to observe that change has occurred after it has occurred; then only because some event happens to demonstrate that, at some previous time, a change must have occurred to have made the event possible. In the present account, changes have been divided into phases, the length of each phase being determined by the occurrence of an event which can be related to identifiable change in the process under study. All the known events believed to have had any effect on the process have been recorded. The phases have been related, so far as has been possible, to such quantitative measures as have been available. This has given a 'four-dimensional' record:

- a chronological phase sequence of the process;
- events directly related to it;
- other events less immediately relevant but which can be shown to have had effects;
- the quantitative data available.

Thus, the analysis in Chapter 14 of the results of the experimental reorganization of non-automatic weaving identifies nine phases of length varying from ten to one hundred and four days. Each phase is identified by social or technological changes in the methods of work organization in the first 'dimension'. The second 'dimension' is characterized by events in the experimental shed itself, and the third by events in the mill and in the external environment. These three 'dimensions' are related to each other for each phase, and the quantitative results of efficiency, damage, and cost are then related to the whole.

The same methods of analysis have been used for all three change processes described, but, whereas in the weaving sheds certain quantitative data could be directly related to the changes introduced, in the reorganization of management no such immediately relevant data were available. Some indications of the overall results of the Company are given, and these can, in the sense that management is responsible for overall results, be considered with caution and reservation as related, however indirectly, to the reorganization.

PLAN OF THE BOOK

The book is presented in six parts. The remainder of the first part is concerned with background information about the Company and its setting in Ahmedabad. The second is a brief statement of the concepts and assumptions used in the work of the project. In the third, fourth, and fifth parts, work in three specific areas of company activity is described. Although for the sake of clarity each sub-project is treated as a separate piece of work, all are accounts of parallel activities which overlapped each other not only in time but as regards the people involved in them. I have tried to indicate the interaction between events in the different sub-projects, but, with so much happening at the same time, the events were not always easy to disentangle from each other; unwittingly, some over-simplification may have occurred. In the sixth and final part further consideration is given to the concepts and assumptions used and some general observations are made about the social and psychological demands of machine technology.

CHAPTER 2

Ahmedabad and its Textile Industry

THE CITY

Ahmedabad is situated on the banks of the river Sabarmati, some three hundred miles north of Bombay. It is in the middle of a wide flat plain only a few feet above sea level and is one of the chief cities of the Bombay state. The climate is hot and, except during the monsoon, dry. Day temperatures range between 80 and 118 degrees Fahrenheit and night temperatures between 40 and 85 degrees, depending upon the season of the year. The cool season which starts in November and lasts until February is delightful—warm days and cool nights with little or no rain. After the beginning of February the weather gets slowly hotter and more humid until the monsoon breaks in June or July. During the monsoon, and immediately after, the countryside is a rich and vivid green, but at other times of the year it is brown, dried up, and dusty.

The present city was founded by the Sultan Ahmed Shah in A.D. 1411 on the site of the more ancient city of Ashawal. Legend associates his choice of site with the ferocity of the rabbits infesting the river bank. When they defied his hunting dogs he felt that a place which could breed such rabbits must have virtues which would be useful to his fighting men. Ashawal, earlier known as Karnavati, had been for many years a centre of *Jain* learning and of a flourishing trade in fine, handwoven textiles. Nothing of Ashawal or Karnavati now remains; but the castle, the fortifications, and much of the wall surrounding the city, all built by Sultan Ahmed, still stand—a source both of pride and embarrassment to the present legislators and citizens of Ahmedabad. The wish to preserve the city's monuments is natural and strong but the wall with its twelve narrow fortified gates was never intended for modern traffic. Part of the wall was destroyed by the Maratha invaders in the eighteenth century, some has fallen down, some has been removed to make roads of access to the city less congested, and some is still falling down. A small part is being repaired and preserved, the rest is being gradually removed to provide space for more useful, if less romantic, purposes. There are still many buildings which date from the fifteenth and sixteenth centuries and the streets in the city itself, except those which have been widened in recent years, are still, for the most part, narrow medieval alley-ways—picturesque but inconvenient.

In its medieval heyday Ahmedabad and its suburbs had a prosperous and thriving population of 800,000. By the time the British arrived in 1818, soon after the Maratha invasion, this had shrunk to a poor and luckless 80,000. The suburbs were dilapidated and abandoned while big game infested the country round the city. By 1942 the population had risen to just over half a million. War-time expansion in the textile industry and the establishment of ancillary industries and of some new industries attracted large numbers of new residents. After independence and partition in 1947 the population was further increased by the arrival of some thousands of refugees from nearby Pakistan. By 1950 the population had increased to nearly a million. No building programme could possibly cope with such an increase, nor could the city services expand at a sufficient rate to meet the demands being made upon them. Six years later, in 1956, building is immensely accelerated; drainage systems have been and are being greatly enlarged; electricity, water, and other services energetically intensified. The problems of growth are gradually being brought into manageable proportions. In the city and surrounding suburbs parks are being created, and along all roads where there is any possible space trees are being planted to give shade.

Driving through the city can be both an art and an exasperation. In the congested streets vehicles of all kinds, cars, lorries, and rickshaws, compete with pedestrians, cows, goats, and dogs for the relatively small passage available, while strings of camels, tied nose to tail and ambling along with regal disregard for other travellers, can make chaos of a busy junction. The confusion is not helped by the continuous hooting and bell-ringing practised by the drivers and riders of all wheeled traffic. That the resultant noise has little apparent effect upon the habits of pedestrians, let alone upon those of the animals, does not appear to discourage the drivers who continue to hoot and to ring even when they have a clear road. To the majority of the inhabitants of Ahmedabad, all life is sacred. Animals

—and, among those who are strict in their observances, even insects—are never deliberately killed. It is perhaps this attitude that accounts for the enviably low road accident rate.

An airport is situated about three miles to the north of the city and the route from the airport to the city runs through the 'Camp' and the Shahibag. They are park-like in appearance; houses of varying size stand in their own grounds and are separated by wide open spaces, some of which are used as a golf course. The majority of the members of the diminishing foreign community, who are mainly employed either in the Electricity Company or are agents for foreign firms supplying many of the equipment needs of the textile industry, live in the 'Camp'. The Shahibag is a residential suburb, where a large number of the millowners and more wealthy citizens live. Their estates are surrounded by high walls, over which can be caught glimpses of large houses and luxuriant vegetation at all times of the year.

Even before independence, Ahmedabad was considered one of the cities of India least under European influence, either architecturally or socially. Ahmedabad, even more than other Indian cities, has become still more Indian since the British left. The greater part of the population still lives in the city under crowded conditions. The climate is such that, in the summer, large numbers elect to sleep out in the streets, and the pavements and traffic islands are usually well occupied from about ten o'clock at night onwards. The capacity of men, women, and children to sleep through the night apparently undisturbed by traffic, pedestrians, scavenging dogs, and insects is remarkable. It is very difficult, however, for those who work at night to get much sleep during the daytime. Some who work in the city or in its surrounding mills live in neighbouring villages and walk several miles each day on their way to and from work. They, at least, can escape from the crowded city, but, as elsewhere in the world, many appear to prefer city life and to be deserting the countryside. However, in an inquiry carried out recently,[1] the majority of workers interviewed expressed the hope that one day they could return to their villages. Retirement gratuities, which are being gradually introduced, may make this hope more realizable than in the past, when few industrial workers appeared able to save, or indeed to keep themselves out of debt.

The streets in the city and suburbs are all tarred, but, so far, only a few of the roads leading out into the country can be anything but deeply

[1] Murphy, Gardner, *In the Minds of Men*. New York, Basic Books, 1953.

rutted tracks—chokingly dusty in dry weather, seas of mud in the monsoon. Buses connect the main nearby villages with the city, but the ruts they leave behind make the busier roads virtually impassable to any vehicle which is not high-slung. Roadmaking, like building, drainage, and electricity distribution, is being pressed ahead, but the problem of supply catching up with demand, as elsewhere in India, is immense.

It was just outside Ahmedabad on the banks of the Sabarmati that Mahatma Gandhi set up his first *Ashram*. The Mahatma, or to give him his full name Mohandas Karamchand Gandhi, known with reverence and affection as 'Gandhiji', did much of his early work in India in Ahmedabad. It was from Ahmedabad that he set out on his famous march in 1933. The *Ashram* is now a place of pilgrimage visited by many thousands annually. Also just outside Ahmedabad, in one of the growing suburbs, is the new Gujarat University which, like other educational institutions in Ahmedabad, is having to expand rapidly to deal with the ever increasing number of students who apply for admission. It is as yet too soon after independence for the greatly enlarged building and other programmes to have had more than a limited effect, but tremendous efforts are being made to deal with the social and economic problems of a growing industrial community.

THE TEXTILE INDUSTRY OF AHMEDABAD

The first textile mill in India is reported severally as having been opened in Broach in 1851 and in Bombay in 1854. The first mill in Ahmedabad was opened in 1861. All the machinery and equipment for the first mill had to travel the seventy-five miles from the port of Cambay by bullock-cart, since the railway did not reach Ahmedabad until 1864. Today with its forty-six thousand looms and nearly two million spindles Ahmedabad is, after Bombay, the second largest textile centre of India, having over a fifth of the looms and just under a fifth of the spindles of the country. The hot, dry climate of Ahmedabad and its location in the middle of a wide, dusty plain make it unsuitable for the manufacture of textiles. Furthermore, under British rule, the encouragement given to the Lancashire export trade led to the imposition of restrictions and duties on the new industry, which were not fully lifted until the 1930s. The growth and success of the industry, despite both the physical and the man-made handicaps under which it worked, must be ascribed, in the first place, to the enterprise of the early millowners and to their tenacity in the face of difficulties. During the latter part of the nineteenth and early part of the twentieth centuries a strong middle-class of shareholders, technicians, and managers grew up with the industry—a middle-class which has been a great force in the civil and political life of the city ever since.

The first world war gave a great impetus to the industry. Many of the older established mills were expanded and a large number of new ones built. The great slump, the first signs of which were visible in 1922, became acute in 1925 and 1926. It was not until 1930, when the movement for the boycott of all foreign imports became widespread, that the rescue came. The second world war gave renewed impetus, and mills throughout India did well. The benefits to the industry of the expanded war production were however accompanied by some disadvantages. So great was the demand for cloth that virtually any cloth could command some kind of sale, and, since prices and production were controlled, both management and workers lost some of their interest in quality. The working habits of nearly ninety years were temporarily forgotten. The period of control extended for some years after the war. When it was finally ended many mills which had previously specialized in fine cottons and high qualities had a struggle to reintroduce their former standards.

Since the war there have been recessions and minor booms; some mills have had to close down, some have had to discontinue shifts in some departments; but the industry, as a whole, has prospered. Most mills in Ahmedabad had a bumper year in 1948, a relatively poor year in 1949, and after a good year in 1951 another poor year in 1952. Since then the general trend has been for the price of cloth to come down and the cost of cotton and of salaries and wages to increase. Not all mills have been affected equally by these trends, since the cost of different qualities of cotton and the prices obtainable for different qualities of cloth have not varied in the same way. In Egypt, in 1954, for example, the cotton crops were such that the price of some medium qualities rose steadily until it was higher than that of some fine qualities and, at the beginning of 1956, the gap between the prices of medium and fine qualities and the prices of coarse qualities was far greater than is usual. In the same way, the demand for good-quality cloths made of medium and fine qualities of cotton in 1951 was such that prices obtainable rose steadily only to fall heavily as compared with prices obtainable for cloths made of coarse cotton in 1952. *Table 1* gives the published results of a group of the recognized leading mills of Ahmedabad since independence in 1947. The bumper year of 1948 has been taken as the base year, and cash turnover and gross profit have all been related to the base year at 100.

Table 1. COMPARISON OF CASH TURNOVER AND GROSS PROFIT OF A GROUP OF LEADING MILLS, 1948–1955

Year	*Turnover*	*Gross Profit*
1948	100	100
1949	90	45
1950	96	52
1951	130	81
1952	115	43
1953	116	63
1954	117	62
1955	127	90

During the same period the total expenditure on wages and salaries in the same mills has risen by twenty-three per cent, and the expenditure on raw cotton, which in 1952 rose to a peak of seventy-nine per cent above the expenditure for 1948, has since fallen, due to an increased use of locally grown cotton, to forty-eight per cent above the expenditure in 1948.

The problems of changing the depressed norms of output and rewards in India are complicated by language and caste differences among the working population. Languages are regional and, although Ahmedabad is in the Gujarat, and the common language of all those who work in the industry is Gujarati, it is not uncommon to find three or even four different languages being spoken in the same department of one mill. On one occasion, in a discussion with a group of eight workers, which was being interpreted in three languages, Gujarati, Hindi, and English, it was discovered after half an hour that one worker had not up to that time understood a word that had been said—he came from South India and spoke only Tamil. Caste groups, which are primarily work organizations, run, for the most part, at right angles to language groups, that is, within each language group most castes are represented, and within one caste most languages are spoken. With rare exceptions broad caste divisions have been carried into mill organizations. Spinning departments are usually staffed by members of the Harijan castes, while weaving departments are staffed by members of middle castes and Muslims. Currently, strenuous attempts are being made by government and other agencies to break down caste divisions. Legally there are now no castes in India, but, as often happens, behaviour lags behind legislation.

The textile industry in Ahmedabad was, in the first place, modelled on Lancashire, and everywhere the models were almost exact. Thus, even the buildings are built in the style of Lancashire mills, multi-storeyed and windowed, irrespective of their convenience or suitability for the country or the climate. The first technicians and workers were brought from Lancashire, so that Lancashire methods and Lancashire organizations were copied in Ahmedabad. Even today, experience in Lancashire or qualifications obtained at Manchester University, although being replaced by qualifications from either Indian or American Universities, are highly valued. Qualifications and experience gained abroad generally lead to faster promotion and higher salaries than would otherwise be obtained.

In recent years the Ahmedabad Textile Industry's Research Association, more familiarly known as ATIRA, has been established. It was started by funds provided by the millowners and Government and is now supported by subscriptions from the millowners and grants from Government funds. Dr Vikram Sarabhai, brother of the Chairman of the Calico Mills, was one of its main architects and was its honorary director until 1956. Sections have been set up for research in physics, chemistry, economics, psychology, and for all aspects of textile production. In 1954, the Prime Minister, Pandit Nehru, officially opened the new building of the Association near the Gujarat University campus. All the mills in Ahmedabad and some from other textile centres as well as organizations from other industries in Ahmedabad are members or associates of the Association and receive service from it. It publishes regular reports on its work for circulation to its members and holds conferences and training courses for technicians and managers.

Wages in the textile industry are paid either on a straight piecework basis, or time rates, plus a cost of living allowance known as 'Dearness Allowance', or 'D.A.' Usually some spinning and finishing processes are paid at time rates, while other spinning and all weaving are paid on piecework. Between 1953 and 1956 dearness allowance has varied between Rs. 78 and Rs. 54 per month with the general tendency in 1954 and early 1955 to be downwards. In December 1955 and early 1956 the trend has been upwards, and in April 1956 'D.A.' was standing at Rs. 64 per month.

Average earnings of mill workers, excluding dearness allowance, vary between Rs. 28 per month for unskilled workers to Rs. 66 for weavers on two looms, Rs. 100 for those on four looms, and Rs. 139 for 'jobbers' in charge of forty looms.[1]

THE MANAGING AGENCY SYSTEM

The managing agency system was first introduced to India by British traders. It has since been widely used by Indian industrialists for the management of their own concerns. The system is one whereby an individual, a group of individuals, or a private limited company manages a business on behalf of the owners. For this service of management the managing agents are usually paid a commission either on turnover or on profit. In effect, the managing agents sell their capacity for management to the owners of the companies they manage and the large managing agencies in India manage anything up to forty different businesses either as a single agency or as a group of agencies all composed of the same individuals. The system assured that managerial capacity was available to the developing commercial and industrial life of a new country. On the whole, the system has been used with integrity. Nevertheless a system which pays to agents a commission on profit or turnover and hands to them complete responsibility and authority for management is obviously open to abuse from those whose only motive is to make money without concern for the long-term stability of the industry. Such abuses have occurred. Because of the abuses and because of the interlocking financial control of large sectors of the economy through the same managing agency, which has led to the building of large industrial empires, the system has not unnaturally attracted the attention of social, economic, and political reformers.

A new Companies Act restricts the financial and economic arrangements of managing agencies. Recent amendments have laid down that by 1960 not more than ten companies can be managed on commission by any one managing agency; also they give Government the power to exclude managing agencies from any particular business or industry. There has, for some time, been a strong movement, particularly among the trade unions, to abolish the managing agency system entirely. Government has resisted this demand for fear of the large managerial gap that might be left if the experienced, scrupulous, and competent managing agencies were

[1] 1 Rupee=1*s.* 6*d.* (or 21 cents U.S.) approx.

removed from control of the majority of the companies they now manage.

The growth of industry in India has been characterized by the success of small businesses started with comparatively little capital, usually supplied by the managing agents themselves, or borrowed on the managing agents' own credit. The big returns on the small capital invested have, in their turn, attracted equity capital and enhanced the capital values of the original holdings. For the most part, the managing agencies are either family units or small private companies dominated by the members of one family. Since a contract to manage a business is made by the agency and not by individual members of the agency, those in charge of the agency can make all appointments, and usually members of the agency family automatically occupy key positions in the control of the companies managed. They are, however, not 'managers' in the sense understood in the west, since their remuneration is not paid by the company managed but comes as a share of the commission earned by the agency. Difficulties have been caused when there have been too many key posts to be filled by members of the one family. The position is not dissimilar to that in other countries when small family concerns have grown beyond the size which can be adequately controlled by the available members of the family. In the United Kingdom the need to admit other than family members into the ranks of higher management has had to be faced in many private companies.

TRADE UNION ACTIVITY

Trade unions in India are not as yet, from the Western point of view, strong unions.[1] Their power in collective bargaining is weakened by the tremendous unemployment that exists throughout India, and by inter-caste and inter-regional differences and conflicts. As recently as 1950 there was a disastrous strike in Bombay that impoverished both workers and unions and brought few compensating gains. In Ahmedabad, in contrast to other large cities, the reputation of the major trade union, the Textile Labour Association, is high, and the history of industrial relations is better than anywhere else in India. A comparison of industrial disputes in Bombay and Ahmedabad shows that over the past twenty-five years (with full allowance for the greater number of workers in Bombay) nearly twice as many workers have lost more than

[1] Murphy, Gardner, *In the Minds of Men*. New York, Basic Books, 1953.

seventeen times as many working days in Bombay as in Ahmedabad.

By law only one trade union may represent the workers in any industrial establishment. To qualify as the 'recognized' union, a union must have as its members at least fifteen per cent of the workers in the establishment, and must represent more workers than any other union. The Textile Labour Association, which is in effect a federation of smaller unions, represents approximately two-thirds of the Ahmedabad textile industry's workers. It is affiliated to the Congress Party. There can be little doubt that Mahatma Gandhi's influence has had much to do with the comparatively good relationships that exist between millowners, the trade union, and the workers. Today, in spite of the many changes that have taken place, the Mahatma's influence is still very strong in the Textile Labour Association, and although other unions, affiliated to other political parties, are active, they are as yet neither 'recognized' nor have they nearly so many members nor so much influence.

The history of the Textile Labour Association starts in 1918 when the workers of the city went on strike against the millowners. During the latter half of 1917 virulent plague broke out and the people of Ahmedabad were afraid of gathering together in crowds. The millowners paid a bonus of from twelve annas to a rupee a day over the current wages (Rs. 23 per month) to those who came to work.[1] When the plague died down the millowners tried to withdraw the bonus, but the workers protested. They were led by Anasuyaben Sarabhai, who during her education in England had taken an active part in the suffragette movement. On her return to India she had become a follower and close friend of Mahatma Gandhi, who had some time earlier established his Ashram just outside Ahmedabad. Her brother, Ambalal Sarabhai, who is the father of the present Chairman of Calico Mills, was, at the time of the strike, the President of the Millowners' Association, and in charge of the Calico Mills. He, too, was a friend of the Mahatma. This dispute, on the Mahatma's advice, was referred to arbitration, but before the arbitration proceedings had started, the millowners declared a lock-out. When after nineteen days the mills were re-opened, the workers demanded a fifty per cent increase in wages before they would start work. The millowners offered twenty per cent (the Bombay average wage was Rs. 28 per month). The Mahatma persuaded the workers to accept a thirty-five per cent increase, but the millowners refused to pay it and the workers went on strike.

[1] 1 Rupee=16 Annas; 1 Anna=1*d.* or 1.25 cents (U.S.) approx.

'I was in a most delicate situation: the millhands' case was strong. Shrimati Anasuyabhai (Anasuyaben) had to battle against her own brother Srijut Ambalal Sarabhai who led the fray on behalf of the millowners. My relations with them were friendly and that made fighting them the more difficult.'[1]

The Mahatma laid down four rules for the worker on strike:

Never resort to violence.
Never molest blacklegs.
Never depend on alms.
Keep firm, no matter how long the strike continues.

After twenty days the workers began to weaken saying that they and their families were starving. The Mahatma declared that he would fast until the workers rallied.

'My fast was undertaken not on account of the lapse of the millowners but on account of that of the labourers in which, as their representative, I had a share. With the millowners I could only plead; to fast against them would amount to coercion. . . . The principal man at the back of the millowners' unbending attitude towards the strike was Seth Ambalal Sarabhai. His resolute will and transparent sincerity were wonderful and captured my heart. It was a pleasure to be pitched against him. The strain produced by my fast upon the opposition of which he was the head, cut me, therefore, to the quick.'[2]

After three days of the fast the millowners accepted the principle of arbitration and the strike was ended.

The settling of this strike by arbitration set the pattern for the future, and when the Textile Labour Association officially came into existence in 1922, its constitution was drawn up in accordance with the Mahatma's instructions. It aims at the peaceful solution of all disputes and always prefers arbitration to violence. Anasuyaben Sarabhai was elected its first President and has remained in that office ever since.

The Association, familiarly known throughout India as the T.L.A., has departments dealing with industrial complaints, municipal, village, and

[1] Gandhi, Mohandas Karamchand, *The Story of my Experiments with Truth*, translated by Mahadey Desai. Ahmedabad, Namjivan Publishing House, 1940.

[2] *Ibid.*

family affairs, and runs cooperative banks and insurance schemes. Its Public Relations department is primarily concerned with propaganda for the principles and teachings of Gandhi. Its 80,000 members elect between them 2,200 *pratinidhis* (shop stewards) who meet monthly and who elect an executive of 76 which, with 15 officers of the Union, meets weekly. Any pratinidhi can have three days' paid leave on request for meetings of bodies of which he is a member.

In common with other trade unions in India, the Textile Labour Association is more effective in dealing with individual grievances than with collective bargaining, but it exercises considerable collective influence through political action in the Congress Party. The present Federal Ministers for Labour and Planning were, formerly, Secretaries of the Association. Their influence on industrial legislation, which has been mainly directed towards protecting workers' interests by reducing the power of employers to dismiss or otherwise punish, has been particularly strong. By law, no reduction in the number of posts in any textile mill is permitted without either the written agreement of the recognized trade union or a court award, and any reorganization that would lead to a reduction or to an increase in the number of workers required for any job has first to be approved either by the recognized union or by an industrial court before it can be put into effect. Moreover, no change in working practice or in working method can be introduced even though it does not result in reduction or increase in the numbers of workers. In 1954 regulations were made that required even experimental changes to be agreed either by the union or the court before they could be introduced.

In India only a very small minority of the working population is employed in industry and a great part of the majority, which is engaged in agriculture, is underemployed. One of the major problems facing both Government and trade unions is the enormous unemployment, actual and potential, that exists. Not unnaturally, the trade unions are, in consequence, strongly opposed to any reorganizations that might result in the introduction of new machinery requiring fewer workers. Mill-owners, on the other hand, are reluctant to replace their older machinery with the same kind of machines, which are outdated. Trade unions are caught in a dilemma between their wish to ensure a prosperous industry with high wages and their fears of having to agree to a reduction in the number of jobs before higher wages can be paid. The situation is complicated by the existence of a widespread and traditional handloom industry which employs over ten million workers, and which is an essential part of village life and economy. One of the Mahatma's precepts was the need for Indian economic self-sufficiency and for the encouragement of important village craft industries, but although the Textile Labour Association subscribes to and actively propagates the precepts it does not organize hand-weavers or other craft workers.

The Association tries to maintain a balance between the demands made upon it, on the one hand, to advance the wages of its members by collective bargaining, and, on the other, to resist the introduction of new kinds of machinery that, while possibly making increased wages more easily obtainable, might also increase the already great unemployment. During prosperous times the Association can claim a higher share of profits; during more difficult times it is driven to demand reduction of costs by better management. But the demand for a reduction of costs by better management invariably leads to a demand for changes of working practice or other kinds of reorganization that would reduce the number of workers required. At present the balance is an uneasy one.

CHAPTER 3

The Calico Mills

EARLY HISTORY[1]

The Ahmedabad Manufacturing and Calico Printing Co. Ltd. was started in 1880 as a mill for the printing of cloth. In 1881 it failed and went into liquidation. The Sarabhai family, whose members are the present managing agents, and who were then bankers, found themselves as the main creditors. The mill was put up for auction, but when the price offered did not reach the amount of the loan given, the banking house decided to take over the company and to run it themselves. They became the managing agents, first as a partnership under the name of Karamchand Premchand, and later in 1942 as the private limited company of Karamchand Premchand Ltd.

Within a very short time the bankers found that one of the main reasons for the failure had been the high cost of cloth. A weaving mill was built to provide the cloth for printing, but the mills still did not prosper because the cost of yarn was so high. A spinning mill was built to provide the yarn. Unfortunately the mills continued to lose money. Investigation showed that the money was being lost on printing, and so printing was stopped and the mill continued to spin yarn and to weave cloth. From that time onwards the company prospered. Gradually, finishing processes, including printing, were restored.

In the early 1920s the mill was doing fairly well but was finding that competition with the other mills was increasing. At that time the Calico Mills, like other mills in India, were making only coarse counts (thick yarn) which when made up into cloth did not compete with imported cloth. The experience of the only Indian mill to have tried cloths of fine

[1] Much of this material, as well as that of the earlier chapter, is taken from or was suggested by a booklet published by the Calico Mills.

counts (thin yarn) was not encouraging. Nevertheless the father of the present Chairman and Managing Agent, who was then in charge of the mills, decided to build a new mill for the manufacture of medium and fine counts and to enter into direct competition with imported cloth. After some difficult years, the new mill started to do well and the whole mill was changed to medium and fine counts. In the early 1930s, when the movement to boycott foreign goods became strong throughout India, many other mills in Ahmedabad and elsewhere changed from coarse to medium and fine counts.

Today the company has 139,120 spindles and 2,400 looms in two mills, the Calico Mill and the Jubilee Mill, and departments for bleaching, mercerizing, dyeing, printing, Sanforizing, and finishing at the Calico Mills. Collectively, as was mentioned in Chapter 1, all are known as the Calico Mills. They produce rather more than 110 miles of finished cloth per day. Except for a small amount of yarn that is turned into sewing thread, and cotton waste that is turned into blankets, the mill uses up all its raw cotton for the production of yarn, all the yarn for the production of grey (unbleached) cloth, and all the grey cloth for the production of finished cloth.

No expansion is now possible since the Bombay State has been declared a surplus zone for the production of cotton textiles. By Government regulation no more than the recorded number of spindles or the recorded number of looms can be worked, or be erected ready for work, on any one day.[1]

FINANCIAL STRUCTURE AND TRADING RESULTS

The company is a joint stock company with an authorized share capital of Rs 32,500,000 (£2,500,000 approx.) of which Rs 15,433,333 (£1,187,000 approx.) is issued and Rs 15,412,213 (£1,185,000 approx.) paid up. Of the issued capital of Rs 15,433,333, shares of the value of Rs 2,200,000 (£170,000 approx.) only have been issued for cash. All other issues have been by way of bonus by capitalizing reserves. The total reserves at March 1956, including a depreciation fund, amounted to Rs 55,810,000 (£4,300,000). The company's mean annual sales turnover, wages and

[1] In the middle of 1956 Government decided that it would grant licences for expansion for the manufacture of cloth for export only. The granting of a licence is for a limited number of new installations only and severe excise penalties will be imposed on any cloth from the new installations which is not exported.

salaries, and gross profits for each five years from 1921 to 1955 are given in *Table 1*.

Table 1. MEAN ANNUAL TURNOVER, WAGES AND GROSS PROFIT OF THE CALICO MILLS, 1921–1955

Years	*Average per year in Lacs of Rupees**		
	Turnover	*Salaries & Wages*	*Gross Profit*
1921–1925	74·0	25·2†	10·4
1926–1930	73·0	26·6†	10·4
1931–1935	66·6	28·8†	11·6
1936–1940	117·6	27·6	18·4
1941–1945	380·4	85·0	107·6
1946–1950	519·4	128·8	91·6
1951–1955	676·2	135·4	99·8

* 1 lac=100,000; Rs 1 lac=£7,576 approx.

† Includes stores purchases

MANAGING AGENCY

Members of the Sarabhai family have been the Managing Agents of the company since they took over the mills in 1881. In 1942, when the managing agency was turned into a private limited company, the articles of association provided that members of the family would not have any hereditary right to employment in the company and that others, not members of the family, could, by agreement, become shareholders and directors. The Managing Agents are appointed by the shareholders of the Ahmedabad Manufacturing and Calico Printing Co. Ltd., who also elect the Board of Directors to whom the Managing Agents report. Gautam Sarabhai is both Chairman af the Board of Directors of the Ahmedabad Manufacturing and Calico Printing Co. Ltd., and Chairman of the Board of Karamchand Premchand Ltd. He is also the member of Karamchand Premchand Ltd. who acts as the chief executive of the Calico Mills. In British terms he is, in effect, the Chairman and Managing Director of the company. Throughout the remainder of this book he will be referred to as the Managing Agent.

The Calico Mills have a wide reputation for being socially and industrially progressive. They were the first mills in India to go over entirely to the manufacture of medium and fine counts, and the first to introduce university graduates into management. The father of the present Managing Agent was a strong supporter of Mahatma Gandhi in his early struggles, particularly against the caste system. On one occasion when many contributors withdrew their support from the Mahatma because he accepted a Harijan family into his Ashram, Ambalal Sarabhai continued his.

'To Gandhi's great surprise a rich man one day drew up in his car near the Ashram quarters and told him that he wanted to give some help. When Gandhi said he would welcome it, the stranger brought the next day Rs 13,000, placed the donation in Gandhi's hands and left.'[1]

The anonymous donor was Ambalal Sarabhai. At the time of the 1918 strike and lockout he was the President of the Millowners' Association. After the lockout he had many discussions with his sister Anasuyaben Sarabhai and with Mahatma Gandhi about the relationships between employees and employers. As a result of these discussions and of his own experience during the lockout, he felt that the workers would always be in an inferior position when it came to any struggle with the millowners and that no fight between workers and millowners could ever be a fair fight. He therefore gave his full support to the trade union movement in its early days and encouraged all the workers in the mill to join it. This was not achieved without some disagreements with other millowners who felt that support of the newly-founded Textile Labour Association was against their interests.

WELFARE ACTIVITIES

Before the first world war the hours of work were from sunrise to sunset. All the mills in Ahmedabad were finding it difficult to get labour and a large number of young boys and girls were employed as 'half-timers'. They were allowed by law to work for half-time in the mill and were expected to attend to their education during the rest of the day. Because of the shortage of labour, it was easy for any boy or girl to obtain two certificates under different names and work half-time in two mills. Wages for 'half-timers' were Rs 6 per month and the parents of half-timers were so poor that they could not afford to send their children to school. The

[1] Tendulkar, D. G., '*Mahatma*'—*Life of Mohandas Karamchand Gandhi*, Vol. 1, published privately by Vithalbhai K. Jhaveri and D. G. Tendulkar, Bombay, 1951.

Calico Mills therefore opened a school for 'half-timers' and offered an allowance of Rs 4 per month to all those who attended.

In 1915 a doctor and a nurse were engaged and a crèche was opened where children of the workers could be treated and could spend their time under supervision while their parents worked in the mill. It was a comparatively short step from this to opening a hospital to deal particularly with maternity cases. A hospital was built and another doctor and more nurses were engaged. This hospital, however, built as a part of the activities of an industrial concern, was such a novelty and so distrusted that it went unused for some time. A prize of Rs 50 was therefore offered for the first woman to have her baby in the new hospital. This did produce one patient, whose confinement was fortunately successful. From then onwards the hospital was well used, so much so that women working in other mills frequently tried to get work in the Calico Mills as soon as they discovered that they were pregnant. By 1916, it had become necessary to introduce a rule making the hospital facilities available only to those who had at least one year's service in the mills.

The total number of workers employed was 8,000 on 31st December 1955, and the total labour wastage is less than ten per cent per annum. Late in 1955, when the length of service of all employees of the mills including all managers and workers had to be calculated for insurance purposes, it was found that the mean length of service in the Calico Mills was fifteen years, and in the Jubilee Mills seventeen years.

PART II

Concepts and Assumptions

CHAPTER 4

Task and Work-Group Organization

The work in the Calico Mills was carried out within a consultant-client relationship. The maintenance of the professional relationship and the work to be described called for the use of concepts, assumptions, and principles derived from several of the social sciences. The Tavistock Institute attempts to combine various disciplines—psychology, sociology, anthropology, medicine, psychiatry, and psycho-analysis. Although each member of the staff shares, to a greater or lesser extent, in the knowledge and experience of his colleagues, he has his own emphasis and prejudices and works in his own way. Chapters 4 and 5 do not pretend to summarize the general concepts, assumptions, and principles that derive from the various disciplines. These have been described elsewhere.[1] Rather they seek to formulate particular concepts and asumptions that were used to analyse the problems encountered in the Calico Mills.

They are given here, and in this form, because I found very early in the work in the Calico Mills that I had to try to formulate them and to write them down both for my own benefit and for that of the managers with whom I was working. On my first visit and within a day or two of tackling the first specific problem—that reported in Part III—we found it difficult to work together because so many of the concepts and assumptions upon which my questions and suggestions were based were implicit rather than explicit. When I tried to make them explicit I

[1] (*a*) Bion, W. R., 'Experiences in Groups, I, II, III, IV, V, and VI', *Human Relations*, 1948, 1949, and 1950, Vols. I, II, and III.
(*b*) Bowlby, Jaques, Kelnar, Menzies, Morris, Sutherland, and Wilson, 'Social Therapy', *The Journal of Social Issues*. Edited by Elliott Jaques, 1947, Vol. III, No. 2.
(*c*) Jaques, Elliott, *The Changing Culture of a Factory*, London, Tavistock Publications, 1951.
(*d*) Wilson, A. T. M., 'Some Aspects of Social Process', *The Journal of Social Issues*, Kurt Lewin Memorial Award Issue, 1951.
(*e*) Wilson, A. T. M., 'A Note on the Social Sanctions of Social Research', *The Sociological Review*, 1955, Vol. 3, No. 1.

found their formulation in coherent and unambiguous terms both difficult and time-consuming. Some, which I had intuitively accepted as obvious and self-explanatory, needed considerable explanation. Others, which I had thought complex and involved, were intuitively accepted by the managers as simple and straightforward. Since those first attempts, the concepts have naturally been added to and modified in discussions with the members of the company and with my colleagues. In the form given here they represent a brief statement of their present development.

Chronologically the first attempts at formulation belong to the later pages of Chapter 6, and their subsequent development at various places throughout Parts III, IV, and V. They are discussed more generally in Chapters 21 and 22, after examples of their application have been described in Chapters 6 to 20.

PRIMARY TASKS OF INDUSTRIAL PRODUCTION SYSTEMS

Industrial production systems perform many tasks at the same time. At the conscious level the most important tasks are the making of profits, the payment of dividends, the manufacture and sale of products, and the provision of employment in a great variety of occupational roles. At both conscious and unconscious levels production systems provide mechanisms for the satisfaction of social and psychological needs and for defence against anxiety.[1] The number and distribution of tasks vary between different systems and between different departments or sections of any one system. They may also vary over time. Each system or sub-system has, however, at any given time, one task which may be defined as its *primary task—the task which it is created to perform.*[2] Thus the primary task of private enterprise in a western economy is to make profits,[3] while that of a public utility is to give services. In making profits the private enterprise may give services, and, in giving services, the public utility may make profits, but their primary tasks remain different and the effectiveness of their performance should be judged by different criteria. In the

[1] Jaques, Elliott, 'On the Dynamics of Social Structure', *Human Relations*, 1953, Vol. VI, No. 1.

[2] Cf. Bion's definition of 'Sophisticated Task' in 'Experiences in Groups V', *Human Relations*, 1950, Vol. III, No. 1. This comparison is discussed in Chapter 21.

[3] The 'making of profit' is used throughout this book in its widest sense, that is, it is used to refer in a brief way to the economic task of ensuring the long term financial stability of an enterprise of which the 'making of profits' is a convenient symbol. It does not mean the 'maximization of profits' at the expense of future investments, future developments or future economic stability.

same way the primary tasks of the different departments of a factory may be to purchase raw materials, to manufacture, to market finished products, to obtain workers or to keep accounts. In so doing each contributes to the tasks of the others, but their *primary tasks* are different and are identifiable in terms of what they are created to perform.

The performance of a primary task invariably requires that other tasks should also be performed. The weaving of cloth requires that yarn should be provided, designs made, weavers employed, looms installed and maintained, and cloth inspected and measured. The ancillary tasks are controls over, and services to, the primary task. Their performance, however important, is secondary to that of the primary task. In making judgments about any organization two questions have priority over all others:

What is the primary task?
How well is it performed?

All other questions are subsidiary to these two.

TASK ORGANIZATION

The members of an organization contribute both to the performance of the primary task and to the emotions associated with what Bion has called 'the hatred of learning by experience'.[1] By this he means the hatred of having to behave as adult human beings in a sophisticated and reality-based manner. The attitudes of individuals and groups towards the effective performance of the primary task vary widely in quality and intensity, but by their continuing membership all must share to a greater or lesser extent in the realization of a common purpose. So far as their behaviour is adult and reality-based it can be said that:

The performance of the primary task is supported by powerful social and psychological forces which ensure that a considerable capacity for cooperation is evoked among the members of the organization created to perform it,

and that, as a direct corollary,

the effective performance of a primary task can provide an important source of satisfaction for those engaged upon it.

[1] Bion, W. R., 'Experiences in Groups V', *Human Relations*, 1950, Vol. III, No. 1.

In other words, there is, among the members of any organization, a need, whether latent or manifest, to get on with the job. They take pride and find satisfaction in doing the job well.

The high degree of cooperation in working groups faced with serious difficulty in the performance of their primary task has often been noted. The respect felt for those who are capable of managing a situation so that effective task performance becomes possible is common knowledge. Equally, inefficient organization, which interrupts the flow of work, or otherwise makes effective performance difficult, is a well-known and frequent cause of dissatisfaction and frustration.

If the satisfaction to be obtained from primary task performance is to be realized, the task must be one that is recognizable and meaningful for those who perform it. Its performance must be felt as something for which responsibility has been taken. The relationships it provides must be satisfactory. Three assumptions may accordingly be made about task organization:

1. *A task should be so organized that those engaged on it can experience, so far as is practicable, the completion of a 'whole' task.*

'Closure', giving a sense of completion, is a well-known source of individual satisfaction. Dissatisfactions caused by job-breakdown that leaves individuals responsible for only small component tasks are familiar. They have frequently been the subject of study, and numerous devices—such as displays or visits to other parts of a factory—have been used in attempts to convey a sense of 'wholeness' to workers engaged on component tasks.

Technological demands may require the number engaged on a 'whole' task to be too large for individuals to have an easily realizable sense of group membership. Yet problems of technological demand are frequently less intractable than they appear at first sight. Although the manufacture of a complete product by a group sufficiently small to provide a sense of group membership may not always be possible, a number of definite intermediate stages can often be arranged whose completion can be accomplished by such a group. At least some of the satisfactions of 'closure' can be so provided.

2. *A task should be so organized that, so far as possible, those engaged upon it can control their own activities.*

Both for individuals and groups, self-government, to the limit of their capacity to control their own activities, is a source of satisfaction. Without such internal self-government the individual or the group is forced into a dependent, child-like role. Though for some purposes this may be welcomed, it must, in those with aspirations to adult maturity, lead either to guilt at its acceptance or to resentment at its imposition. The capacity of individuals and of groups to take control of their own activities varies with their abilities as individuals and with the situation in which they find themselves. The 'situation' includes the whole structural and cultural complex of the society to which they belong. In some societies, notably those of the West, individualism is an established ideal; in others, of which Indian society is one, greater emphasis is placed on group membership and group leadership, particularly when the group is that of the family or community. Within the context of the structure and culture of the particular society, too much responsibility provokes anxiety, too little causes frustration.

Delegation of responsibility for 'government' can be made easier when tasks performed by individuals or groups can be performed within definable physical boundaries. Those responsible for the task can then 'own' their 'territory'. They can identify easily what is theirs and who belongs in it. They can raise questions about the rights of others not engaged on the task to be there. 'Territory', in this sense, includes such obvious boundaries as a room or an enclosed section of a department, but it may also include less obvious boundaries such as those provided by a telephone communication network.

3. *Related tasks should be so organized that those performing them can have satisfactory relationships.*

When complaints are made about the quality of work at particular stages of manufacturing it is not uncommon for those responsible to find fault with the work of those engaged on the previous stage. In a textile mill, when the quality of weaving is called in question, the weavers will blame the preparation departments for poor warp beams, or the spinning departments for poor weft yarn. The process of passing the blame can easily be continued until it appears that the only fault lies with the man who planted the cotton.

This third assumption will hold for the relationships between individuals engaged on interdependent tasks, for the intra-group relationships of primary working groups, and for the inter-group relationships of groups engaged on different parts of a total process. Difficult relationships between members of a work organization may be caused by indifferent work in any one part of it; equally, but not necessarily so obviously, indifferent work may be caused by difficult relationships. It follows that component tasks should be so organized as to provide those engaged on them with satisfactory interpersonal relationships and that the relationships of those performing component tasks will have important effects on productivity.

WORK-GROUP ORGANIZATION

The three assumptions stated above apply to the organization of tasks rather than to the organization of work-groups, in that they can be made both about individual and about group task organization. By mechanization and job-breakdown modern industry makes it increasingly difficult for 'whole' tasks to be performed by self-governing individuals, and some form of collective organization, in which those who perform component operations can have relationships with those on related operations, is imperative. It follows from the assumption about primary task performance that:

If task performance is efficiently organized, then there will be neither fewer, nor more, engaged on a 'whole' task than can efficiently perform it.

If there are too few engaged on 'whole' task performance, stress and strain are inevitable, with resulting poor performance and loss of satisfaction. If there are too many, then sooner or later there will arise a need to deny or otherwise to deal with the guilt involved in the mutual investment in inefficiency. It can be expected as a corollary to the above proposition that:

A group consisting of the smallest number that can perform a 'whole' task and can satisfy the social and psychological needs of its members is, alike from the point of view of task performance and of those performing it, the most satisfactory and efficient group.

In every society there is obvious biological support for a productive group of two. Within the limits set by particular cultures, clinical experience, largely derived from psychological, psychiatric, and psychoanalytic practice, suggests that:

1. *The smallest productive and satisfactory group is a pair, and the next most satisfactory a group of from six to twelve, with perhaps the most satisfactory of these a group of eight.*

With fewer than six members, the importance of individual contributions is so great that the fear of casualties, however caused and however temporary, may be such as to produce disruptive strain. With more than twelve, the complexities of the multiple relationships to be maintained become too great to be carried by every member, and the group tends to split into sub-groups. It follows that in those societies in which work-group organization is a desirable means of obtaining the satisfactions to be derived from group activities, tasks which can be performed by pairs or by groups of from six to twelve are likely to provide the most satisfactory relationsnips. Groups engaged upon tasks performed by three, four, or five or by more than twelve, are likely to require special conditions if the group is to build stable and cohesive relationships. Among these special conditions can be those in management groups in which each manager, although a member of a small group of colleagues, has a field of work for which he is responsible as an individual and which is therefore organized as a 'whole' task for him as an individual. By contrast, the members of a primary working group have only their own group task and have no other source from which to obtain the satisfaction of effective task performance.

The most appropriate form of internal organization for any work group will depend upon the structure and culture of the society from which the members come, particularly upon the prevailing attitudes towards leadership élites. Few societies are completely egalitarian, few of those that are developing industrially are not today at least suffused with ideas about equality of opportunity. If group stability is to be maintained the contribution of each individual member towards the task of the group must be accepted by all as valuable and the reward as equitable. Neither contributions nor rewards may necessarily be the same in quality or in quantity but both must be felt by the group to be appropriate. More formally, the assumption may be stated:

2. *Group stability is more easily maintained when the range of skills required of group members is such that all members of the group can comprehend all the*

skills and, without necessarily having, or wanting to have, them, could aspire to their acquisition.

The greater the differences in skill between group members (whether the skills are comparable in level or not), the more difficult is communication likely to be between group members. The less likely therefore are they to form a cohesive whole.

Where the performance of the group task requires a range of skills so that all members cannot, by the nature of the task, share them all, acceptance of all skills as contributing to the task of the group is essential for satisfactory group life. Specialization of function in management groups made necessary by the increasing complexity of modern industry, or specialization of task in workers' groups brought about by increasing mechanization, usually calls for some skill differentiation among the members of these groups. When this occurs the need for the recognition of the appropriateness of contributions may be stated as:

3. *The fewer differences there are in prestige and status within a group, the more likely is the internal structure of a group to be stable and the more likely are its members to accept internal leadership.*

Inequalities of responsibility and authority in management commands, for example, can lead to considerable difficulties in relationships between colleagues unless the inequalities are accepted and adequately structured into the group organization.

Consideration of the highly structured character of Indian society, of the industrialization and urbanization which is occurring, and of current attempts to increase social mobility, suggested that for Indian conditions the second and third assumptions could be stated together:

The tasks performed by members of a group should be differentiated according to the skills required and the equipment used, and tasks requiring different levels of skill should be hierarchically structured. The task organization should provide opportunities for change in status within the group, and, as a corollary, tasks requiring comparable skills should provide some opportunities for interchange of task between members of the group.

The greater the value attached to group membership as an end in itself, the greater the fear of its loss and, hence, the greater the danger that the group, as a group, will become more important than the task it was created to perform.[1] If this occurs and, as a result, task performance suffers, then the whole group may suffer such loss of satisfaction because of ineffective performance that, even as a group, it may be unable to continue. It is important therefore that:

4. *When members of small work groups become disaffected to the extent that they can no longer fit into their own work group, those disaffected should be able to move to other small work groups engaged on similar tasks.*

The possibility of transferring to other similarly structured work groups reduces the emotional investment in membership of a particular group and the chance of exclusion is not so threatening as to be itself disruptive. Recent work on labour turnover[2] has suggested that where individuals go when they leave an institution and how they are assisted to get there deserve at least as much attention, for the sake of the institution, as where they come from and how they are inducted when they enter.

[1] Adams, S., 'Status Congruency as a Variable in Small Group Performance', *Social Forms*, 1953, Vol. 32. In this American study it was shown that the performance of groups with high as well as with low status congruence was poor; that is, the highly congruent groups appeared to have put group membership before group performance. It may be surmised that the formation of highly congruent groups was a neurotic mechanism unrelated to primary task performance. See also Likert, Rensis, 'Developing Patterns in Management', *Personnel Management*, 1956, Vol. XXXVIII, No. 337.

[2] Rice, A. K., 'The Relative Independence of Sub-Institutions as illustrated by Departmental Labour Turnover. (The Glacier Project—VII)', *Human Relations*, 1952, Vol. V, No. 1.

CHAPTER 5

Operating and Managing Systems of Industrial Organization

From the physical point of view the characteristic state of the living organism is that of an open system. A system is closed if no material enters or leaves it; it is open if there is import and export, and, therefore, change of its components. Living systems maintain themselves by the exchange of materials with their environment and by the continuous building up and breaking down of their components. An open system may attain a time-independent steady state where the system remains constant as a whole, and in its phases, though there is a steady flow of materials through at A characteristic of an open system is that the system exerts forces to attain, and then maintain, a steady state. Self-regulation is a general property of open systems.[1] In field theory the self-regulated steady state is referred to as a quasi-stationary equilibrium.[2]

Any industrial organization may be likened to an open system. It imports capital, raw materials, equipment, and supplies; it exports dividends, investments, waste products, and finished goods. It maintains itself by the exchange of these materials with its environment. If there is neither import nor export, the organization dies. Elsewhere the labour turnover of an industrial organization has been shown to display many of the characteristics of organic metabolism.[3]

[1] Bertalanffy, Ludwig von, 'The Theory of Open Systems in Physics and Biology', *Science*, 1950, Vol. III, p. 24.

[2] Lewin, Kurt, 'Frontiers in Group Dynamics', *Human Relations*, 1947, Vol. I, No. 1. For fuller accounts of the field theory concepts and approach to problems of change see *Field Theory in Social Science*, Kurt Lewin, ed. Dorwin Cartwright, London, Tavistock Publications, 1952.

[3] (*a*) Hill, J. M. M., 'A Consideration of Labour Turnover as the Resultant of a Quasi-Stationary Process', *Human Relations*, 1951, Vol. IV, No. 3.

(*b*) Rice, A. K., and Trist, E. L., 'Institutional and Sub-Institutional Determinants of Change in Labour Turnover', *Human Relations*, 1952, Vol. V, No. 4.

OPERATING SYSTEMS

Any production system may be defined by reference to what is imported into and exported from it. By a special use of the word 'production' it could be said that the import into the simplest form of production system is a piece of property which is bought, and export the same piece of property which is sold. There is no other system activity than the work required to produce the change in ownership. Indeed, in transactions such as those of the Stock Exchange and some commodity markets, the property bought and sold need never be handled or even inspected between import and export. More complex industrial systems import raw materials, convert them into a variety of products, and export the products by selling them.

For a textile mill such as the Calico Mills, the import is raw cotton; conversion is the manufacture of finished cloth from raw cotton; export the selling and delivery of finished cloth to customers. Similar identifications and definitions may be made at every level of an organization. Thus, for the Weaving department of the Calico Mills, the import is cotton yarn on bobbins from the Spinning department and cotton yarn on beams from the Preparation department; conversion is the manufacture of grey (unbleached and undyed) cloth from cotton yarn; and export is the delivery of grey cloth to the Bleaching and Finishing departments.

The process of changing import into export may require the carrying out of either sequential or simultaneous operations, or of both. Where different operations are carried out discretely, a production system may be differentiated into *operating systems.*

Two stages of increasing differentiation may be distinguished:

1. Where export and import are so differentiated that they are carried out in discrete operating systems.
2. Where between import and export such changes are made in the property that they lead to the differentiation of a discrete system or systems of conversion (conversion in this sense may include the transport of property from a position of import to a position of export).

In the most general case production systems may be differentiated into three kinds of operating systems concerned with:

1. import—the acquisition of raw materials;
2. conversion—the changing of raw materials into products;

3. export—the disposal of the finished results of import and conversion.

In a complex organization there may be more than one system of each kind. In a simple organization there may be incomplete differentiation, more than one operation being carried out in the same operating system.

MANAGING SYSTEMS

When a production system is differentiated into discrete operating systems, its management cannot be contained in any one operating system, and a system external to the operating systems is required to control and service their activities. This is the *managing system*. As a minimum it contains the management of the total production system and of each discrete operating system. Where controls and services are differentiated from the management of the total production system, the managing system contains these in addition. In more usual terms, 'top' management consists of the 'line' managers—the 'general' manager, and the managers of operating departments—and the 'functional' managers in charge of the control and service departments. *Figure 1* shows a diagrammatic representation of a production system, differentiated into three operating systems. The managing system contains the management of the total system, one discrete control and two discrete service functions, and the management of each operating system. The management of the total system is shown on the boundary of the system, since all production systems, however comprehensive, must be related to their environment, and the management of the total system is the mechanism for the mediation of relationships between the system and its environment. Similarly management of each operating system is shown on the boundaries of the managing and operating systems, indicating membership of both.[1]

ORDERS OF DIFFERENTIATION OF OPERATING AND MANAGING SYSTEMS

The differentiation of any given production system into operating systems and a managing system is the first order of differentiation, and the systems may be defined as *first-order operating and managing systems*. In a complex production system, one or more of the first-order operating systems may be further differentiated. This is the second order of differentiation and the sub-systems may be defined as *second-order operating systems*. These

[1] The diagrammatic representations used are based on Lewin's topological notations.

FIGURE 1 *OPERATING AND MANAGING SYSTEMS*

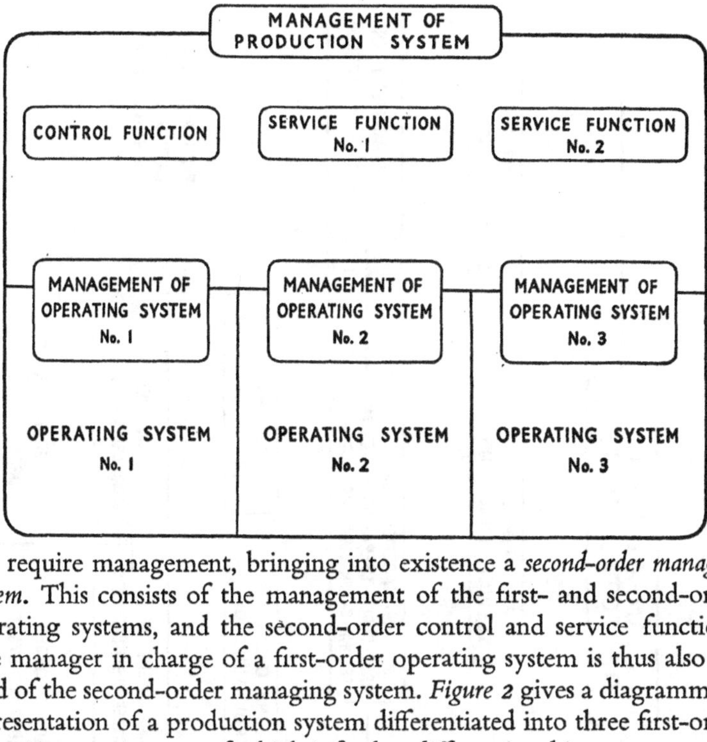

also require management, bringing into existence a *second-order managing system*. This consists of the management of the first- and second-order operating systems, and the second-order control and service functions. The manager in charge of a first-order operating system is thus also the head of the second-order managing system. *Figure 2* gives a diagrammatic representation of a production system differentiated into three first-order operating systems, one of which is further differentiated into two second-order operating systems and a second-order managing system.

Second-order operating systems may be differentiated into *third-order systems*, third-order systems into *fourth-order*, etc. The differentiations can be continued until separate operating systems cannot be discretely identified, and *primary production systems* are reached, in which management, control, and service are internally structured.

The number of orders of differentiation will depend both upon the complexity of the system and upon the frame of reference of the analysis. By definition, with a primary production system as frame of reference no differentiation is possible. With a department of a factory containing more than one primary production system, at least a first order of differentiation may be made. With a large and complex industrial organization, five,

FIGURE 2 OPERATING AND MANAGING SYSTEMS OF THE FIRST AND SECOND ORDERS OF DIFFERENTIATION

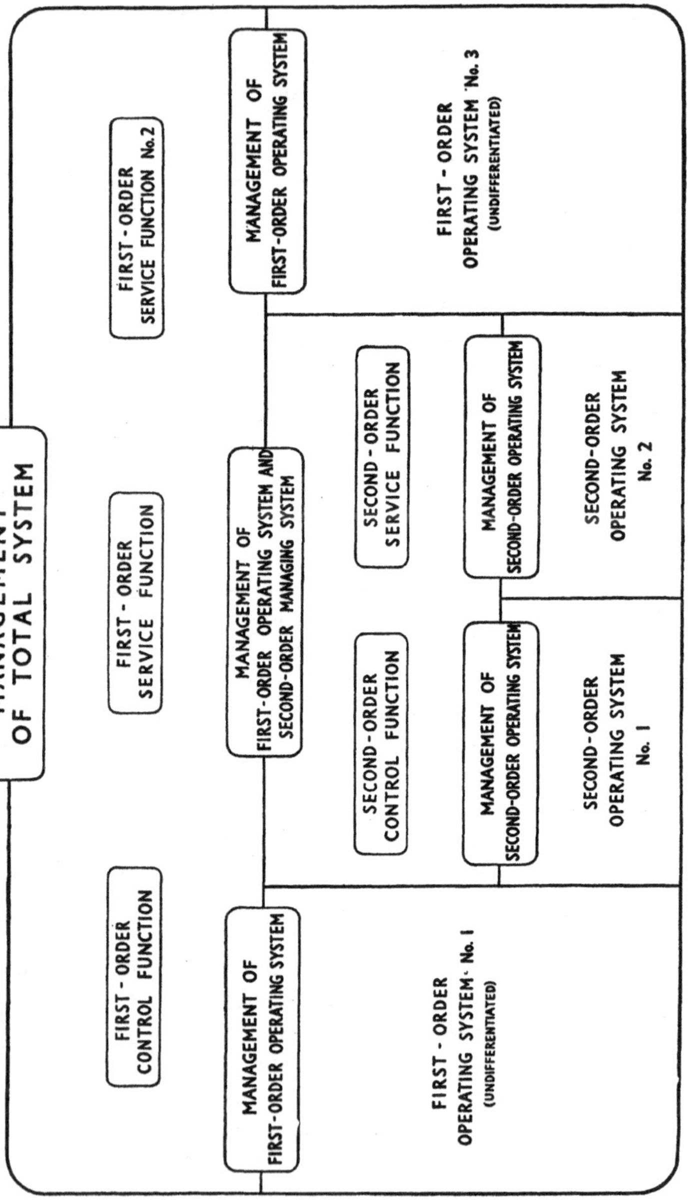

six, seven or even more orders of differentiation may be possible.

For example, with a factory managed by a 'general manager', there may be first-order operating systems (frequently called divisions) concerned with purchasing (import), manufacturing (conversion) and selling (export). The divisional managements of the three first-order operating systems together with the general management of the factory as a whole and such service and control functions as are established at top management level (say, personnel, finance, and research) form the first-order managing system. If the divisions are also divided into departments, and the departments into sections, then the departments will form second-order operating systems, and the sections third-order operating systems. Where, within sections, there are primary working groups, they will form the undifferentiated fourth-order primary production systems.

Other forms of differentiation are common. In a company manufacturing diversified products, the first order of differentiation may be into divisions each of which is responsible for different products or different groups of products. In a combine, the first order of differentiation may be into discrete companies, with a first-order managing system which may or may not contain differentiated control and service functions for the whole concern.

CONTROL AND SERVICE FUNCTIONS

The Control and Service functions exercised by a managing system must be directed towards the effective performance of the primary tasks of the operating systems controlled and serviced—functions which do not serve this purpose have no meaning in organizational terms. It follows that a managing system should contain all the controls and services necessary for the adequate management of the operating systems. More formally:

The greatest operational efficiency is achieved when the functions of control and service are contained in the managing system of the same order as the operating system controlled and serviced.

If, for example, maintenance engineering services are required only by the departments of a manufacturing division, they will be most efficiently located if contained within the divisional managing system and therefore within the command of the manager responsible for manufacturing. Similarly, if inspection is required to control the quality of production, it is most efficiently located as a control function of the same system. Two assumptions follow from this proposition:

1. *The inclusion of a control or service function in a managing system of a different order from the operating systems controlled or serviced, implies an organizational weakness.*

Less formally, the inclusion of a control or service function in a managing system of a higher order than the operating system controlled or serviced implies a vote of no confidence in the management of the system in which the function should be included. Conversely, the location of a control or service function in a managing system of a lower order than the operating system controlled or serviced implies either a vote of no confidence in the control or service function, or only partial differentiation of the function from system management.

If production engineering is regarded as a control and service function of a manufacturing division, then production engineering is most efficiently located as a function of the divisional managing system. A management organization that includes a chief production engineer who reports to the managing director (or general manager) implies that the manager in charge of manufacturing is not trusted to control his own division. A frequent cause of difficulty arises, however, when one operating system is dominant (because of its complexity or because of the relatively high capital investment involved) and the managing director gives so much of his attention to it that the manager nominally in charge of it is in effect only a deputy manager—the real responsibility for operational management being carried, in practice, by the managing director. In these circumstances, it may be appropriate for those responsible for control and service functions of the manufacturing division to report to the managing director. They do not, however, report to him as the head of his own managing system but as the undisclosed head of a lower-order managing system.

Where such difficulties arise it is important that multiple roles taken by members of management should be adequately recognized and the functions carried out located in their appropriate system. Unless this is done, meetings of a management group, in which a managing director meets his subordinates, are in reality two simultaneous meetings. One meeting is between the head of a first-order managing system and his subordinates in that system, the other is between the head of a second-order system and his subordinates in the latter system. Such meetings not infrequently become confused as to purpose and meaning with consequent lack of resolution of the problems. The second assumption may, therefore, be stated:

2. *Effective meetings for the initiation of executive action should be held between members of the same order system.*

When meetings include members of different order systems, there will be risk of confusing roles and, therefore, role relationships. The last assumption should not be taken to suggest that members of different order systems should not attend meetings together, but rather that when they do so, their roles, responsibilities, and authorities, and in particular the terms of reference of the meeting, should be made as explicit as possible, so that confusion about roles does not lead to by-passing in the executive command. Nor should the assumptions about the location of control and service functions be taken to suggest that the members of one managing system should necessarily all have the same rank in the hierarchy of management. In accordance with the third assumption about work-group organization, the fewer ranks there are, the more likely are the members of a system to form stable relationships; but, provided that the ranks are in accordance with the responsibilities and authorities of the tasks performed, and that the hierarchical structure of ranks is accepted, more than two ranks can be tolerated.

PART III

The Experimental Reorganization of Automatic Weaving

THE SOCIAL REORGANIZATION OF A TECHNOLOGICALLY DISTURBED PRODUCTION SYSTEM

CHAPTER 6

Before Change

Before the second world war forty-eight automatic looms were introduced into the Jubilee Mill, being absorbed into a shed containing some hundreds of ordinary non-automatics. So far as running and staffing were concerned they were treated as non-automatics with labour-saving attachments. Though fewer workers were required—twelve as against twenty-six—occupational roles were unchanged and work organization remained the same.

In June 1952, more automatics were introduced, and by March 1953 an experimental shed containing two hundred and twenty-four new looms had been set up. Work was reorganized on British and American lines with different workers allocated to different operations,[1] numbers being based on American and Japanese[2] standards modified by time studies under Indian conditions. The experimental shed started working with twelve looms. During the first eight months, new machines were brought into production as soon as they had been erected and workers trained. By March 1953 stable conditions had been established and further erection was halted pending the completion of the building.

The results, though better than for the first automatics, were still disappointing. Neither productivity as measured in terms of efficiency nor quality as measured in terms of damage was as high as expected. Neither was appreciably better than, or always as good as, on ordinary looms. Technological change had not led to the expected productive change.

The morale of the shed appeared good, supervisors and workers getting on well together and enjoying a reputation for competence and hard work. The shed was new, specially designed to obviate the worst features

[1] Smith, E. D., *Technology and Labour*, New Haven, Yale University Press, 1939.

[2] The looms in the shed are of Japanese manufacture and figures of worker allocation of similar installations in Japan were supplied by the manufacturers.

of tropical conditions, with the latest type of lighting and humidification.[1] Hours of work were the same as for the rest of the mill: two eight-hour shifts, from 7.0 a.m. to 3.30 p.m. with a half-hour break from 11.0 to 11.30, and from 3.30 p.m. to midnight with a half-hour break from 7.30 to 8.0. Higher management paid considerable and continuous attention to the shed, because it was new and experimental.

During a discussion at a management meeting[2] various reasons were put forward for the disappointing results, but no agreement was reached. Every known technological difficulty had been tackled and those few that remained unsolved could not explain either the short-fall in efficiency or the high damage rates. Erratic variations in individual weavers' efficiencies together with the general perplexity about what might be wrong did suggest, however faintly, that relationships were not so good as they appeared and that there might be some hidden resistance to the way the new looms were being worked.

I directed my attention first to the primary task of the shed—the weaving of cloth.

THE AUTOMATIC SHED

Automatic Weaving Activities

Import into an automatic weaving shed is yarn on *beams* and *bobbins*. Conversion is the manufacture of *grey* cloth. Export is the delivery of the grey cloth to a cloth department, external to the weaving shed, where it is inspected, measured, and made up into lots for subsequent processing.

The operations of automatic weaving are carried out by bobbins containing *weft* (threads across the length of cloth) and beams containing *warp* (threads along the length of cloth). An automatic loom set up for weaving is represented in simplified form in *Figure 1*. The loom is prepared for weaving by *gating*. A beam is gated into brackets at the back, and each warp thread is passed through the eye of one of several *healds*, then through a *reed* to keep it in place. Finally it is connected to a roller on the front which takes the woven cloth. A bobbin containing weft is placed in a *shuttle* from which it is ejected when empty or when the thread breaks. Empties are automatically replaced by full bobbins stored in a *battery*.

[1] Under the climatic conditions in Ahmedabad, relative humidity in the loom shed has to be artificially maintained at 80 to 85 per cent to enable yarn to stand up to the strain in the weaving process. For this purpose a plant is installed that humidifies the whole shed.

[2] These meetings are described and discussed in Part V.

When the loom is weaving the shuttle is knocked backwards and forwards by *pickers* on a *slay* in front of the reed. The shuttle passes through a *shed*

FIGURE 1 *REPRESENTATION OF AN AUTOMATIC LOOM SET UP FOR WEAVING*

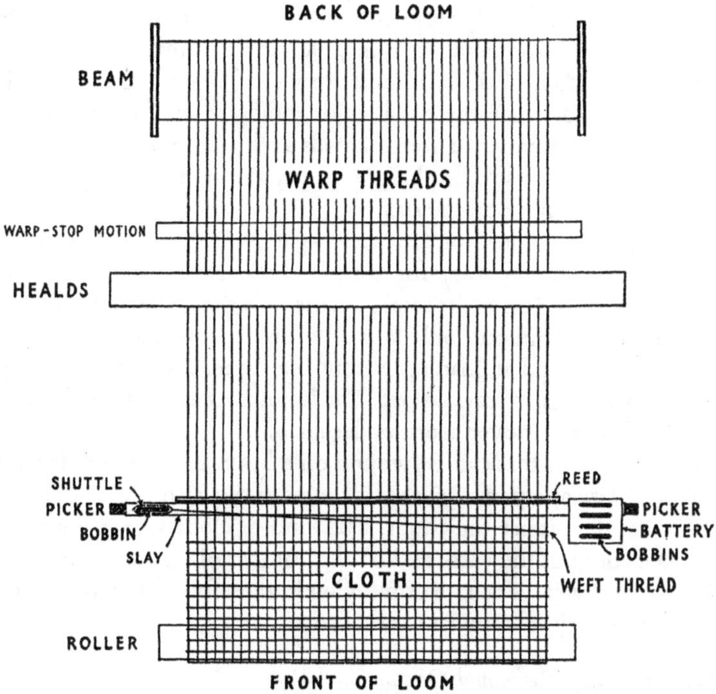

formed by the rise of certain healds and the fall of others, thus separating the warp threads from each other in an ordered pattern. As the shuttle travels through the shed it leaves behind a weft thread unwound from the bobbin. Each weft thread is banged into place by the reed. The weaving ceases when the warp yarn on the beam has all been converted into cloth on the roller; the loom is then unloaded, the finished cloth taken off (this may occur at intervals during weaving) and the empty beam removed.

The looms are fitted with a mechanical device called a *warp-stop motion*. In the warp-stop motion used, each warp thread passes through a weighted wire which drops into a slot and so stops the loom whenever a warp thread breaks. When this occurs, the stopping of the loom is observed, and its cause must be investigated. The mending of a broken warp thread involves knotting a short piece of spare yarn to the broken end and drawing it through the appropriate place in the heald and reed. The loom is then restarted.

The normal time for mending a single warp thread is thirty to sixty seconds. Stops of this duration also occur when there are minor entanglements in the warp threads and when there are short or missing threads on the warp beams. Stops of thirty minutes to several hours occur when the beam is exhausted or when there is a major entanglement or a *smash*—the breaking of a large number of warp threads at the same time. A smash is usually caused when the shuttle ploughs its way through the warp threads, owing to untrue running on the slay.

The activities of a single loom are cyclic—gate, weave, unload. But since weaving time (including stops for yarn breaks) always greatly exceeds loading and unloading time, the total activities of a shed containing a number of looms are continuous, only a small proportion of the looms being stopped for gating and unloading at any one time. During these stops maintenance activities are carried out. The loom is tuned and oiled and all accumulated fluff is removed from underneath.

The length of yarn that can be wound on a beam or a bobbin depends partly on their size and partly on the thickness of the yarn (the *count*). The finer the yarn, the higher the count. The kind of cloth woven (*sort*) depends on the count of the yarn, and on the number of threads to the inch in both warp and weft. The rate of weaving is, therefore, a function of the speed and continuity of loom run and of sort.

Automatic Weaving Tasks and Occupational Roles

Twenty-nine workers manned the two hundred and twenty-four looms in the automatic shed. Once looms were loaded and set up, eight *weavers* were responsible for keeping them running, discovering reasons for stoppages, mending broken warp threads, and dealing with minor entanglements. Three *smash-hands*, regarded as weavers in training, dealt both with major entanglements and smashes. Five *battery-fillers* kept batteries full of new bobbins. Two *gaters* removed exhausted beams and gated in new ones, and two *cloth-carriers* cut and removed the finished cloth.

Two *jobbers* and two *assistant jobbers*, responsible for loom maintenance, adjusted looms while running and tuned them when new beams were gated. One *oiler* kept all moving parts oiled and went over the whole loom during gating. A *feeler-motion fitter* specialized in the maintenance of the automatic device that ejected empty bobbins, and a *humidification fitter* maintained the plant that kept the humidity of the shed at the necessary level. Other ancillary tasks were performed by a *bobbin-carrier* who removed all empty bobbins and returned them to the Spinning department, and a *sweeper* who removed all dirt and fluff from the shed and cleaned under the looms during gating.[1]

The whole shed was under the control of a *Top Supervisor* who had a *Shift Supervisor* in charge of each of two shifts.

The Measurement of Productivity and Wages

Productivity is measured by two figures—*efficiency* and *damage*. Efficiency is reckoned in terms of the number of *picks* (weft threads) inserted in any shift, expressed as a percentage of the number of picks that would have been inserted had the loom run continuously for the whole shift—no allowance being made for loading, unloading, or any other stops. Damage is the percentage of cloth not accepted as of standard quality by inspectors and viewers. The higher the efficiency and the lower the damage, the greater the productivity.

The wage system adopted gave jobbers and weavers a piece-rate determined by efficiency. The piece-rates were based on an average standard of efficiency of eighty-five per cent per month. Higher or lower efficiencies resulted in a proportional increase or decrease in the amount of pay (excluding dearness allowance). For percentage increases over ninety-two the proportional increase was doubled, ninety-three being paid as ninety-four, ninety-four as ninety-six, and so on. All other workers were paid on time rates.

THE OPERATING SYSTEM

Interdependent Tasks and Independent Roles

The production process of a loom shed, in contrast with that of a single loom, is continuous rather than cyclic. All activities must be directed to maintaining a *steady rate* of multiple loom weaving. This requires the simultaneous carrying out of all activities. In spite of the interdependence

[1]The tasks of automatic weaving and their related occupational roles, as found at the beginning of the investigation, are shown in *Table 1* of Appendix 1. *Table 2* of the same Appendix shows these roles related to the numbers employed on each shift, the lines of responsibility, and the average wages per month, less dearness allowance.

of the tasks, only the jobbers and assistant jobbers had any form of stable internal work-group. The others formed an aggregate of individuals, a number of whom were virtually independent. Though jobbers had some authority over most of the others, and weavers over smash-hands, the lines of authority were confused and undefined. The oiler could be directed by a jobber, but the relative authority of the two jobbers was not established and, though the smash-hands could be instructed by a weaver, the order in which the eight weavers could demand their services had never been stated. Difficulties about priorities had to be referred either to a jobber or, because there were two jobbers and three smash-hands, to the Shift Supervisor.

The activities of the shed having been broken down into component tasks with the number of workers determined by work studies of the separate components, those in different occupational roles worked on different numbers of looms. Weavers operated twenty-four or thirty-two, depending on their skill and on sort, while battery-fillers charged the batteries of from forty to fifty. Smash-hands served on average seventy-five. The number of workers and the average number of looms per worker for each occupational role are shown in *Table 1*. This method of determining the number of workers required to carry out a production process is the normal production engineering corollary of job-breakdown and work study. Katz and Kahn have included it as a major factor in their concept of the 'Machine Theory of Organization'.[1]

The number of looms on which any individual worker was engaged did not remain constant, since a change of sort could change his work-load. A change involving a higher number of threads per inch in the warp might decrease the number of looms allocated to a weaver, because the greater number of threads could cause more frequent warp breaks. On the other hand, a change involving yarn of higher count could increase the number of looms allocated to battery-fillers and gaters because more yarn could be wound on bobbins and beams, which would therefore last longer. Without necessarily changing the total number or the kinds of workers, each change of sort, by varying the number of looms that some individuals operated, tended to change their pattern of relationships and to add to the confusion of the lines of authority.

Each weaver had on average the services of one-quarter of a pair con-

[1] Katz, Daniel, and Kahn, Robert L., 'Human Organization and Worker Motivation', *Industrial Productivity*, L. R. Tripp (Ed.), Industrial Relations Research Association, 1951.

Table 1. THE NUMBER OF LOOMS PER WORKER AND THE NUMBER OF WORKERS IN EACH OCCUPATIONAL ROLE IN THE AUTOMATIC LOOM SHED

Occupational Role	*Number of Looms per Worker*	*Number of Workers*
Battery-filler	48–50	5
Gater	80–112	2
Weaver	24–32	8
Smash-hand	60–80	3
Cloth-carrier	112	2
Jobber	112	2
Assistant jobber	112	2
Oiler	224	1
Feeler-motion fitter	224	1
Bobbin-carrier	224	1
Sweeper	224	1
Fitter	224	1
Totals	24–224	29

sisting of a jobber and his assistant, five-eighths of a battery-filler, three-eighths of a smash-hand, and so on. But any change of sort altered these proportions. Battery-fillers served on average one and three-fifths weavers, though with some sorts a particular battery-filler might be able to serve two. There was then opportunity for the two weavers and their battery-filler to build interdependent relationships (albeit of an awkward kind) consistent with the interdependence of their tasks. Occasionally one smash-hand might find himself working continuously on the looms of two or three weavers. But these patterns were not common.

The Pattern of Relationships

The overall picture is of a confused pattern of relationships among an aggregate of individuals for whom no stable internal group structure could be discerned. This picture may be both compared and contrasted with that found by Trist and Bamforth in the longwall system of coal-mining.[1] On a longwall face the effect of job-breakdown and task allocation led, especially on the filling shift, to a similar aggregate of individuals with no stable internal group structure; but the sequential nature of the process resulted in splitting and isolation and in the segregation of those engaged on component tasks both between and within shifts. In the automatic shed the continuous nature of the process and the simultaneous performance of all component tasks led to confusion.

Of the assumptions about task and work-group organization stated in Chapter 4, few could be satisfied by the conditions in the automatic shed. According to production-study figures, there were neither more nor fewer engaged in the shed than were required, yet there were disappointment and varying opinions about the effectiveness of performance. Because the workers formed only an aggregate and not a group, and because jobs were broken down into component operations, none experienced either as an individual or as a group member the completion of a whole task. Nor could they have stable and secure relationships. Far from promoting any chance of self-government, the multiple lines of executive communication and the varying numbers of looms resulted in a confused pattern of authority and responsibility, with few being sure about the boundaries of their own and others' 'territories'.

With the exception of the pairs of jobbers and assistant jobbers, there was no group but only an aggregate of twenty-nine workers on each shift. The only differentiation was into two shift operating systems and the only equivalent aggregate to which disaffected members could be transferred was the other shift. Though the range of skills was comprehensible to all members of the aggregate and tasks were hierarchically structured, with some provision for promotion from one grade to another, there were far too many grades—nine—as represented by levels of pay. There was no interchange of task.

THE MANAGING SYSTEM

The Management Organization

Another consequence of allocating one task to one role together with variation in loom allocation was that the workers could not be conveniently grouped for supervision. So many were the jobbers' techno-

[1] Trist, E. L., and Bamforth, K. W., 'Some Social and Psychological Consequences of the Long-wall Method of Coal-Getting,' *Human Relations*, 1951, Vol. IV, No. 1.

logical tasks and so undefined their supervising responsibility that the Shift Supervisor had to assist them by dealing directly with their nominal subordinates. In spite of the supposed responsibility of the jobbers for other workers and of the weavers for smash-hands, the Shift Supervisor was in fact directly responsible for twenty-seven different individuals. Only the assistant jobbers did not report to him. A chart of the organization of one shift is shown in simplified form in *Figure 2*. It was not possible to represent all lines of communication and theoretical authority.

The Top Supervisor was the Company's specialist on the erection, maintenance, and running of automatic looms. With the assistance of an erection engineer from the suppliers, he had installed the looms and got the shed going. He had trained the first workers and the first Shift Supervisors, and adjusted and tuned the first looms. By March 1953 these development tasks were finished and others could perform them as routine operations. Formally, he now had little to do, for while in the shed he had only one immediate subordinate (the Shift Supervisor) to direct. His other work (that of coordinating with the departments from which he imported 'raw materials' and to which he exported 'finished products') took little of his time. Yet the Shift Supervisor had so much to do in handling work allocations and relationships that the Top Supervisor had to deal directly with jobbers and other workers; thus, in formal terms, by-passing his own subordinate.

This breakdown of the formal organization placed a high premium on the quality of the relationships between the Top Supervisor, the Shift Supervisors, and the workers. The absence of overt difficulties was a tribute to their capacity for tolerating the confusion of responsibility and authority. In addition, the Managing Agent, the Mill Manager, and the Works Manager,[1] were giving considerable attention to the shed. While this attention had helped to strengthen shed and shift management and to maintain morale, their frequent presence had helped also to increase the confusion of the executive organization.

The Control and Service Functions of the Managing System

Formally, the managing system contained only the Top Supervisor and his two Shift Supervisors, representing shed and shift management. Two major control functions, inspection and production study, were carried out by other departments external to the shed. The lack of internal struc-

[1] These roles and their relationships are discussed in Part V.

FIGURE 2 OUTLINE ORGANIZATION CHART OF ONE SHIFT OF THE AUTOMATIC LOOM SHED

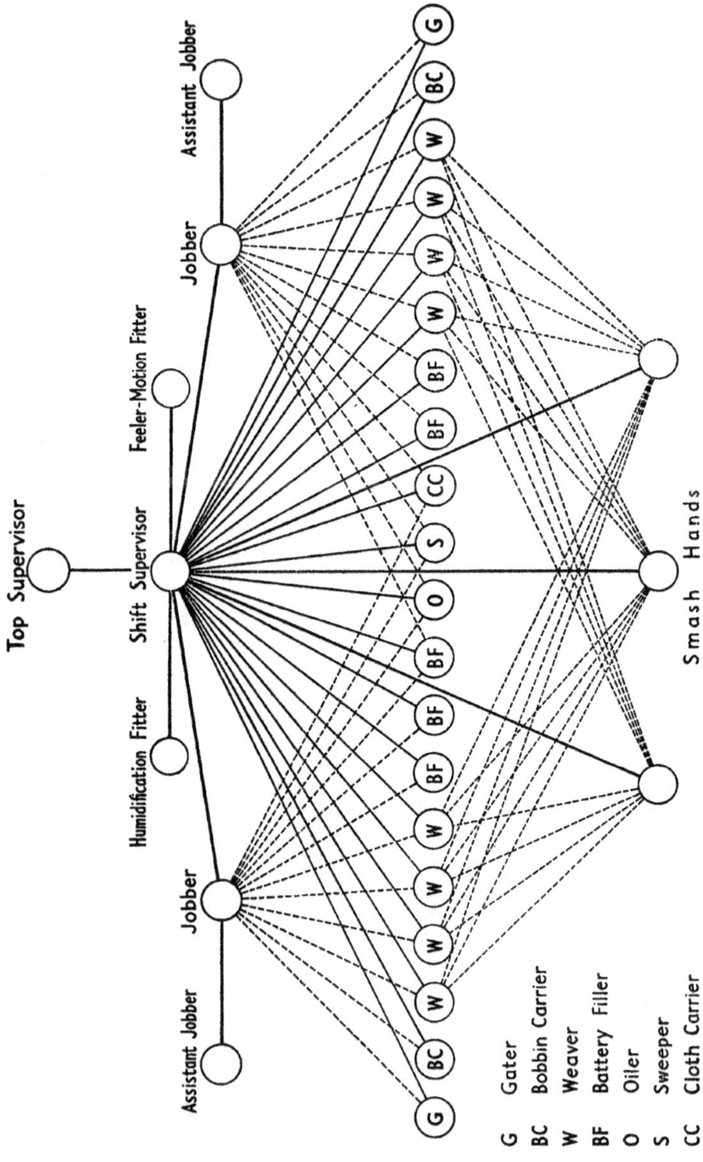

ture in each of the two operating systems had been counterbalanced by the reinforcement of shift management by the Top Supervisor, while higher management attention compensated for the organizational weakness of shed management. In practice the managing system included members of higher management in addition to its formal members, but did not include two of the control functions essential to it. In spite of apparently good relationships, there was an unacknowledged implication that higher management had insufficient confidence in the capacity of the shed managing system to control and service its own operating systems.

Faced with the short-fall in expected productivity there appeared to be, apart from minor technological improvements, two possibilities. The first was still further to strengthen the shed managing system and the external controls by increasing the number of supervisors and tightening inspection. The second was reorganization: to transform the managing system by adding appropriate control functions while creating some kind of stable internal group structure for the working aggregates on the two shifts. The danger of increasing the number of supervisors and of tightening inspection without reorganization was that the implicit vote of no confidence in shed and shift management would be reaffirmed. The workers would not only continue to experience the discomfort of their unstructured confusion but would feel further coerced and policed. In consequence, they might be expected to increase their resistance to greater effort and productivity.

CHAPTER 7

Reorganization

Examination of the existing system of automatic weaving had shown that all tasks in the shed were interdependent, but that many of the individual workers were independent. They were linked only through the Shift Supervisor. Even those with interdependent relationships had varying degrees of interdependence on overlapping numbers of looms. The shed was too big and there were too many workers to permit stable, cohesive relationships between the members of shift aggregates. The confusion of task relationships precluded the formation of small, structured, and internally led work-groups consistent with the interdependence of tasks.

Job-breakdown and consequent specialization had reduced the quality and range of skills in the automatic as compared with other loom sheds. Weavers, unlike those on non-automatic looms, no longer had to service their looms, refill shuttles, or stop the looms to prevent damage. The automatic loom itself had become the weaver. In spite of the persistence of the title, 'weaver', the weaver's task could more accurately be described as warp-mending, and the weaver himself as a warp-mender.

Specialization of task had restricted the possibilities of task and role rotation. Labour turnover was low; only the prospect of completion of the shed and the installation of more looms held out any real hope of promotion or transfer. Even such an event offered no more than the opportunity of transfer from one specialized task to another. Mobility was further restricted by the many different grades and, since the grades were allied to rates of pay, almost any exchange of task would have involved a change of pay—easy to accomplish only in one direction. In effect, the workers were chained to their roles and tasks. Attention was therefore directed to the work organization, and the tasks and roles of the loom shed were re-examined.

A NEW LOOK AT ROLES AND TASKS

Roles

Smash-hands were already accepted as weavers in training; and the weaver depended on the efficiency with which the battery-filler performed his task. The battery-fillers in their turn had aspirations to become weavers. Assistant jobbers were already members of a pair, and gaters sometimes assisted jobbers to get looms running. The feeler-motion maintenance fitter was responsible for a specialist part of general loom maintenance. The oiler was under the nominal control of both jobbers, and although the sweeper, the bobbin-carrier, and the cloth-carrier had each a special task and were not considered interchangeable, they and the oiler were all graded as unskilled.

In spite of the breakdown of tasks into component operations there appeared to be occupational roles closely allied to each other in terms of the skills required and the operations performed. Such roles could be considered as at least partially interchangeable.

Tasks

The primary task of the automatic loom shed—the conversion of yarn to cloth—is only carried out when the looms are running. All operations in the shed, therefore, have to do with keeping looms weaving. But individual tasks may be differentiated by reference to the directness of their relationships to the overall primary task. Thus warp-mending, battery-filling, and smash-tenting are directly concerned with the weaving loom, while gating, maintaining, and oiling are directed to getting the loom ready for weaving and keeping it repaired. Sweeping, bobbin-carrying, and cloth-carrying, while being essential services, were less closely related to actual weaving in that some delay in their performance would not immediately cause a hold-up in production.

Individual tasks and workers could also be differentiated according to loom stops. Loom stops are of two kinds: short stops of from half a minute to a minute for simple yarn breaks, and long stops of from one to two hours for gating, or of from half an hour to a whole day for smashes. Also to be counted as long stops were the half-hour meal breaks, and the seven hours between the second and first shifts. During actual shift hours workers could be divided into those whose tasks were directed to keeping the looms running through short stops and those whose tasks were to get the looms weaving again after a long stop. Thus weavers were concerned with restarting looms after short stops, while gaters and jobbers entered the picture when the loom was stopped for replacing exhausted with full beams. At the same time, the jobber, assistant jobber, feeler-motion fitter and oiler had to use the opportunity of a long stop to obtain access to the loom for maintenance work. Even the sweeper had to use that time as his only opportunity to get under the loom to remove accumulated fluff. Smash-hands were concerned with long stops, but they had aspirations to become weavers, and their training was directed to their being able to perform the more rapid operations of short stops. Only battery-fillers, bobbin-carriers, and cloth-carriers were not dependent in some way upon loom stops since their tasks could be carried out on the running loom; but so far as battery-fillers could be considered as able to become assistants to the weavers, they too become concerned with short stops. The humidification fitter was the only one not concerned directly with looms. He was, therefore, ignored in the subsequent analysis.

Two analyses of tasks concerned with looms therefore appeared possible: a temporal analysis according to the state of the loom—whether running or stopped for a short or a long period—and an activity analysis according to whether the tasks being performed were concerned directly with weaving, with gating and maintenance, or with ancillary services. The two analyses with related occupational roles are given in *Table 1*.

For gating and maintenance they yield exactly the same and for ancillary services virtually the same result. Only in weaving does a discrepancy appear, but the underlying unity of the grouping is indicated by the fact that both battery-fillers and smash-tenters were training to become weavers and were therefore concerned with short stops.

It was therefore suggested that three task and worker groupings might be brought into being: one for weaving, one for gating and maintenance, and one for ancillary services. Each of these groupings would be consistent as to activity and would not be so inconsistent as to tempo as to make personal relationships impossible.

Such groupings would not however provide any one group with a 'whole' task. Moreover, apart from the numbers that might be required, they would have to work over the whole shed. Only if a group of appropriate size could be formed at least combining the duties of weaving and of gating and maintenance, would its members experience 'closure' in terms of the total task they performed. How this might be obtained was the next question to be taken up. Could there be formed a group of workers for a group of looms?

Table 1. ANALYSIS OF AUTOMATIC LOOM SHED TASKS

Activity	*Tasks*	*Tasks Concerned with* *Short Stops*	*Long Stops*	*Running Looms*	*Occupational Roles*
Weaving	Warp-mending	X			Weaver
	Battery-filling	(X)		X	Battery-filler
	Smash-tenting	(X)	X		Smash-hand
Gating and Maintenance	Gating		X		Gater
	Maintaining		X		Jobber / Assistant Jobber
	Maintaining (special)		X		Feeler-motion Fitter
	Oiling		X		Oiler
Ancillary Services	Sweeping		(X)	X	Sweeper
	Bobbin-carrying			X	Bobbin-carrier
	Cloth-carrying			X	Cloth-carrier

A GROUP OF WORKERS FOR A GROUP OF LOOMS

Variations in Numbers Required with Change of Sort

The problem was complicated by two variable conditions that occasioned change in the number of workers employed in the different occupational roles. These variables were the frequency of short stops and yarn count. Warp-thread breakages, which cause short stops, are mended by weavers, so that the frequency of short stops determines the number required. The amount of yarn carried on beams and bobbins varies directly with yarn count; the higher the count, the more is it possible to wind; the longer therefore will beam and bobbin last. Work studies showed that variations in yarn count required variations in the numbers of battery-fillers and gaters. On the other hand little change was required in the number of cloth- and bobbin-carriers, and virtually none elsewhere.

Variations in yarn count are determined by the sort woven. Current performance suggested that the frequency of warp-thread breakages, and therefore of short stops, could also be standardized for different sorts. Hence the number of workers required for all the various roles where change occurs (weavers, battery-fillers, and gaters) could be related to sort.

To examine the limits of these changes in the number of workers required, the theoretical number of looms that could be attended by these grades was calculated for each sort likely to be woven. The results were then converted to show the number of workers theoretically required to attend 960 looms. The figure 960 was chosen arbitrarily to give a large enough number to avoid too much approximation.

It was found that there were considerable variations in the numbers required for warp-mending, battery-filling, and gating over the whole range. Nevertheless they could be grouped into three main categories. In these comparatively little variation occurred in the numbers required for warp-mending and battery-filling taken together or for gating. These main categories corresponded to coarse, medium, and fine yarn counts.[1]

Provided warp-mending and battery-filling could be regarded as partly interchangeable tasks, two kinds of workers would be required, whose numbers would vary with change of sort: those concerned with warp-mending and battery-filling and those concerned with gating. The numbers required for all other tasks would remain the same.[2]

Theoretical Work-Group Organization

Inspection of the loom shed showed that wide gangways and pillars divided the loom shed most conveniently into blocks of sixty-four looms. An outline plan of the shed is shown in *Figure 1*. Further constructional work and the installation of more looms would turn the block of forty-eight looms marked '*c*' into another block of sixty-four. If, therefore, any experimental reorganization was to be tried, it seemed appropriate to start with a group of sixty-four looms as an easily recognizable 'territory'.

The results of the calculations of the numbers required for 960 looms were combined with the results of the re-examination of roles and tasks, and the figures reduced to show the numbers required for a block of sixty-

[1] The detailed figures for these calculations are given in Appendix 1, *Tables 3* and *4*. Variations in the numbers required for cloth-carrying and bobbin-carrying with change of sort even over so large a number of looms as 960 were found to be too small to merit consideration.

[2] The numbers required for other tasks were calculated on the assumption that the numbers in the existing shed would be adequate for two hundred and forty looms. For details of these calculations see *Tables 5* and *6*. Appendix 1.

FIGURE 1 *PLAN OF AUTOMATIC LOOM SHED*

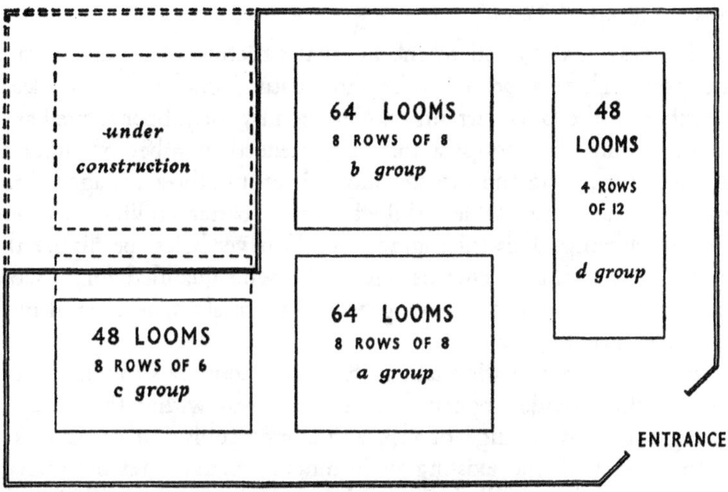

four looms. These are given in *Table 2*, in which, since as yet the exercise was purely theoretical and based on existing production studies, no rounding-off was attempted. It was noted, however, that the total numbers required for a block of sixty-four looms for coarse, medium, and fine

Table 2. THEORETICAL NUMBERS OF WORKERS REQUIRED FOR 64 LOOMS

Sub-Group	*Tasks*	*Numbers Required for each Main Sort* *Coarse*	*Medium*	*Fine*
Weaving	Warp-mending and Battery-filling	4·0	2·8	2·5
	Smash-tenting	0·8	0·8	0·8
Gating and Maintenance	Gating and Maintaining	2·1	2·1	1·5
	Oiling	0·3	0·3	0·3
Ancillary Services	Sweeping	0·3	0·3	0·3
	Bobbin-carrying	0·3	0·3	0·3
	Cloth-carrying	0·5	0·5	0·5
Totals		8·3	7·1	6·2

counts, alike fell within the range (6–12) that satisfied the assumption about the appropriate size of work-groups.

Grades, Wages, and Titles

Attention was next turned to the internal structure of a possible small work-group. There appeared to be three natural grades: a group leader responsible for the tasks currently undertaken by the jobber as well as for those of leading the group; a fully experienced member of either the weaving or the gating and maintenance sub-group; those engaged almost entirely on the relatively less skilled jobs of battery-filling, sweeping, oiling, or carrying. This third grade should nevertheless be higher than that of a new unskilled entrant since those who qualified for it would already have been accepted, having proved themselves, as integral members of a working group.

It was taken as axiomatic that any form of internally structured work-group should provide opportunities for progress within the group by allowing some interchange of task and some acquisition of new skills. This together with the existing wide differences in wages between the fully skilled and the unskilled suggested that another grade should be interpolated between the second and third. This new grade was reserved for those who had earned promotion from the third but had not yet acquired sufficient skill for the second.

Higher management felt that some increase over the current jobber's rate should be given to any worker appointed as a group leader. There was also, at the time, an outstanding request from the weavers for a rate yielding Rs. 132 at eighty-five per cent efficiency. It was further agreed that if any experiment were carried out, all members of a group should be paid on the same basis. Whereas previously only jobbers and weavers had been paid piece rates, all members would now participate. Tentatively, five grades and five monthly wage rates based on eighty-five per cent efficiency were suggested for discussion with the supervisors and workers. These are given in *Table 3*. Provided eighty-five per cent efficiency could be reached, all members joining an experimental group, with the exception of those previously employed as battery-fillers, would receive some small rise in pay.

It was recognized that current titles given to occupational roles would not be appropriate in a reorganized internally-led small work-group, since so many tasks had been made interchangeable. Various possible titles were

Table 3. GRADES, SKILL, AND WAGES FOR EXPERIMENTAL WORK GROUP

Grade		*Monthly Wages* Experimental Group*	*Equivalent Monthly Wages Existing Grades*
		Rs	*Rs*
A	Overall group leader, working head of gating and maintenance sub-group	170	153
B	Fully skilled member of either weaving or gating and maintenance sub-group	132	88–128
C	Not yet fully skilled member of sub-group but has acquired enough skill to help with main sub-group tasks	90	–
D	Full members of group mainly engaged on less skilled jobs, battery-filling, oiling, etc.	45	28–45
E	New unskilled entrant not yet accepted as group member	28	28

* All wage figures exclude Dearness Allowance.

suggested, but the danger of expressing, consciously or unconsciously, hopes, expectations, doubts, and fears about the outcome of the experiment led to a decision to await discussion with the supervisors and workers before trying to define further either the new grades or the new roles.

IMPLEMENTATION

Spontaneous Acceptance of Reorganization

The Managing Agent, with the consent of the Mill Manager and the Works Manager, decided to discuss the proposed experiment with the Weaving Master, the supervisors, and the workers. Provided the discussions were satisfactory and volunteers forthcoming, an experiment would be started on one block of sixty-four looms on one shift. The Weaving Master was called into the meeting. As soon as he heard of the notion of *a group of workers for a group of looms* he spontaneously accepted the proposed reorganization. His acceptance of the idea in this way, which took higher management by surprise, provided a first validation of its 'goodness to fit' with the 'felt needs' of those working in the automatic shed.

The Works Manager started discussions with the supervisors the same evening. It had been expected that it would take some time for the discussions to be held. There would be meetings first with the Top Supervisor, then with the Supervisors of each shift, and finally with the workers. It appeared likely that several discussions would be needed at each level. It was also expected that the first experimental group would be chosen by the Top Supervisor in consultation with the Shift Supervisors and the Works Manager. In the event, the supervisors and workers immediately took possession of the system. By the next day, through a complex process of mutual choice far too rapid to permit investigation,[1] the workers had themselves organized two experimental groups—one for each of the two blocks of looms ('*a*' and '*b*') on the first shift. By the following day two more groups had been organized by the workers of the other shift for the same two blocks of looms. There were only medium counts on the looms and each spontaneously chosen work-group consisted of seven workers, four in the weaving sub-group and three in the gating and maintenance sub-group. Between then they said they could cope with all the ancillary services. The composition of the groups is given in *Table 4*.

Table 4. COMPOSITION OF SPONTANEOUSLY FORMED EXPERIMENTAL GROUPS

	Number in each Sub-Group		
Grade	*Weaving*	*Gating and Maintenance*	*Total*
A		1	1
B	2	1	3
D	2	1	3
Totals	4	3	7

This spontaneous acceptance and formation of internally-led small work-groups was both surprising and reassuring. But it worried as well as pleased members of higher management, who felt that they had lost control of the situation. The actual members of the groups, as chosen by the workers, were not those who would have been picked by the Works

[1] Moreno, J. L., *Who Shall Survive?*, Washington, Beacon House, 1934.

Manager. Was the spontaneity displayed by the workers more important than the actual group composition? After much discussion higher management accepted, though not without misgivings, that it was. They decided to allow the groups as chosen by the workers to carry on for an experimental period whose length would be determined by events.

Other Aspects of the Analysis

There were a number of other questions to which answers could not immediately be obtained. Some of these concerned the uniformity of the level of mechanization in the various shed operations. Others would have involved changes in other parts of the total textile manufacturing process. Changing the level of mechanization in some operations required the solution of engineering problems by the invention or development of further mechanical devices. Some alterations—for example, those related to the removal of fluff—were awaiting the arrival of equipment already ordered.

One outstanding question was that of the long stops caused by meal breaks and by intervals between shifts. The purpose of an automatic machine is to run without attention. I decided, however, not to suggest for the present any alteration in the current practice during meal breaks. The question of intervals between shifts was affected by current attitudes to third-shift working. Sleeping during the daytime is so difficult for most people in Ahmedabad that the third shift was unpopular both with workers and with management. By practice and by law no rotation of shifts was possible. Management believed that neither good workers nor good supervisors would consent to work on the permanent third shift. Experience had shown that when third shifts had been worked efficiency became lower and damage higher. Again, apart from insisting that full machine utilization was desirable, I left for future consideration any question of altering current practice.

The surprisingly rapid acceptance of the experimental work organization, and the decision to allow the experimental groups to start immediately, gave no time for adequate consideration of shift management or the proper location of production study and inspection. The formation of two experimental groups on each shift represented the beginning of a second order of differentiation in the loom shed production system. Each shift supervisor would have reporting to him two group leaders responsible for their own working groups, but, as the other looms in the shed would still be working on the old system, an undifferentiated aggregate would persist alongside the new groups. Not unnaturally, both higher and shed management felt that enough change was taking place for the present, and even that not sufficiently controlled. Further reorganization was left until the outcome of the first experimental groups could be known and the results studied.

CHAPTER 8

The First Results

The four experimental groups started work on 30th March and the experimental period, extending over fifty-nine working days, lasted until 7th June, when the rest of the shed was reorganized in the same way and a partial third shift started on the *a* and *c* blocks of looms.

I left India to return to London on the seventh day of the experimental period and was able to observe for myself the results of the reorganization for only the first few days. The quantitative results and the account of the remainder of the period were sent on to me by the Works Manager. I discussed them with the Managing Agent during his visit to England in the summer of 1953, and with the Works Manager on my return to India in the autumn, when, as will be described later, a further investigation became necessary.

EVENTS AND INDICES
30TH MARCH TO 6TH JUNE 1953

Four Phases to the Experimental Period

The experimental period can be described in four phases characterized by changes in the experimental conditions, the beginning and end of each phase being marked by events which showed that a change had occurred.

The first phase covered the eleven working days immediately following the formation of the four experimental groups. There was an increase in efficiency but at the cost of an increase in percentage damage and of neglect of loom maintenance. On the second day a breakdown in the humidification plant flooded a part of the shed, spoiled twenty-five beams in the experimental groups, and halted the whole shed for just over an hour. In spite of this breakdown, efficiency was higher than before reorganization. The increased damage and neglect were discussed by the Works Manager with the supervisors, group leaders, and workers, who expressed their worry but said that they were unable to keep damage down and efficiency up and also attend to maintenance while working with short stops at the current rate. A check showed that short stops were between 1·5 and 2·0 per loom per hour, whereas for the sorts being woven a mean rate of 1·4 was standard.

Observation of the experimental groups during the first few days gave a remarkable picture. Members of the weaving sub-group ran to stopped looms; even gaters carrying beams weighing over two hundred pounds on their shoulders were seen trotting. Except when members of the gating and maintenance sub-group were actually engaged on their assigned tasks, they too ran to stopped looms to help the weaving sub-group. The workers in the rest of the shed asked for permission to reorganize themselves in the same way as the experimental groups. They were asked to wait until more results were available.

The second phase lasted three working days, during which the Top Supervisor personally took over the leadership of one of the groups in order to investigate the possibility of keeping up efficiency while avoiding increased damage and decreased maintenance. As a result, extra help at the rate of half an extra Grade D worker was given to each group.

The third phase of eight working days started when the Top Supervisor relinquished active group leadership. A general resettlement followed his investigation. Efficiency climbed, damage remained less than before the experiment started, and loom maintenance was restored.

Discussions took place between the Works Managers, supervisors, group leaders, and workers about the running of looms during meal intervals. The fourth phase started when looms were not stopped by the workers at the beginning of the meal break but were allowed to run on until they stopped automatically when yarn broke. Because industrial legislation lays down that no worker shall remain in his workplace during a meal break, and because enthusiasm was so great, a supervisor had to remain in the shed during meal breaks to make sure that members of groups neither stayed at work after the beginning of the break nor returned before it ended. The extra help given in the third phase was withdrawn, although checks showed that short stops still averaged 1·6 per loom per hour.

After thirty-seven days the request of the workers in the rest of the shed to reorganize themselves in the same way as the experimental groups was granted. A partial third shift was started on one of the blocks of sixty-four

Table 1. PHASES OF THE EXPERIMENTAL PERIOD AND EVENTS OF THE CHANGE PROCESS

Phase	*Period*	*Number of Working Days*	*Events of the Experimental Process*	*Events related to the Experimental Process*
1.	30 March–10 April	11	The four groups, *a*I, *a*II, *b*I and *b*II, formed spontaneously by the workers started work. Loom stoppage rates over standard. Increase in efficiency and in damage. Loom maintenance neglected. Discussions between Works Manager, supervisors, group leaders, and workers about damage and maintenance.	Other workers in shed request similar reorganization. Breakdown in humidification plant.
2.	11 April–14 April	3	Top Supervisor acted as leader of one group. Investigation of reasons for increase in damage. Extra help given to groups. Fall in efficiency and in damage. Loom maintenance restored.	
3.	15 April–23 April	8	Top Supervisor relinquished group leadership. Recovery in efficiency to level of first phase.	Discussions between Works Manager, Top Supervisor, group leaders, and workers about investigation and about running during meal breaks.
4.	24 April–6 June	37	Looms not stopped at beginning of meal breaks. Extra help withdrawn. Increase in efficiency without increase in damage.	Beginning of reorganization of other looms in shed on same system as in experimental groups. Preparations for starting third shift, and new workers engaged.

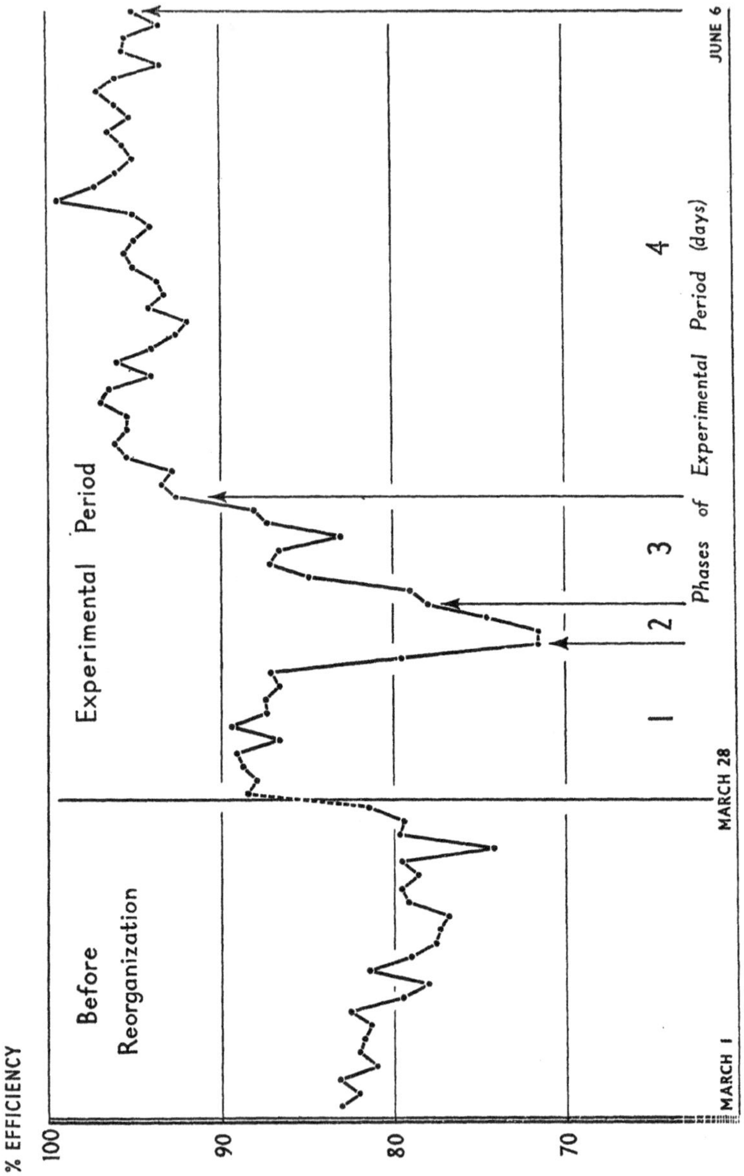

FIGURE I PERCENTAGE EFFICIENCY BEFORE AND AFTER REORGANIZATION

FIGURE 2 PERCENTAGE DAMAGE BEFORE AND AFTER REORGANIZATION

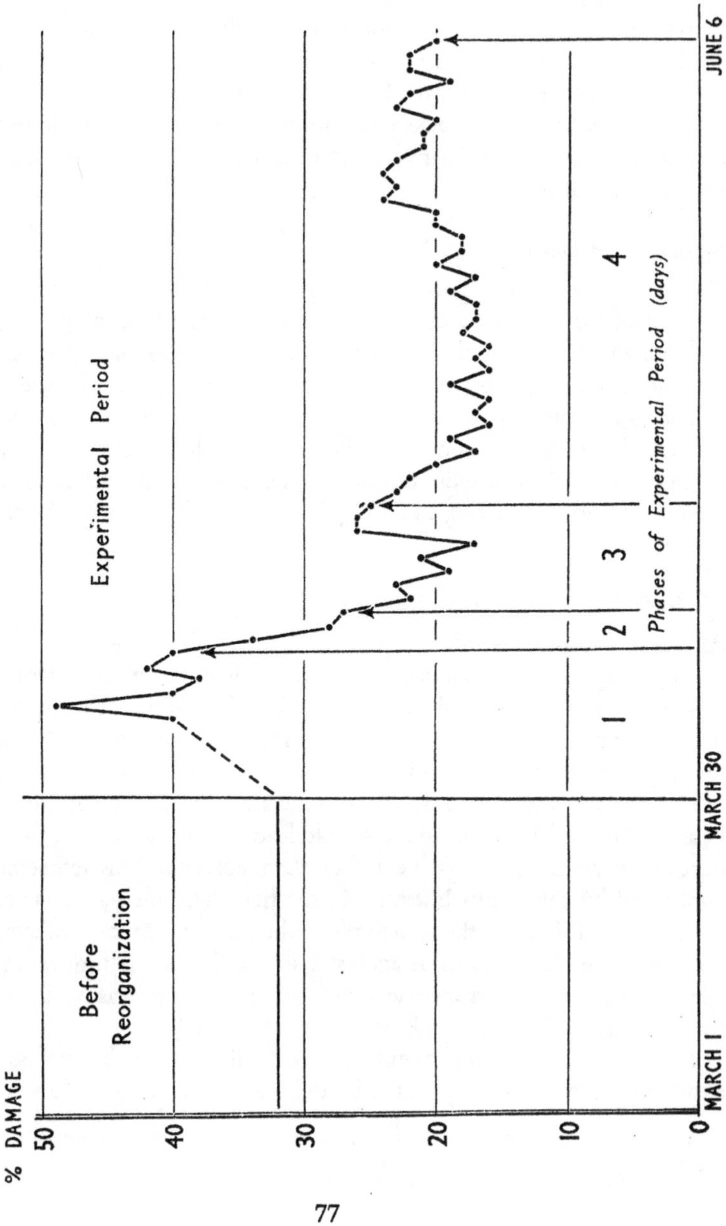

looms and on one of the blocks of forty-eight. Results thereafter are not, therefore, directly comparable with those of the experimental period.

The phases of the experimental period, the events of the experimental process and other events directly related to it are shown chronologically in *Table 1*. In this table blocks of looms are designated by the letters *a*, *b*, etc., and shifts by the Roman numerals I and II. Work-groups then become *a* I, *a* II, etc.

Efficiency and Damage

The results of the comparison of the mean percentage efficiencies and damage of the experimental groups with the mean percentage efficiency and damage of the shed before reorganization are shown in *Figures 1* and *2*.[1] The increase in efficiency due to running through meal breaks is included in the fourth phase results. The period before reorganization, from 1st March to 28th March, was chosen as the longest period available during which allowance did not have to be made for disturbances, resulting in lowered efficiencies, caused by building activities or by the erection of new looms.

Efficiency and Damage in the Rest of the Shed

An examination of the efficiency and damage results in the rest of the shed strongly suggests an induction effect from the experimental groups.

Theoretically, the rest of the shed continued with the previous form of organization during the experimental period. The formation of the experimental groups, however, had a disturbing effect and involved a reallocation of tasks and work-loads. This disturbance, apart from any feelings of being left out of the experiment, would lead one to expect that the induction effect would be negative rather than positive. This expectation is confirmed by the results but only in the first three phases of the experimental period. During the fourth phase the mean percentage efficiency of the rest of the shed was 81 as against a shed efficiency before reorganization of 80 per cent, and the mean percentage damage was 23 as against a shed damage before reorganization of 32 per cent.[2]

The view that this improvement was a reflection of the success of the experimental groups is supported by the requests from those concerned to

[1] Detailed results and comments for each experimental group are given in Appendix 1, *Tables 7*, *8*, *9*, and *10*.

[2] The full figures are given in *Table 11* of Appendix 1.

be allowed to reorganize themselves in the same way as the experimental groups.

SOME IMMEDIATE CONSEQUENCES

Short Stop Frequencies and Absenteeism

The experience during the first phase directed attention to the consequences of variations in the conditions under which the groups were working. Work-load calculations, and hence calculations of the number of workers required for any of the three main categories of sorts, had been made on the assumption that standard frequencies of short stops would be maintained. Increase in the standard frequency would clearly increase the work-load of the task of warp-mending. While this might reduce other work-loads, since high efficiencies would not be possible with high stoppage rates, any such decrease could not possibly balance the increased load in warp-mending. Theoretical calculations of the variations in overall work-load caused by an increased frequency of short stops were not practical without further studies under the new experimental conditions. It was agreed that studies should be made and that extra assistance would be given to the groups as required.

Moreover, change of sort, even within the main categories, did cause some variations in work-load as between the different tasks of the working group, and it was agreed that, so far as possible, the same sort should be kept continuously on all the looms of each group.

Partly because of the climate, and partly because of the accepted importance of religious festivals, absenteeism in India tends to be higher than in Great Britain and the United States. A marriage ceremony, for example, is more complex and lasts longer than its equivalent in the West, and attendance by even distant relatives is almost obligatory, however inconvenient it might be, or however much travelling it might entail. The taking of two weeks' leave to attend a distant cousin's wedding in a remote village is accepted by both management and workers as reasonable and normal. Against this higher absenteeism, it must be remembered that the working week is of six full days. Average absenteeism in the mill as a whole was twelve per cent. It was agreed that sufficient additional workers would be kept in the shed to provide replacements for normal absenteeism.

Spare members entering groups to make up either for a higher frequency of short stops or for absentees might be difficult to assimilate as temporary members. It was hoped to obviate some, if not all, of these difficulties by creating a highly skilled group of spare workers who would be welcomed for their technical contribution, if for no other reason.

Management

The immediate effect on shift management after the shed had begun to settle down to the reorganization was that the number reporting directly to the Shift Supervisor was reduced. Although those workers not included in the experimental groups still continued as before reorganization, those in the experimental groups were now responsible to their group leaders. In addition, workers requiring training, instead of being spread over the whole shed, could now be concentrated on one block of forty-eight looms. Here they could receive more direct attention. When, at the end of the fourth phase, the other two blocks of looms were reorganized, the Shift Supervisor was left with only four group leaders and the humidification fitter reporting directly to him. Instead of the shed needing more supervision, there was every chance that the present supervisors would become under-employed.

By the end of the experimental period two courses of action previously regarded as being unlikely to succeed had been initiated. The first was to allow looms to run on during meal breaks without attention; the second, to start a third shift. It had always been felt that the return after the meal break with the majority of the looms stopped would prove so disheartening as seriously to reduce efficiency, and a third shift had come to be thought of as too troublesome to be worth while. Yet when the first measure was put into operation during the fourth phase, far from reducing efficiency, it increased it. As the starting of the second marked the end of the fourth phase, results were not available in the experimental period. The shift was started however with far fewer misgivings than usual about low efficiencies and high damage.

During the experimental period higher management began to take a less active part in shed management, not so much as part of a consciously determined plan, but as a result of increased confidence in the ability of those in the shed to solve their own problems. Some months later, the Managing Agent, when in England, said, 'Whereas I always spent some time in the automatic shed every time I went to the Jubilee Mill (on average twice a week), I don't think I've been in more than two or three times since it was reorganized, not because I've lost any of my interest in it, but because I know it is going well.'

THE END OF THE EXPERIMENTAL PERIOD

Because of language difficulties and of the speed at which the reorganization was implemented, it was not possible to discover from the workers themselves just why they accepted the new organization with such spontaneity and with so little question. There had been no overt complaints about the existing system and the first discussions about the new, which, on the management's side, were intended to be tentative only, were short and by no means exhaustive.

Neither supervisors nor workers had had any previous experience of the new work organization, nor were they apparently concerned with any of the theoretical reasons for thinking that they might find it more satisfying or more productive. It seems reasonable to infer that their acceptance of 'a group of workers for a group of looms' was the result of an intuitive recognition that it provided a means of satisfying needs of which they had been, and probably still were, largely unaware. Such intuitive acceptance brooked no argument. Nor did it require any reasoned questioning.

Even in the first few days, when they had no real experience on which to base a judgment, their behaviour showed an unmistakable determination to make the new system work. On the second day, when the humidification plant broke down flooding a part of the shed, the Works Manager said that even seventy per cent efficiency would have been creditable but the group most affected achieved over eighty-three per cent. The pace of work of all groups in the first few days was obviously too fast to last. It would have been remarkable under any conditions and in any country. In India, with an outside temperature of over 100 deg. F. and an artificially maintained humidity of 85 per cent, it was extraordinary. Although the pace of work inevitably slowed down after the first phase, the determination remained as evidenced by the need to station a supervisor in the shed during the meal breaks. It was as though the workers had recognized, again intuitively, that the new system so satisfied some of their felt but unexpressed needs that they were afraid that they might lose what they had gained.

The spontaneous creation of four groups as against management's intention of starting with only one, and the immediate request by the workers in the rest of the shed to organize themselves in the same way, were not only further evidence of the satisfaction that was felt to be obtainable but also suggested that the workers' acceptance of the new system was in advance of management's. This was to be expected since management's acceptance was based, not on intuition, but on argued assumptions and on theoretical calculations. In the event, management was distinctly worried by the way the workers 'grabbed' the new system for themselves. Although the immediate increase in efficiency was gratifying, the parallel increase in damage was not reassuring. Only towards the end of the third phase did management begin to accept the internal structuring of small work-groups as a method of management, alternative to that of imposing additional external structure.

The sophisticated behaviour of management, first in permitting the workers to reorganize themselves and then in taking no immediate action when damage rose so sharply, increased the workers' confidence in their capacity to create satisfying conditions for themselves. It probably also increased their fears that unless productivity rose and stayed at a new level, they would have to revert to their former, less satisfying organization. This view was supported to some extent by the workers' attitudes to job descriptions and occupational titles. In discussion with the supervisors, they expressed a positive desire to avoid the old titles of their jobs but no enthusiasm for any new titles other than the 'A', 'B', and 'D' grade designations. Tasks became known as 'A', 'B', and 'D' jobs and those in the appropriate roles as 'A', 'B', 'C', and 'D' workers. This clinging to arbitrary titles suggests that the members of groups not only valued their group membership but also wished to avoid any definitions which might limit the content of the various tasks they performed. It was as though any title or description might jeopardize their new-found freedom by giving rational content to what was only intuitively accepted.

CHAPTER 9

Follow-Up

At the end of October 1953, seven months after the original reorganization and five months after the end of the experimental period, the efficiency of the automatic shed started to fall and the rate of damage to rise. By the middle of November levels were near those of the shed before the experiment. During November and December an investigation was made into the cause of the setback and, as a result, action was taken in the following months to restore the situation—this time permanently.

The investigation was made during my second visit to the Calico Mills from October 1953 to June 1954. For a large part of this time I was accompanied by a colleague, George M. Stalker, who was responsible for the field work of the investigation, and for much of the consultancy activities that followed.

THE COURSE OF EVENTS JUNE TO NOVEMBER 1953

Expansion of the Shed and Extension of the Group System

In accordance with the plan made during the experimental period, one block of forty-eight looms (the *d* block) had been designated a training group. All newcomers went to this before becoming members of a production group. Members of production groups also went to it to be trained for up-grading. By 8th June eight groups were working as self-contained, relatively autonomous primary production systems, with two groups—on the first and second shifts—as training-groups. By the middle of July another training group had been started on the third shift. In October the building of the shed was completed; sixteen more looms were added to the *c* block, turning it into a block of sixty-four looms. The workers of one of the training-groups became a working group, so that there were now three blocks of sixty-four looms (*a*, *b*, and *c*) each working three shifts, and a training block of forty-eight looms (*d*) working two shifts.

During November, December, and January, the *d* block of looms was transferred to the newly constructed part of the shed in order to make room for the forty-eight automatic looms that had been working in another part of the Jubilee Mill since before the war. The final layout is shown in *Figure 1*.

Mixed Sorts

Starting in the summer and continuing through the autumn of 1953, there was a trade recession. In Ahmedabad seven mills closed down. In October twenty-one others were for some time in danger of having to discontinue one of their two shifts. During this recession production planning in the automatic shed was dominated by a capricious and erratic market. Long runs of the same sort could not be arranged. Different sorts had to be put

FIGURE 1 *FINAL LAYOUT OF AUTOMATIC LOOM SHED*

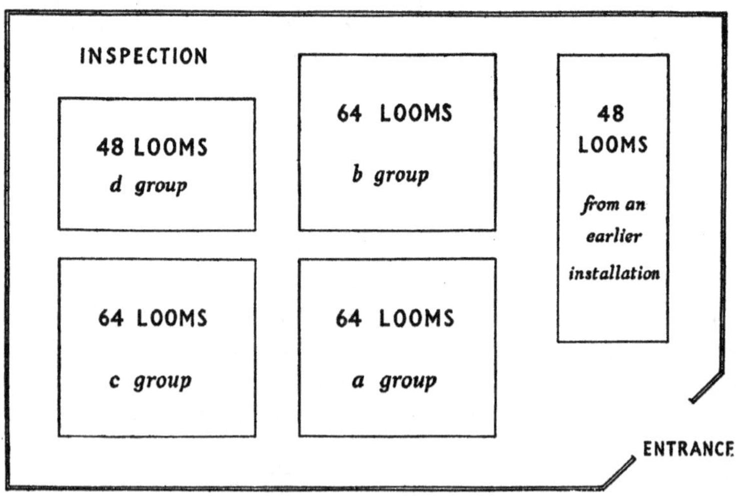

into production as looms became available, every group having a mixture which varied every two or three days. Although all sorts being woven were of medium counts, change from one to the other altered the balance of component tasks in the weaving process. This made it difficult for groups to settle down to a steady rhythm of work.

At the same time the success of the reorganization had encouraged management to experiment with more complex sorts of higher reed and pick than had previously been woven on this kind of loom. It was hoped that the increased efficiency and the better quality now expected would help to satisfy the capricious and discriminating market. To avoid upsetting any one group these experimental sorts were spread among all. They gave rise to special technological problems, particularly in loom-tuning, and stoppage rates differing from those of looms on standard sorts. They thus interfered still further with the settling down to a steady rhythm.

Working-Group Strength

The forty-eight automatic looms that had been working in the Jubilee Mills since before the second World War had been staffed by numbers far in excess of those in the new automatic shed. Their transfer to the new shed had always been intended as soon as construction was completed. The workers on these looms, like those not included in the experimental groups, had also asked to be reorganized but not at the expense of redundancy—a condition that management had accepted. Because of the impending transfer it had been necessary to keep the number of workers in the new shed to a minimum. Only in this way could the expected surplus be absorbed without causing redundancy. In consequence there had been no spare workers either to give the extra help required for higher stoppages or to replace absentees. The condition caused by these shortages became acute in October when both loom stoppage rates and absenteeism were at their highest. The figures for the period June to November are given in *Table 1*.

Table 1. MEAN LOOM STOPPAGE RATES AND LOST TIME PERCENTAGES

Month	*Stoppages per Loom per Hour*	*Lost Time Percentage*
June	2·0	8·1
July	1·7	8·2
August	1·4	8·5
September	1·5	10·7
October	2·1	11·5
November	1·7	9·4

FIGURE 2 PERCENTAGE EFFICIENCY, MARCH — NOVEMBER 1953

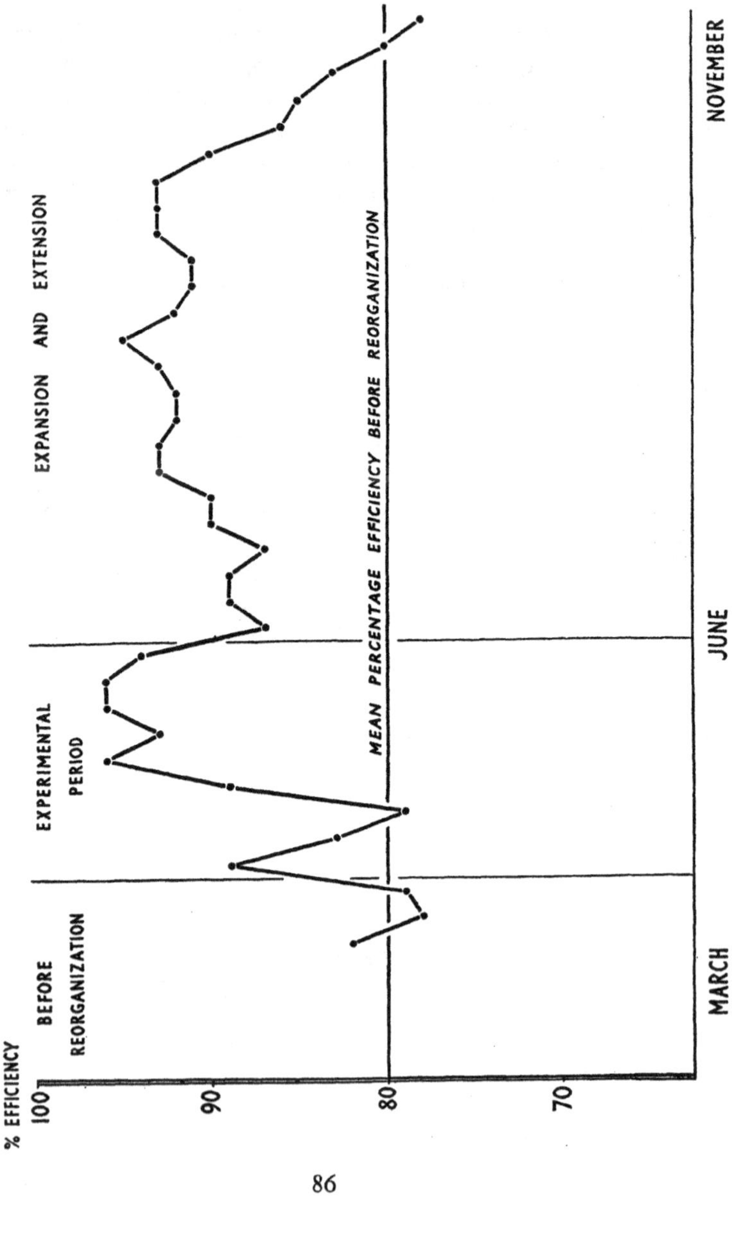

FIGURE 3 PERCENTAGE DAMAGE, MARCH – NOVEMBER 1953

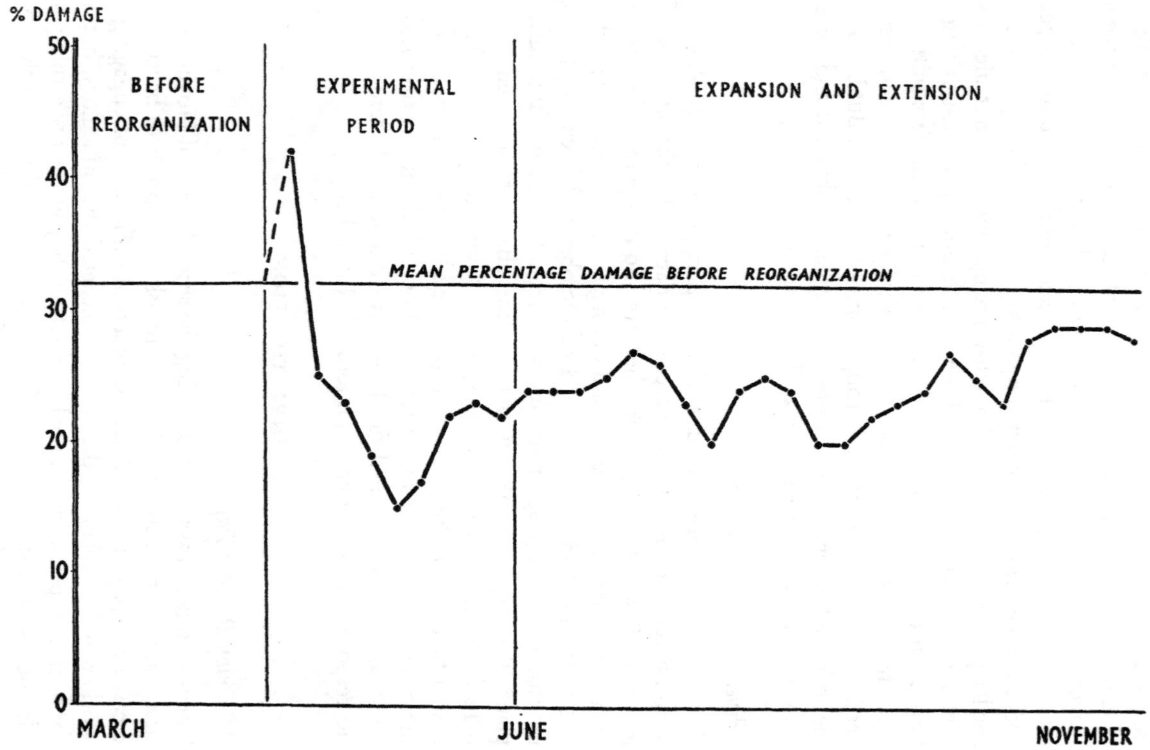

The theoretical numbers of workers required for a group of sixty-four looms for medium sorts (7·1) had been calculated on a standard efficiency of eighty-five per cent and a frequency of loom stoppages for the sorts woven of 1·2 to 1·6 per loom per hour, with a mean at 1·4. In all but two months, stoppage rates had been in excess of the maximum expected.

Some relief had been obtained by taking away from the groups certain ancillary tasks. Sweeping and bobbin-carrying, which did not affect loom-running, had been made shed services; similarly cloth-carrying—the Inspection department continued to work only in the first shift and all cloth had to be removed then. Theoretically these stops withdrew the need for 1·1 workers for each group of sixty-four looms. But by October the increased absenteeism had offset any relief so obtained and no extra help was available for the increased stoppage rate.

Efficiency and Damage Results

The weighted mean efficiencies of all working groups from 8th June to 22nd November 1953 and the percentage damage for the same period are given in *Figures 2* and *3*, where they are also compared with the results obtained before reorganization and during the experimental period.

The fall in efficiency at the end of October had been ascribed to an increase in the stoppage rate caused by trouble with the humidification plant. This explanation, however, became unacceptable when efficiency fell still further in November, in spite of a lower stoppage rate. This suggested that the workers had been stretched beyond their capacities. The increased stoppage rate for October, although little higher than had been dealt with in June, seemed finally to have discouraged them. There was no response to the better conditions of November.

INVESTIGATION

Minimum Rates of Pay

The investigation was started during the second week of November. The first reaction from the workers was to ask for more help because of increased stoppage rates. When the practical difficulties of engaging extra workers were explained, the workers accepted the difficulties, but asked for some compensation for the lower wages they were now earning. Their earnings were tied directly to efficiency and they did not feel that the fall was their fault. After a full discussion it was agreed by management that the basic rates should become minimum rates, and that no deductions would be made for falls in efficiency below eighty-five per cent. What had particularly impressed management was that the spontaneous reaction of the workers to a first inquiry about the fall in efficiency had been task-centred. They had asked for more help. Only when this was found impracticable had they asked for compensation.

Work-Group Composition

The composition of the working and training groups was compared by grades with the establishment for the first experimental groups. The grades were taken as an approximate indication of the skills and capacities of group members. The comparison could not have favoured the working groups since the need for more skilled members was so urgent that workers were put in a higher grade more quickly than they would have been had there been more time for training. Even so only one group was fully manned as regards skill. One group had no leader at all; two had only acting leaders; three out of the nine working groups had C grade workers in place of B and four had only D instead of B. Nine E grade workers, new entrants in training, were working as group members in either the gating and maintenance or the weaving sub-groups. It was the gating and maintenance sub-groups that were particularly understaffed. One had only a group leader, and two D grade workers. Another had only an acting leader with two workers of Grades D and E against an establishment of one A, one B, and one D.[1]

The rapid expansion of the shed and the extension of the group system occurring simultaneously, had necessitated the engagement of new and the upgrading of existing workers. As one consequence, the intended concentration of training in the *d* block of looms had not been maintained; training had become diffused through all groups. A second and even more important consequence was that seven new group leaders had to be found. So far only six had been produced and four of these came from the B grade workers of the gating and maintenance sub-groups of the original experimental groups. The other two had recently completed their training for B grade work.

A check showed, as might have been expected, that maintenance had not been adequately performed for some time. One of the reasons for the higher stoppage rates was inadequate maintenance. But the increase in

[1] The full analysis is given in *Table 12* of Appendix 1.

the stoppage rate had overloaded the weaving sub-group, who required assistance. This could be given only by the group leader and other members of the gating and maintenance sub-group, since no spare workers were available. Inadequate maintenance arose therefore not only from inadequate skills in the gating and maintenance sub-group, but also from their having to neglect their real tasks to help with loom-running. There was no apparent solution other than to allow efficiency to fall while the gating and maintenance sub-group learnt and performed their real tasks and got the looms back into condition again.

The theoretical calculations made for the first experimental groups were re-examined. Two variations were found:

1. Whereas smash-tenting had been regarded before the reorganization as a job that could be performed by 'weavers in training', it was found to require full loom-running skills. B grade workers had to do it. The low status given to smash-tenting resulted in looms, stopped because of a smash, being kept out of commission much longer than was necessary—the B grade workers were too busy, the D grade had insufficient skill.
2. The original calculations had not allowed the group leader any time to perform the task of leading.

Since no one group of looms had been continuously on one sort, final standards of the number of workers required for given stoppage rates could not be established. It was, however, possible to agree temporary standards. In these a theoretical 0·6 of a worker was allowed for the task of group leadership, and from three to six workers were allowed for different stoppage rates.[1]

Sorting Out the Working Groups

It appeared certain that maintenance was so easily neglected in favour of loom-running, and with such harmful consequences, that the maintenance sub-groups had to be trained and adequately staffed as soon as possible. To do this, spare workers had to be provided immediately so that the weaving sub-groups would not continuously milk the maintenance sub-groups. It was decided, as a temporary measure, to sacrifice some production and to close down certain groups. One group on the third shift was accordingly stopped on 20th December, and its workers, with their approval, made available to other groups. This provided some immediate relief, but when

[1] The full table of temporary standards is given in *Table 13*, Appendix 1.

in February 1954, because of market demands, more experimental cloths, not previously woven in the automatic shed, had to be tried, the position once more became difficult and another group on the third shift was also closed down and its members reallocated.

The level of all workers was re-examined. After full discussion with the group leaders it was decided to divide the groups into three classes:

1. Production groups—fully staffed with adequately skilled workers, whose results would be judged by efficiency and damage.
2. Transition groups—still short of some skills but capable of being fully staffed within a comparatively short time—also to be judged on efficiency and damage.
3. Training groups—to be judged on the output of skilled group members rather than on the output of good quality cloth.

The sorting out of the groups into these three classes was carried out by the group leaders. They found, on the one hand, that their choices of individuals frequently overlapped and, on the other, that they sometimes chose workers who, in the opinion of the supervisors, were not yet adequately trained. Skill levels were reconsidered by supervisors and group leaders together. After discussion the supervisors drew up a list of approved gradings for all workers. Group leaders' choices, however, still overlapped. The suggestion that the worker concerned might then be allowed to choose his group leader was received with surprise, but ultimately adopted.

The sorting out took some time, not being complete until the end of March 1954. On 1st April there were only two fully staffed production groups, five transition, and two training groups. Four months later there were still only five production groups. Not until December could the two groups closed down be restarted. A new group was also added then and the expansion at last completed.

Training and Promotion

While the provision of two groups as training groups would serve to give practice in the group system of working, they would hardly provide adequate training opportunities for the basic skills of maintenance, gating, tuning, and loom-running. Two looms were therefore erected in a small room off the main loom shed as training looms. Training was then designed as a two-phase process:

1. The first phase would cover training in basic skills either for newcomers or for those about to be up-graded. The principles and conditions of work in the automatic loom shed would be discussed.
2. The second phase would provide practical experience in the new production system on a group of looms where the establishment of good work habits and the production of good quality cloth would be considered more important than high efficiency.

As soon as the immediate needs of the working groups had been satisfied, it was proposed that the training group would operate on one shift only, and that the first appointment to a production group should be to the permanent third shift. Vacancies in the first and second shifts would be filled by transfer from the third shift. It was also agreed that promotion would follow the same route.

Regular meetings of group leaders with their supervisors, and of the supervisors with my colleague were also instituted. These meetings were not run as formal training sessions, but as discussions directed to the concrete problems of the shed. The exercise of sorting out the production, transition, and training groups was taken as a model.

Labour Turnover

An examination was made of labour turnover from the beginning of the experimental period to the end of the year. The results showed that thirty-eight new workers had been engaged, mainly during the period of expansion, and that eighteen had left within a few weeks of engagement. An analysis of the eighteen leavers showed that four were skilled workers transferred from another shed in an attempt to reinforce maintenance skills. After one week's trial they decided that they did not like work in the automatic shed and returned to their old jobs. The other fourteen were all E grade workers engaged to train for D grade work. Six were found unsuitable and discharged. Eight had left of their own accord before the completion of training. No trained members of the working groups had left during the year.

The urgent need for skilled workers was such that there had been a tendency to engage, as E grade workers, applicants whose qualifications were too good for D grade work, but who showed promise of quickly becoming B or even A grade workers. Because of the high level of unemployment in India, matriculates formed the majority of applicants for work of this kind. While at the time of applying they were anxious to get work, they soon became dissatisfied if the prospects of promotion beyond D grade were not immediate. It was decided to select the next recruits specifically for the heavy work involved in the D grade of the gating and maintenance sub-groups.

Mixed Sorts

An examination of the cloths produced during the recession of the summer and autumn showed that in spite of the capricious market demands it would have been possible to have worked two blocks of sixty-four looms on the same sort, and to have confined the necessary changes to one block only. While spreading changes equally through all looms ensured that all groups of workers were fairly treated, it also ensured diffusion of the problems raised. This diffusion could not but interfere with the settling down of all the groups, already having a difficult enough time from other causes.

It was recognized that market demands might require more complex sorts to be put into the automatic loom shed from time to time. To introduce a new sort required two kinds of data:

1. The suitability of the loom for the manufacture of the particular sort;
2. The changes in the balance of work-group skills required.

It was decided to use some of the looms of the training block *d* for experimental testing. If the looms were found suitable, then a whole production block would be turned over to the new sort to test the effect on work-groups.

By the end of the first week of February the experimental sorts had been concentrated on twenty-four looms of the training block. At the insistence of market demand, certain production and transition groups had to be used for sorts for which the looms were not ideally suited. Against this, the experimental testing in the *d* block and then the conversion of a production group into an experimental group resulted in some sorts not previously woven being accepted as regular production lines.

REGRESSION

Working Habits

When in November the behaviour of members of working groups towards each other was examined, a contrast was found between the gating and maintenance and the weaving sub-groups. While the former helped with loom-running, the latter neither assisted with maintenance and gating, nor helped each other. During the experimental period and for some months afterwards members of the weaving sub-group had worked as a team over their whole group of looms, but in the last few weeks they had regressed to individual work habits. The B grade workers had begun to take the warp-mending on thirty-two looms each. As the efficiency fell, they expressed resentment about the group bonus and the participation in it of other group members. They took the view that the former B grade workers of the gating and maintenance sub-group had obtained promotion at their expense. Not only were the replacements inadequately skilled and the work-load of loom-running thereby increased, but even the help they obtained in loom-running was not as efficient as formerly. As the relationships in the weaving sub-group became strained, the D grade workers, whose tasks included helping B grade workers by doing simple warp-mending, reverted to battery-filling only, each taking thirty-two looms. This left them underloaded despite the general overload.

In this situation the group leaders, especially the new ones, attended increasingly to production work. They regressed to the role of worker and neglected the leading of their groups. On the surface the situation was not so confused as before the experimental reorganization. Although the groups had regressed to aggregates of individuals, the confusion was still restricted to groups on sixty-four looms. Indeed, the reluctance to give up belief in 'our group system' was so strong that the regressions that had occurred were largely ignored.

Supervisor-Worker Relationships

Faced with the lack of group leadership and the regression to earlier work habits but, like the workers, reluctant to renounce belief in the new system, the supervisors themselves tended to regress to earlier patterns of management behaviour. They by-passed the group leaders and dealt directly with workers. To solve the problem of group overload they seized on the underloaded battery-fillers, putting one D grade worker of the weaving sub-group exclusively on battery-filling for forty-eight looms (thus fully loading him) and the other on battery-filling for sixteen looms, assigning him to cleaning and oiling duties for the rest of his time. Apart from the resentment felt by the D grade workers, the intervention by the supervisors in the organizing of group tasks tended further to destroy the internally structured leadership of the groups.

When to the inadequate skill in the groups is added the constant confusion due to mixed and experimental sorts, the shortage of spare workers, the increased work caused by the greater absenteeism from August onwards, and the disturbance of building and loom erection, the surprising thing is not that efficiency fell at the end of October, but that it did not fall much sooner. There is small wonder that, after the effort had been prolonged for so long, the fall, when it came, was rapid, and the regression complete.

CHAPTER 10

Later Results

EVENTS AND INDICES
NOVEMBER 1953 TO APRIL 1956

Nine Phases of the Follow-up Period

The first phase lasted four weeks and covered the period of the investigation. Working and training groups remained virtually undifferentiated and no spare workers were available to compensate for absenteeism or for any increases in loom-stoppage rates. At the beginning of the phase management agreed to pay minimum rates—a decision taken within a day or two of the start of the investigation. The building was completed and a start was made on the transfer of the *d* block of looms to its new site.

The end of the first phase and the beginning of the second were marked by the closing down of one working group, thus making its members available for training and as spares. The second phase, from December 1953 to February 1954, was largely taken up with the observation of the effects of making the spares available and with discussion with the group leaders about sorting out the groups. As a result of the observations another group was closed down, marking the end of the phase. The transfer of the *d* block of looms was completed.

Phase three, which lasted only four weeks, was a period of considerable activity and disturbance. Further discussions were held about the sorting out of groups, and many transfers were made. The various experimental cloths scattered round the shed were concentrated on twenty-four looms of the *d* block; the sorts on the *a*, *b*, and *c* blocks were redistributed so that the *a* and *b* blocks had one sort each on all looms, leaving a mixture of sorts on the *c* blocks only. A start was made on the transfer and re-erection in the space vacated by the *d* block of the forty-eight automatics from the other shed of the Jubilee Mill. The phase ended with the differentiation of working groups into production and transition groups.

During the fourth phase one of the sorts experimentally tested on the *d* block of looms was woven on the *c* block. The beginnings of the fifth and sixth phases were marked by the 'graduation' of transition groups into production groups and by the testing of more experimental sorts on various blocks of looms.

During the seventh and eighth phases, which lasted fifteen and sixteen weeks respectively, production planning was considerably disturbed by changes in market demand. Because of the better quality woven in the automatic as compared with the non-automatic sheds, it was decided, with considerable reluctance, to weave high reed sorts in the automatic shed. It was known that the looms would not be ideally suited to this kind of cloth but, since new machinery was being installed in the preparation departments, it was hoped that improved preparation would offset some of the disadvantages. The *a* and *b* blocks of looms were changed to the more complex and difficult sorts. In consequence, the normal sorts woven in the shed were all concentrated in the *c* block, giving it a very mixed range.

The experiment was not as successful as was hoped and in the eighth phase *b* block was put back on to normal production. One of the main reasons for persisting with the high reed sort on *a* block longer than results justified was the attitude of the supervisors, group leaders and workers. While they regretted the continued low efficiency, they felt challenged by the technological problems involved. In the face of quite strong evidence that the looms were not suitable they persisted doggedly, making modifications to the looms, changing the preparation of beams, and trying different kinds of work organization. At the end of the seventh phase, after fifteen weeks' trial, they were so reluctant to admit defeat that they were allowed to carry on for another period.

The ninth phase, from March to June 1955, saw all groups on normal production. There were, of course, changes of sort that caused confusion, and experimental sorts still had to be put on some looms, but, compared with 1953 and 1954, the changes were less erratic and less disturbing. During the eighth phase one new group was started and the two groups closed at the beginning of the year were restarted, thus completing the planned expansion of the shed to twelve groups.[1]

[1] The detailed differentiation of working groups into production, transition, and experimental groups, and the number of groups working in each phase, are given in *Table 14*, Appendix 1.

At the beginning of the seventh phase a member of the Production Study department was 'attached' to the automatic shed, and during the ninth phase an inspection section was started under the control of the Top Supervisor, who from then on took full responsibility for the inspection of the cloth woven.

Table 1. PHASES OF FOLLOW-UP PERIOD AND THE PROCESS OF EVENTS

Phase	*Period*	*Number of Working Weeks*	*Events of the Process of Investigation and Follow-up*	*Related Events*
1	Nov.–Dec. 1953	4	Investigation of causes of drop in efficiency and rise in damage. Minimum rates of pay agreed.	Completion of building. Start of transfer of *d* group of looms.
2	Dec.–Feb. 1954	10	One working group closed down. Discussions about re-structuring of groups.	Transfer of *d* group of looms completed.
3	Feb.–Mar. 1954	4	Second group closed down. Experimental cloths concentrated in *d* group. Cloth on *a*, *b*, and *c* groups redistributed. Differentiation of working groups into production and transition.	Erection of looms from other shed started.
4	Mar.–June 1954	10	Experimental cloth put on *c* group.	Erection of other looms continued.
5	June–July 1954	7	Graduation of two groups from transition to production. Experimental cloth on *b* group. Experimental cloth on *c* group accepted as production line.	Erection of other looms completed.
6	July–Aug. 1954	4	Graduation of two groups from transition to production. Experimental cloth on *b* group accepted as production line.	Difficult market conditions. Demand for high quality.
7	Aug.–Dec. 1954	15	*a* and *b* groups on experimental cloth.	Work Study man allocated to Top Supervisor.
8	Dec.–Mar. 1955	16	*b* groups back to normal. New groups restarted.	New machinery installed in preparation departments.
9	Mar.–June 1955	14	Normal production on all groups.	Inspection put into shed under control of Top Supervisor.

The phases of the follow-up period and the course of events related to them are shown chronologically in *Table 1*.

Efficiency and Damage

The mean percentage efficiency and damage for the working, production, and transition groups are shown in *Figures 1* and *2*. They are also compared with the efficiency and damage before reorganization, in the experimental period, and in the period of expansion and extension. The percentage efficiency and damage of the experimental groups and training groups are not included in these figures, but are shown in the detailed tables in Appendix 1.[1]

In the first phase there was rise in efficiency coinciding with the beginning of the investigation. A further rise in the second phase coincided with the closing down of a group to provide spare workers. This rise was maintained in the third phase in spite of the changes which occurred. During the seventh phase the considerable mixing of normal sorts on *c* block resulted in a slightly lower efficiency, which recovered in the eighth phase when more looms went back to normal production.

In the detailed figures given in the Appendix it will be seen that third shift efficiencies were as high as, if not higher than, those of the first and second shifts for most of the phases. Whatever else may have happened, any doubts or misgivings about poorer performance in the third shift had been dispelled.

Since June 1955 other experimental cloths have been tried in the automatic shed, and mixed sorts have frequently had to be tolerated, but the overall efficiency of the whole shed, including experimental and training groups, between June 1955 and April 1956, was 93 per cent, and damage over the same period was 11 per cent.

DIFFERENTIATION OF THE PRODUCTION SYSTEM

First-Order Managing and Operating Systems

The starting of a third shift brought the number of discrete first-order operating systems up to three. The managing system, which had formally contained only the Top Supervisor and two Shift Supervisors, was thus enlarged by one member. It was further enlarged during the seventh and

[1] Figures for each group are given in *Tables 15*, *16*, *17*, and *18*, Appendix 1.

FIGURE I EFFICIENCY: EXPERIMENTAL WORKING, PRODUCTION, AND TRANSITION GROUPS

MARCH 1953 — JUNE 1955

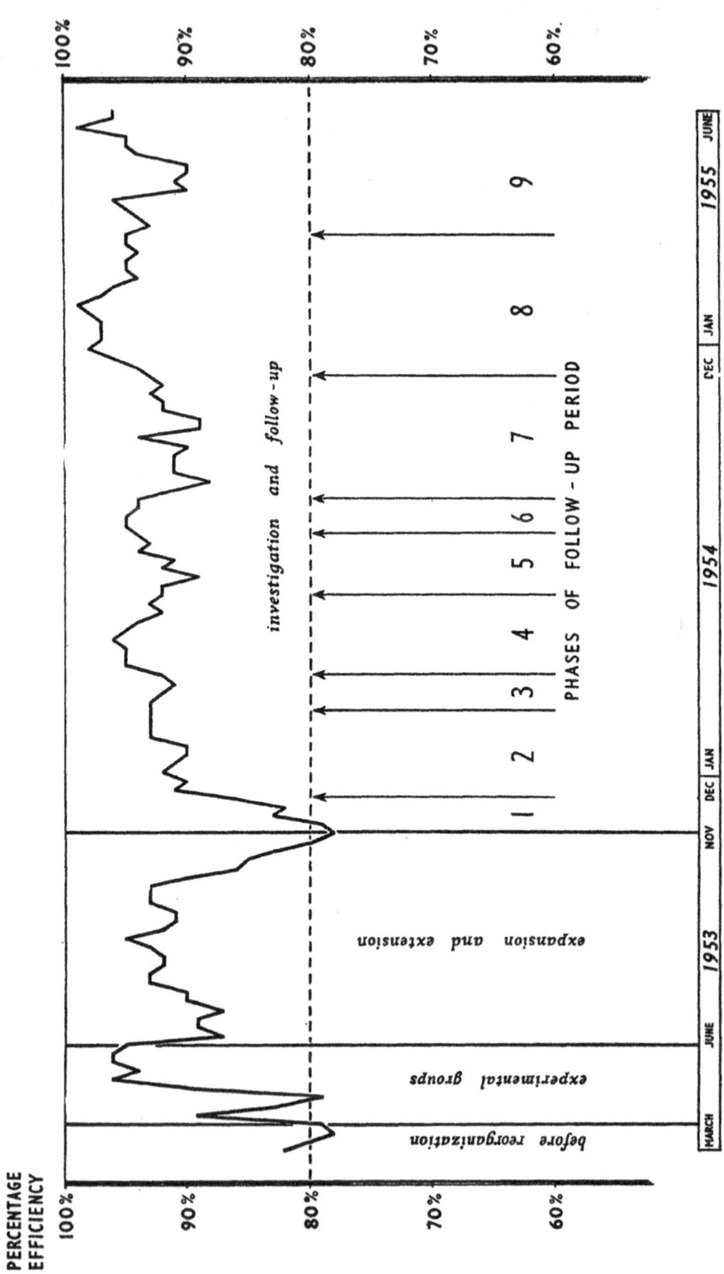

FIGURE 2 DAMAGE: EXPERIMENTAL, WORKING, PRODUCTION, AND TRANSITION GROUPS

MARCH 1953 — JUNE 1955

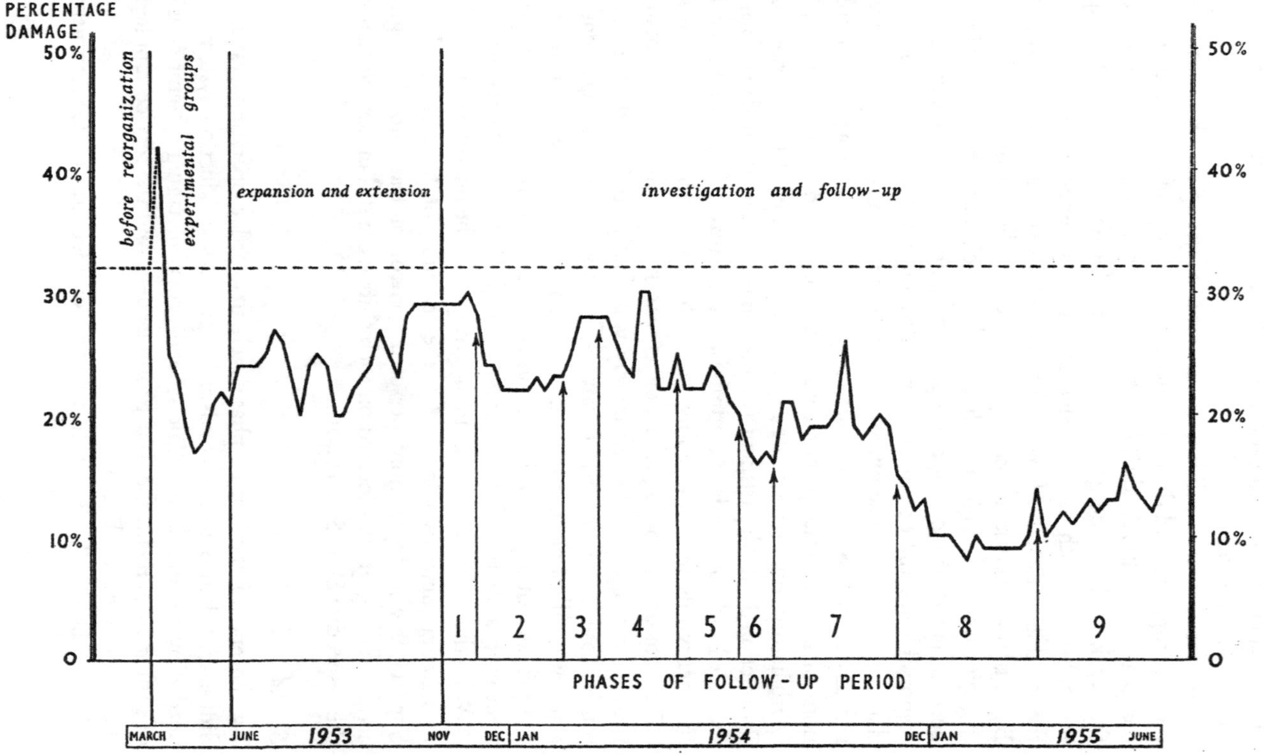

ninth phases of the follow-up period by the introduction of production study and inspection.

The decision to establish new standards of group numbers for varying rates of stoppage, and the experiments in weaving different sorts, required constant checks by Production Study officers both on the looms and on the work-loads of the groups. When, in the seventh phase, the experiments became both more numerous and more widespread a member of the Production Study department began to work full-time in the shed. By this time, work in other parts of the mills, particularly in the reorganization of management, had reached the point where the policy had been accepted of locating appropriate functions in the managing system responsible for the operations controlled and serviced. This is not to say that control and service functions were automatically located in the theoretically correct system, but that, in the work of the project, the implications of not so locating them, when that occurred, were made explicit. With hardly any discussion or any question being raised, the member of the Production Study department working in the automatic shed was formally seconded and came under the administrative control of the Top Supervisor. In other words he became a member of the first-order managing system.

The confidence of higher management in the ability of shed management to manage the shed effectively was finally confirmed when, in the ninth phase, inspection also became a function of shed management. Because any roll of cloth inspected, in whichever shift it was inspected, was the product of all shifts, inspection became a function of the first order managing system under the direct control of the Top Supervisor.

With the stabilization of training groups and the building of the training room containing two looms for the teaching of basic skills, the Top Supervisor also took more personal control of training, although the actual training groups located on each shift were still under the charge of the respective Shift Supervisors.

Second-Order Systems

By the end of the eighth phase each first-order operating system was differentiated into four second-order primary production systems, each headed by a group leader. The second-order managing systems consisted of shift management, the four group leaders, and the service supplied by the Humidification Fitter.

The Calico Mills already had under consideration by Government an application for a licence to import more automatic looms. This, if granted, would mean a further rapid expansion of the shed and it was important to consider the flexibility of the present management organization and its capacity for dealing with expansion. Examination of a Shift Supervisor's responsibilities suggested that, provided reasonably stable conditions could be maintained with respect to change of sort, he could manage up to seven or eight primary groups. If, however, his command became so enlarged, he would need to be relieved of any responsibility for training. Since expansion would not only mean larger commands for the Shift Supervisors, but also a great number of new workers, training would become a separate service function of the managing system with a specialist supervisor in charge. It appeared therefore that the present organization could expand to rather more than double its present size without much further change. The managing and operating systems of an expanded automatic loom shed, with first-order operating systems differentiated into seven second-order primary production systems and a separate training function, are shown in *Figure 3*.

FIGURE 3 *MANAGING AND OPERATING SYSTEMS OF AN EXPANDED AUTOMATIC LOOM SHED*

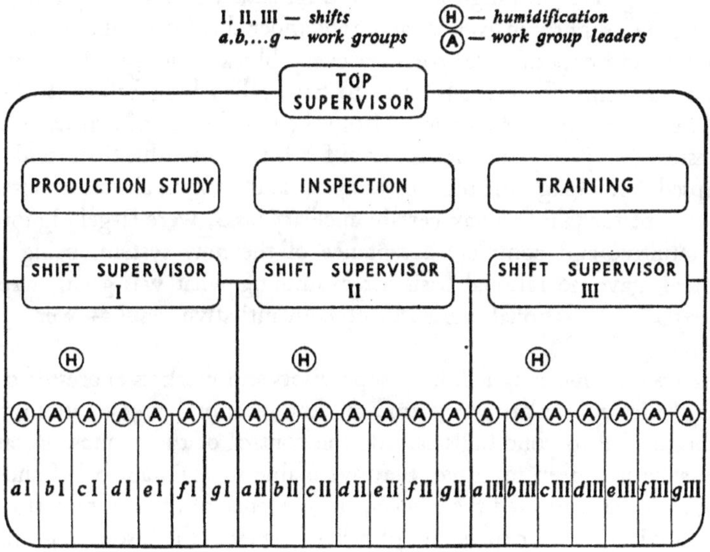

CHAPTER 11

Interpretation and Conclusions

It has been suggested that one possible explanation of the spontaneous acceptance of the new system was to be found in the workers' intuitive acceptance of it as a means of satisfying needs of which they were largely unaware. Such intuitive acceptance would need no rational arguments but would be complete and unquestioning. It was argued that the workers' remarkable determination to make the new system succeed, and their fears of losing what they had gained, were evidence supporting this explanation.

There was further evidence in the sustained effort following the setback caused by the rapid expansion and extension at the beginning of June. The stoppage rate was high in June and remained nearly as high in July. When it fell slightly in August and September there were the difficulties of mixed and experimental sorts on every block of looms. There were reasons in plenty for the efficiency to have fallen long before it did. It might easily never have recovered from the initial stress of expansion and extension. Yet it stayed at a high level for several months, then suddenly collapsed. For a long time the increasing difficulties went almost unnoticed and, except for taking away certain ancillary tasks, were largely ignored. The intuitive and complete acceptance of the new system, being unreasoned, gave no rational basis for examining what was going wrong while the only rational measures—the quantitative results—were still good.

Even when efficiency fell, both supervisors and workers expressed continued belief in 'our group system', the first reaction being an attempt to ascribe the fall to conditions outside the control of the groups. Because acceptance had been intuitive, they were able to maintain belief and to deny, as far as it affected their belief, the evidence of their own performance. In spite of these expressions of belief, however, there were regression to former working habits and a breakdown of the group relationships that had been built up. It may be inferred that the regression was a defence against having to admit any failure of the system. They could not tolerate the guilt of having destroyed something on which they had come to place such value. Nor could they admit that what they had so unquestionably accepted as wholly good might be turning out after all to be partially, if not wholly, bad.

When, in November, the trouble with humidification no longer provided an adequate explanation of the fall in efficiency, management was brought face to face with its own share in the collapse. Spare workers had not been provided for the weaving sub-groups when stoppages had increased. Management seized on poor maintenance as the cause of increased stoppages and hence of the lower efficiency. Since maintenance was a group task, the fall could then be blamed on the workers. To avoid its own sense of guilt, management had to distort the previously agreed policy about spares and it was remembered as an intention to give help only when efficiency fell, not when stoppages increased. Although during the summer stoppages rose, efficiency remained high and, by the distortion, no spares were required; when efficiency did fall it was the workers' own fault. They did not deserve help. In this way management preserved its own belief in the reorganization in spite of the performances.

One other incident gives strong support to the view that acceptance of the new system by both supervisors and workers was more intuitive than reasoned. When the groups were being sorted out, and several group leaders all chose the same worker, they were surprised at the suggestion made by my colleague that the worker be allowed to choose his own leader. Considering that the first four experimental groups all chose themselves, there was nothing novel about the suggestion in itself. But the fact that it was made in a setting in which rational action was being discussed caused surprise.

If during the period of the setback the workers were feeling guilty and despondent about their results, it becomes understandable why the agreement to pay minimum rates at the beginning of the investigation coincided with a halt in the fall of efficiency. The supervisors' and workers' previous experience of an investigation had resulted in the experimental reorganization from which they had obtained so much satisfaction. Another investigation at least promised help, while the immediate agreement to pay minimum rates was an expression of confidence in the supervisors and workers by higher management. It was an acceptance that blame for the failure could not be entirely laid at the door of those in the shed. Their self-confidence was sufficiently restored to enable them to take advantage of the slightly better conditions of November.

Subsequent management actions not only removed most of the causes of difficulty but consistently confirmed the worker's views of their own worth. When experimental cloths were tried average, piece-work earnings were paid while the cloths remained experimental. From March 1954 onwards, when the reshuffling of the groups was completed, the number of stoppages per loom per hour was regularly sampled. This was done to provide the supervisors with evidence upon which to base the allocation of spares and to check standards.[1] In particular, management's drastic action in closing down whole production groups to provide spares confirmed the view that the workers' spontaneous requests for more help were justified.

The basic question, however, still remains unanswered. What was it in the new system that the workers and supervisors accepted as so satisfying to their unexpressed needs?

The pace at which they started, the obvious pleasure in the high efficiency, the worry about the damage rates, the request for more help when productivity fell, the sustained effort, and the generally good performance for over three years suggest that certain assumptions made about task organization have at least some truth for the members of the automatic shed. These were that effective performance of the primary task is an important source of satisfaction and that there is, however latent, a considerable capacity for cooperation available to achieve it. There was further evidence to support these assumptions in the persistence with high reed sorts, long after higher management was prepared to accept that the looms were, for technological reasons, unsuitable.

There was some evidence too to support the further assumptions about group numbers, 'whole' tasks, and the importance of inter-personal relationships. That the workers themselves chose a group of seven, as against theoretical calculations of 7·1, suggests that they did not want to have

[1] The results of the samplings, together with the mean number of workers per group, are given in *Table 19*, Appendix 1. The new machinery introduced into the preparation departments in the seventh phase not only virtually standardized the warp-end breakages but also provided rewound weft yarn, thus improving still further the loom stoppage rates. The new agreed standard of numbers of workers for varying loom stoppage rates resulting from those improvements is given in *Table 20*, Appendix 1.

more than could effectively perform the task. They had indeed underestimated the number rather than played safe, as might have been expected. As regards the satisfaction attendant on the completion of a 'whole' task, it is noteworthy that even at the worst time neither supervisors nor workers suggested that any of the operations directly concerned with the primary task of weaving should be removed from the groups. Finally, the link between personal relationships and effective task performance is demonstrated by the regression to individual work habits as performance declined and its immediate recovery when confidence was regained. The group started working again as a group following the granting of minimum rates of pay.

There is less detailed evidence to support the other assumptions upon which the reorganization was based, although it may be noted that the regression to individual work habits and the resentment about group bonus coincided with supervisor interference in the allocation of tasks, and therefore with group autonomy. The clinging to the letter grades A, B, C, and D—which still continues—suggests that the unambiguous definition of status, and hence of group hierarchy, was more important than descriptive titles of task or role.

Indian culture places great value on community and family membership. The traditional Indian village is divided into communities, which are basically task-determined, and the communities into families which undertake traditional tasks. Families are joint families—they include the wives and children of the male descendants of a given pair of parents who own property and live and work together. Children are often as close to their uncles and aunts as they are to their own parents and have numbers of brothers, sisters, and cousins to live and play with. The family provides the individual with an important source of security and protection deriving from the membership of small, face-to-face, internally structured home- and work-groups. Working and social life provide a consistent pattern of status and authority that gives everybody a place, a task, and a defined role. Industrialization and urbanization divide communities and families, and thus destroy a part, at least, of an important source of protection and security. It seems fair to conclude that the creation, in the automatic shed, of internally structured, internally led, relatively autonomous small work-groups replaced something of what had been lost—and that it was this replacement that the workers welcomed so spontaneously and worked so hard to retain.

SUMMARY OF PART III

1. The weaving process of an automatic loom shed had been broken down into component tasks and the number of workers allocated to each separate component had been determined by work-studies.

2. The resultant pattern was that of an aggregate of individuals with confused task and role relationships and with no discernible internal group structure.

3. Higher management had reinforced the management of the shed. This, together with the quality of the relationships among the supervisors, and between them and workers, had prevented any overt difficulties arising from the lack of group structure. Nevertheless efficiency was lower and damage higher than target figures. Productivity was, in fact, no better than with non-automatic looms.

4. In spite of the persistence of 'weaver' as a title for an occupational role, the weaver was now the loom, and all workers including the 'weavers' serviced machines.

5. The tasks performed could be differentiated into two main groups: those concerned with weaving, and those concerned with loading (gating) and loom maintenance. There were in addition only minor ancillary services.

6. An analysis of changes in the number of workers according to sort woven showed that stable numbers could be maintained for each of three main categories—coarse, medium, and fine. Provided some tasks could be made interchangeable, no changes in work-group numbers would be required for changes within a main sort. The theoretical numbers required for blocks of sixty-four looms into which the loom shed was divided by physical boundaries were calculated.

7. Three natural grades within a work-group for sixty-four looms were found instead of the nine grades existing. They were designated by letters only; rates slightly in excess of existing rates were fixed, and it was decided to pay piece rates to the whole group.

8. Shed supervisors and workers spontaneously took possession of the reorganization, the workers themselves immediately organizing four experimental groups. Higher management took no part in the discussions with supervisors and workers, and permitted the experimental groups so chosen to start work.

9. The immediate results of the experiment were:

(a) The creation of internally-structured and internally-led small work-groups.

(b) A reduction in the number of those reporting directly to the supervisors and a consequent strengthening of the executive command.

(c) The beginning of the withdrawal of higher management from the managing system of the shed.

(d) The abandonment of old titles but without the emergence of new; letter grades only being used.

(e) After an immediate increase in efficiency in the experimental groups at the cost of increased damage and inadequate maintenance, a settling down at a new level of performance in which efficiency was higher and damage lower than before reorganization.

10. When the form of organization was extended to the rest of the shed, and a third shift started, the efficiency was maintained for several months, but in October and November 1953 it dropped steeply through a period of five weeks. At the same time the figures for damage rose steadily.

11. Investigation showed that:

(a) Each group had had to contend with variations in the sort woven.

(b) There had been insufficient spare workers to provide extra help for increased loom stoppage rates and lost time.

(c) Extension and expansion at the same time had given insufficient opportunity for adequate training either of new or of existing workers in the new methods of organization.

(d) The intended concentration of training in two groups had not been possible, and training had been diffused throughout all groups.

(e) The basis on which the original experimental groups had been formed had not allowed sufficient time for group leaders to perform the task of leading.

(f) As a result of the difficulties caused by these factors, group members had regressed to earlier working habits more appropriate to individual than to group working.

12. Action was taken

(*a*) to establish basic rates of pay;

(*b*) to reshuffle the groups into production, transition, and training groups;

(*c*) to close down enough groups to allow adequate time for training, and to provide spare workers for increased stoppage rates;

(*d*) to erect two looms apart from the shed to train new and existing workers in the basic skills of loom running and maintenance;

(*e*) to implement the policy of keeping a group on the same sort for as long as possible, confining experimental sorts to whole groups, rather than spreading them over all groups;

(*f*) to locate in the shed managing system appropriate and necessary control functions.

13. The beginning of the investigation and the establishment of minimum rates of pay coincided with a halt in the drop in efficiency and in the rise of damage. Thereafter the efficiency of production and transition groups rose and quality showed continuous improvement.

14. During the follow-up period various groups had to be used for experimental sorts because of difficult market conditions. As a result of these experiments some sorts, not previously woven in the automatic shed, became normal production lines.

15. By December 1954 the groups which had been closed down earlier to provide spare workers had been restarted, and the shed was working to maximum capacity.

16. It was concluded that the first spontaneous acceptance of the new system and the subsequent determination to make it work were due primarily to the workers' intuitive acceptance of it as one which would provide them with the security and protection of small group membership which they had lost by leaving their villages and their families to enter industry. At the same time the new system allowed them to perform their primary task effectively and thus provided them with an important source of satisfaction.

PART IV

The Experimental Reorganization of Non-Automatic Weaving

THE CREATION OF A NEW SOCIO-TECHNICAL SYSTEM

CHAPTER 12

A Non-Automatic Loom Shed

Part III has described the social reorganization of a production system already disturbed by the introduction of a new technology—automatic looms. Part IV will describe an experimental reorganization of non-automatic weaving in which technological differentiation and social reintegration of tasks and roles were accomplished in one process.

In November 1953, when the investigation in the automatic loom shed was being carried out, management became very concerned about the quality of the cloth woven in non-automatic sheds. Government reluctance to license the installation of more automatics made it necessary to effect an improvement with existing equipment. Experience in the automatic shed had shown that disturbance by technological innovation without adequate attention to social consequences had led to lower productivity than had been anticipated. It had also shown that attention to the social as well as to the technological organization could assist in realizing the potential advantages of the new technology. This was achieved against the background of an already disturbed traditional system. By contrast in non-automatic weaving there had been no disturbance of the traditional system which was working much as it had when first established. It was supported by customs, attitudes, and habits of several generations of weavers and other loom shed workers. To those in the mill it seemed scarcely credible that the required change could be achieved without some radical innovation such as the introduction of automatic looms.

In Lewin's[1] terms, the situation in the automatic shed had already been 'unfrozen' by the introduction of automatic looms. In the non-automatic sheds the situation was frozen. No major technological innovation was available to bring about 'unfreezing'.

After certain preliminary studies in various sheds it was decided to set

[1] Lewin, Kurt, 'Frontiers in Group Dynamics', *Human Relations*, 1947, Vol. 1, No. 1.

up an experimental non-automatic shed in the Calico Mill in which a new system giving a higher quality might be discovered and established as a pilot model. In this shed, with the active co-operation of management and workers, experiments were carried out with various kinds of work organization involving radical changes in work habits. Finally, a pattern was found that enabled internally-structured small work-groups to be formed, each capable of performing all the tasks of running, maintaining, and servicing groups of forty looms. After considerable technological and organizational difficulties in the early stages, the experimental shed became an efficient working unit and the quality of cloth produced showed a significant improvement over that coming from other sheds.

It became rapidly evident during the course of the experiments that they were not only experiments in socio-technical reorganization but also in the building up of permissive and collaborative relationships between workers, supervisors, middle management, and top management. The test of the acceptability of technological or social innovation was dependent not only upon the intrinsic merit of the innovation but also upon the relationships which existed between all those concerned.

THE PRODUCTION SYSTEM

Non-automatic Weaving

The A and B loom sheds of the Calico Mills contain 760 and 640 looms respectively—all non-automatic Lancashire looms. The weaving process is similar to that already described for automatic looms. The important difference is that whereas on an automatic loom the empty bobbin in the shuttle is automatically replaced by a full bobbin stored in a battery, on non-automatic looms the loom stops when a bobbin is empty and the bobbin has to be removed and replaced by hand. The actual operation, *shuttling*, is a short one, taking approximately twenty seconds only. It occurs at intervals of from three to twelve minutes depending upon the amount of yarn which can be wound on the bobbin. The need to perform this operation severely limits the number of looms which a weaver can attend, since he has to keep them all under constant observation. Moreover, when he is occupied with any other task, looms awaiting shuttling have to stand idle.

The non-automatic looms of the Calico Mills were not fitted with warp-stop motions (the mechanical or electrical device that stops the loom automatically when a warp thread breaks). Their installation had always been resisted by the workers on the grounds that it made their work much harder and reduced their opportunities for earning the piece-work bonus that was paid on quantity only. Without warp-stop motions, a break in a warp thread has to be observed—and the observation is often quite difficult to make—and the loom stopped by hand. Any cloth woven on the loom after the break should be unwoven and the warp thread mended. The basic time for mending a warp-thread break without un-weaving is approximately the same on non-automatic as on automatic looms. Much more time is required, however, if the break is not observed at the instant it occurs, and the unweaving is carried out.[1]

On any day approximately forty main sorts (kind of cloth), each with seven or eight sub-varieties, were being woven in the two mills and a new beam was assigned to a loom irrespective of the previous sort woven on it, provided only that the kind and size of the loom was appropriate to the new beam, and that the claims of particular weavers to work on certain kinds could be satisfied.

Weaving Tasks

Once his looms were gated, a weaver became responsible for the total task of weaving on two looms. Weavers even collected their own weft yarn from the weft store. They were not only responsible for running their looms and for warp-mending, but for fault prevention and for minor mechanical adjustments. They were also responsible for repairing all faults in the cloth caused during weaving, for removing woven cloth from the looms, and for delivering it to the Cloth Department where it was measured and inspected.

Each weaver was under the nominal control of a line jobber who in turn was responsible to a head jobber and a weaving supervisor. The line jobber's tasks were to maintain forty looms, to keep them fully loaded by gating new beams, and to supervise the weavers. Other workers performed ancillary or specialist tasks. Beam carriers, who were members of the Preparation department, carried warp beams from the sizing department to the weaving shed warp store, and thence to the looms. Oilers lubricated moving parts while the looms were running and cleaned them during long stops. A few looms were fitted with special attachments

[1] A diagrammatic representation of a non-automatic loom set up for weaving is given in *Figure 1*, Appendix 2.

turning them into jacquard, drop-box, or towel looms. For these specialists were employed. Other specialists—fitters, carpenters, and cobblers—were employed for major overhauls and repairs. As none of the specialists was affected by the experimental reorganization, they are not included in the subsequent analysis.

The detailed data about tasks, related occupational roles, numbers on shift, lines of responsibility, and average wages per month, listed as for automatic looms, are given in *Tables 1* and *2* of Appendix 2. The positioning of looms and the ambits of weavers when engaged on tasks of loom running are shown in *Figure 1*.

The Measurement of Productivity and Wages

Cloth was cut from the looms at cutting marks placed on the warp during the preparation of beams. The length between cutting marks varied with the sort woven. Productivity was measured by efficiency and damage. But efficiency was reckoned in yards of cloth produced rather than as picks inserted, as in the automatic loom shed. The wage system gave the line jobbers and weavers a bonus for quantity based on complex allowances for sorts, colour, and widths of cloth. But there was no bonus for quality. Bad quality was punished by warnings, fines, and in the limit by suspension or discharge. Suspension was infrequently used; discharge almost never. Labour legislation makes discharge for anything except gross misconduct a lengthy, difficult, and complicated process. Fines, limited by law to one thirty-second of the total wage, were imposed by a clerk in the Cloth department on the reports of *folder-inspectors*, all of whom were under the authority of the Sales department. The total of the fines which could be imposed on any weaver for bad quality was less than the bonus he could earn by not unweaving damaged cloth or even by not stopping the loom to repair damage which he saw occurring.

The difficulty of good quality weaving increases with the fineness of the yarn and with the complexity of the colour combinations used in the design. The finer the yarn the more difficult it is to handle; the more threads there are to the inch, the more exacting becomes the task of finding the correct healds and reeds for broken ends. Coloured yarn is more difficult to see than 'grey' yarn, and complex patterns, requiring yarns of different colours, demand the greatest accuracy in all warp-mending operations to avoid getting threads crossed, so changing the pattern and producing faults. Attention to quality is thus more important on the

FIGURE I POSITION OF LOOMS AND AMBIT OF WEAVERS IN A BLOCK OF 40 LOOMS

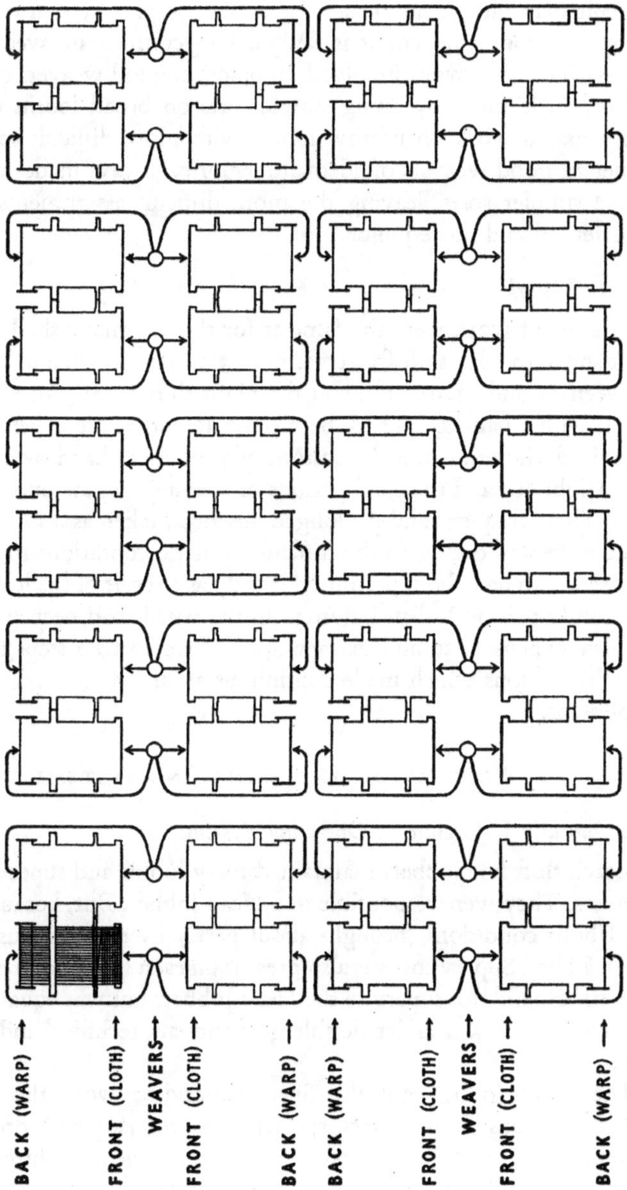

difficult than on the simple sorts and the complex system of allowances for sort, colour, and count is designed to compensate weavers for the necessarily harder work involved. In practice, good weavers could always make a little more by doing simple sorts on broad looms than by the compensated work on narrow looms with more difficult sorts. In consequence, good weavers of adequate seniority always made strong claims to the simpler sorts, leaving the more difficult assignments to the less experienced and more junior.

Hours of Work

The hours of work were the same as for the automatic shed—two eight-hour shifts, the day shift from 7 a.m. to 3.30 p.m., with a half-hour break between 11 and 11.30 a.m., and the night shift from 3.30 p.m. till midnight, with a half-hour break between 7.30 and 8. No other breaks were organized, though it was the custom of weavers to hand over their looms to a neighbour and to spend periods of varying lengths outside the loom shed. These frequent and prolonged absences, taken as a right, were held to be necessary owing to the difficult climatic conditions in India. They can be said to have been permitted largely as a result of the low wage rates previously paid in Indian industry. In the past it had been perhaps easier and less expensive to add extra workers than to take steps to deal with those conditions which made continuous attention to work difficult and unpleasant.

OPERATING AND MANAGING SYSTEMS

The Partially Differentiated Operating Systems

On each shift line jobbers maintained forty looms and supervised twenty weavers. They were responsible to a Head Jobber. But, because of changing labour conditions (brought about partly by recent industrial legislation), a Shed Supervisor was also present on each shift and in charge of the jobbers. He did not supervise the Head Jobber, but was equal in status, so that every shift was under double government, technical and administrative.

The Head Jobber and the Shed Supervisor were also jointly and directly responsible for oilers, specialists on the jacquard, drop-box, and towel looms, weft store workers, sweepers, carpenters, fitters, and cobblers. Sixty-six different workers of varying skill and status reported directly to them. Nevertheless they were not responsible for all workers in their shed. Beam-carriers, who performed certain tasks in the warp store and in the loom shed, were members of the Preparation department. Folder-inspectors, who examined and measured the cloth produced, and the Cloth department clerk, who imposed fines for bad quality, belonged to Sales.

Shift operating systems could only be partially differentiated into primary production systems composed of Line Jobbers and weavers, since the Shift Supervisor dealt directly and executively with the weavers on all personnel and administrative matters. Shift organization is outlined in *Figure 2*, where all lines of communication are shown as joint, and where for simplicity weavers have had to be omitted.

The Managing System

Weaving was contained in a production system differentiated into four discrete operating systems whose managing system contained the Weaving Master (assisted by a staff of record clerks) and the Shift Supervisor and Head Jobber from each shift of the A and B loom sheds. The Weaving Master, who reported to the Works Manager, was also responsible for Preparation (Winding, Warping, and Sizing).

Inspection, exercised by the Cloth department under the control of Sales, was outside the managing system not only of weaving but also of the total manufacturing system. Since the fines for bad quality were also imposed by the Cloth department, a major personnel control was also outside the managing system. The exclusion of this major control left mill and shift management powerless to exercise full authority over the performance of the primary task for which they were responsible. At the same time it enabled them to avoid the hostility inevitable when full authority is exercised in the face-to-face groups of an executive command.

CONCLUSIONS OF A FIRST EXAMINATION

Outstanding Characteristics of the Existing System

The outstanding characteristics of the existing system may be summarized as follows:

1. The primary task was carried out entirely by the weaver who experienced the conversion of cotton yarn to cloth as a 'whole' task, but bonus payments were for quantity only and favoured simpler sorts.

FIGURE 2 OUTLINE ORGANIZATION CHART FOR ONE SHIFT

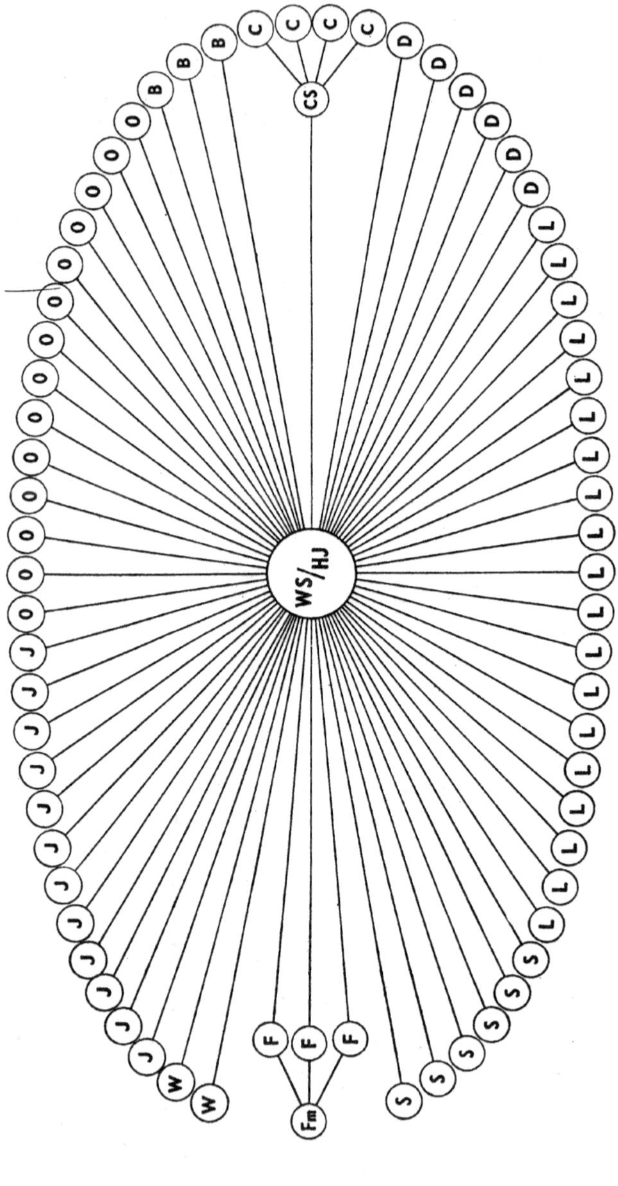

HJ HEAD JOBBER
WS WEAVING SUPERVISOR
L LINE-JOBBERS
D WEFT-DISTRIBUTORS
CS CARPENTER SUPERVISOR
C CARPENTERS
J SPECIALISTS IN JACQUARD, DROPBAR, DROP-BOX, &c
B BELT-REPAIRERS
O OILERS
W WATER-CARRIERS
F FITTERS
Fm FITTERS' MATE
S SWEEPERS

2. Formally the weaver was an independent isolate, working on his own and making his own individual relationships with those in authority over him. Informally, he made mutually helpful relationships with his near neighbours who would take over his looms in his absence expecting him to do the same for them.

3. This pattern of formal isolation and informed mutual support was characteristic of all occupational roles.

4. To perform some tasks the weaver had to move away from his looms—to the weft store or the cloth department. This movement beyond the department was characteristic also of beam-carriers and line jobbers and is shown in *Figure 3*.

5. The Head Jobber and Shift Supervisor carried undifferentiated joint responsibility, a situation which created confusion.

6. The Head Jobber and Shift Supervisor, while having direct responsibility for sixty-six workers at varying levels, had no authority over some of those working in their department.

7. The beam carrier, under the authority of the Preparation department, not only performed carrying duties within the loom shed, but was also responsible for one of the loading tasks on the looms.

8. Disciplinary procedures for damage evoked an executive relationship between the Sales department and the weaver, by-passing not only the Shift Supervisor, Head Jobber and Line Jobbers, but the Weaving Master and the Works Manager.

Such a first analysis immediately suggested that some change was necessary in the methods of bonus payment—with the elimination of fines for bad quality, and better compensating rates for difficult sorts. Change seemed no less demanded in the managing system that left multiple authorities responsible for weaving and its control. The traditional system had however worked fairly well for many years and it was dangerous to assume without special testing that changes appropriate in a western setting would have the same effect in India. In particular the diffusion and confusion of authority suggested that there was a deep-seated collusion to avoid accepting full responsibility for the primary task.

Framework for Reorganization

The amount of time they spent outside the shed suggested that the workers derived no more than a very moderate satisfaction from the efficient performance of their tasks. They appeared only too prepared to allow a

FIGURE 3 RANGE OF MOVEMENT OF LINE-JOBBER, WEAVER, AND BEAM-CARRIER IN PERFORMING LOOM-SHED TASKS

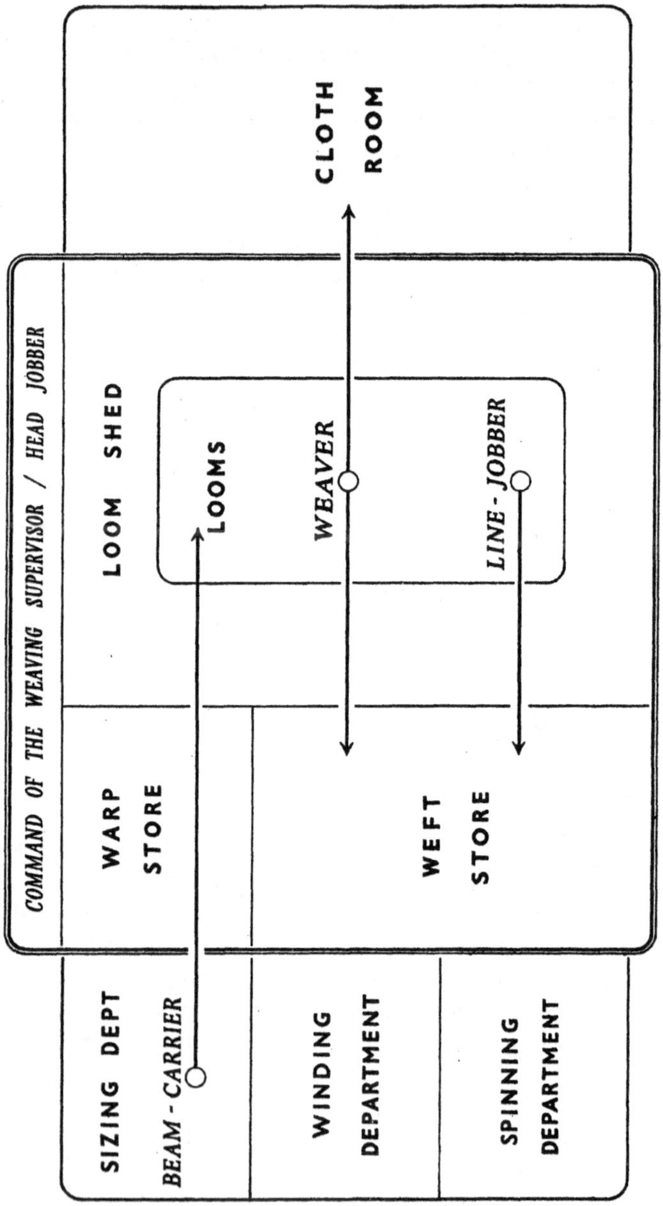

neighbour to run damaged cloth on their looms. Moreover, from the extent to which the right of 'going outside' was used, it was apparent that more workers were engaged in weaving than were needed to perform it efficiently.

The sense of task completion did not apply to the many ancillary workers except through their membership of the shift aggregate, though it applied to weavers and hence, to some extent, to line jobbers. Weavers were also allowed a degree of 'self-government' in that they were paid on piece-rates and could make their own informal arrangements for absence.

Nearly all workers were in roles that formally required them to be independent isolates in a situation in which industrialization and urbanization were leading to a breakdown of the close-knit family and village community which formerly provided traditional opportunities for the satisfaction of group needs. The precursor of the mill, hand-loom weaving, was, and is, carried out in a village home as a family activity. So far as their work organization was concerned it appeared likely that the workers on non-automatic no less than those on automatic looms were being deprived of the satisfactions they needed to obtain from the membership of small groups.

A socio-technical system that could be operated by internally structured, small work-groups might provide these satisfactions so that, like the workers of the automatic shed, they would prefer it to their present system. Even weavers might, in consequence, be expected to welcome the greater potential efficiency obtainable from job-breakdown since it would allow them to produce and to earn at a higher level. A reorganization into relatively autonomous primary groups would enable a further differentiation to be made of the shift operating system, and thus provide an opportunity for reorganization of the managing system consistent both with effective performance and with the needs of shed and shift management.

CHAPTER 13

Setting Up the Experimental Shed

Reorganization is always subject to limitations imposed by the situation in which it takes place. In India certain restrictions are imposed by industrial legislation. No reduction in the number of jobs is permitted without the written permission of the recognized trade union or an award of an industrial court. One of the major problems is the enormous unemployment, both real and potential. Because of this, 'rationalization' embarrasses the Government and is resisted by workers and trade unions. Shortly after the experimental shed had started, an agitation directed against 'rationalization' flared up all over India. Members of Parliament and prominent labour leaders made speeches demanding the banning of all new machinery that required fewer workers. In Ahmedabad, processions of protest were held daily.

No change in current work practice except in an experimental situation is permitted by law without agreement with the recognized union.[1] Agreement with the recognized union, however, does not automatically ensure that a change can take place. Most agreements are enabling only, neither management nor union having the power to compel workers to accept. Only when the workers themselves have consented is change permitted. Some months earlier, in July 1953, an agreement had been reached between the Millowners' Association and the Textile Labour Association to allow weavers to work four looms. In spite of increased wages (Rs. 100 as against Rs. 66 exclusive of dearness allowance) only two mills, of which one was the Calico Mills, had succeeded in getting the agreement implemented for the first and second shifts. In the Calico Mills only 48 looms were working at four looms to a weaver, and that

[1] During the experimental period the law was amended to include experimental changes among the changes requiring agreement.

only after great difficulty and at low efficiency and high damage rates. In the other mill the agreement was implemented only under the threat of closure.

Another restriction is that only a given quota of looms is allowed to any mill. India is divided into surplus and deficit areas, and where production exceeds consumption the number of machines is limited. Ahmedabad is in a surplus area for cotton textiles and the quota of looms in the Calico Mills was already being fully used. Before an experimental shed could even be erected looms had to be obtained from other sheds. They could be transferred only when vacant on both shifts either through prolonged absence or retirement of the workers concerned. Because of certain retirements on gratuity it became possible to erect twenty-four looms in an experimental shed. Over the next few months further retirements made other looms available.[1]

WEAVING TASKS

Standardization of Sort

An examination of the production records of the loom sheds showed that, in spite of more than three hundred varieties and sub-varieties of cloth, some sorts were in regular production. A proportion of the looms could therefore weave the same sort continuously. If looms and workers could be kept always on the same sort, not only would loom tuning, maintenance, and adjustment become more efficient, but workers would become more skilled in the handling of the kind of problems raised by a specific sort. A first suggestion for an experiment to improve quality therefore was to work a group of looms and a group of workers continuously on the same sort—apart from certain changes which might be forced by market demand. This would entail adjusting the wage system to prevent experienced weavers from claiming simpler sorts.

Work-load in weaving can be controlled in three main ways: by mixing sorts of different complexity for a fixed number of workers on a fixed number of looms; by varying the number of looms for a fixed number of workers; and by varying the number of workers for a fixed number of looms. The need to standardize sorts for a given group of looms suggested

[1] In the middle of 1956 Government announced a relaxation of this rule for the manufacture of cloth for export only. The number of extra looms allowed will, however, be small and strictly rationed.

that the first should be kept to a minimum. The consideration that efficient production requires all looms to be continuously manned suggested that the third should be preferred to the second, though it was recognized that variation of the number of workers for a fixed number of looms has been the subject of frequent disputes between management and workers, not only in India but in most countries faced with problems of development and re-deployment.

Loom Shed Tasks

The tasks of the loom shed could be differentiated with respect to

a. TASK AREA: the area over which the task was performed.

b. TIME PERIOD: *Long stops*—smash-tenting, gating, maintaining, oiling (gating), and warp-mounting; *Short stops*—shuttling, fault prevention, and warp-mending; *Running*—oiling (routine), weft-distributing, and cloth-removing—and other tasks (warp-, weft-, and cloth-carrying) for which loom running or stopping is irrelevant.

c. SKILLS: *Fitting*—the capacity to maintain, adjust and tune looms; *Full weaving*—the capacity to take full charge of a running loom and carry out all tasks of weaving, in particular warp-mending at high speed without making errors in the pattern or leaving readily detectable knots; *Part weaving*—the capacity to undertake shuttling and fault prevention, but not to carry out warp-mending at high speed; *Minimal*—unskilled in any of the above senses.

d. CONDITION: the handling of yarn requiring *clean* hands and the handling of machinery involving *dirty* hands.

The tasks of the loom shed were reordered to this classification and the results are given in *Table 1*. The range of skills could be comprehended by a worker performing any one task. There were a number of tasks with allied skills, similar time periods, and the same condition. In any new system, therefore, depending on job-breakdown there would be scope for role interchange. Further, if warp and weft stores could be located close to looms, and cloth, once removed from looms, could be delivered to a nearby point, all tasks could be confined to the loom task area, thus providing a recognizable territory for a group of workers engaged on a group of looms. Failing this, the tasks of warp, weft and cloth carrying could be taken away from any group and still leave it with an easily recognizable 'whole' task.

Work-Load Studies

To discover whether an internally structured group of appropriate size could be formed to deal with all tasks, work-load studies were made. It was assumed that one worker would perform only one task over the

Table I. RE-CLASSIFICATION OF LOOM-SHED TASKS

Task Area	*Time Period*	*Task*	*Skill Required*	*Condition*
Loom	*Short-stop*	Shuttling	*Part Weaving*	*Clean*
Loom	*Short-stop*	Fault Prevention	*Part Weaving*	*Clean*
Loom	*Short-stop*	Warp-Mending	*Full Weaving*	*Clean*
Loom	*Long-stop*	Smash-Tenting	*Full Weaving*	*Clean*
Loom	*Long-stop*	Gating	*Part Weaving and Fitting*	*Clean*
Loom	*Long-stop*	Maintaining	*Part Weaving and Fitting*	*Dirty*
Loom	*Long-stop*	Oiling (Gating)	*Minimal*	*Dirty*
Loom	*Long-stop*	Warp-Mounting	*Minimal*	*Dirty*
Loom	*Time not Significant*	Oiling (Routine)	*Minimal*	*Dirty*
Loom	*Time not Significant*	Weft-Distributing	*Minimal*	*Clean*
Loom	*Time not Significant*	Cloth-Removing	*Minimal*	*Clean*
Loom Shed	*Time not Significant*	Warp-Carrying	*Minimal*	*Clean*
Loom Shed	*Time not Significant*	Weft-Carrying	*Minimal*	*Clean*
Outside	*Time not Significant*	Cloth-Carrying	*Minimal*	*Clean*

maximum number of looms rather than all tasks over a small number of looms. Work-loads could be divided into four major categories:

1. Those which varied with the intervals between gating, caused by different sizes of beams: gating, warp-mounting, and warp-carrying.
2. Those which varied with the count of weft yarn (which affected the amount of yarn that could be wound on bobbins): shuttling, weft-distributing, and weft-carrying.
3. Those which varied with the quality of beams (hence, with the number of warp-breakages per loom hour): fault prevention, warp-mending, and smash-tenting.[1]

[1] The variations were not linear for any of the tasks since, regarded as specialized tasks, the fewer the number of breakages, the more walking required between mendings. At more than four breakages per loom hour there also appeared to be a limit to what could be achieved by fault prevention. Beyond four breakages per loom hour the number of looms to which a worker could theoretically attend remained approximately the same, since giving him fewer looms produced no better results.

4. Those which remained relatively constant: maintaining,[1] oiling, cloth-removing, and cloth-carrying.

Standardization of sorts on given looms would standardize 1 and 2, so that only those work-loads that depended upon warp-breakages would remain variable.[2]

The first studies were made on looms on which the workers were unaccustomed to work with warp-stop motions,[3] and adjustments were subsequently made in the experimental shed. The figures were intended to give only a first approximation of the number of workers for a given number of looms.[4]

Experience of non-automatic weaving suggested that an efficiency of 85 per cent could be considered attainable. The figures obtained from the studies were compared with figures of similar studies made in the United States and Great Britain. When allowance was made for sort, count, package size, and variation in methods of measuring efficiency, they were found to be comparable.[5]

Theoretical Small Work-Group

It was decided that the most economical method would be to put the first groups on to the most difficult sort commonly woven. If they could manage that with improved performance, they should be able to manage any other. The most difficult regular sort was multi-coloured, single-ended, striped shirting, in which the warp threads varied in shade from thread to thread. With this sort a warp-breakage rate of four per loom hour was expected.

Twenty-four looms were known to be available. The figures of the work-load studies were therefore converted to give the theoretical num-

[1] Although regular maintenance was carried out when new beams were gated, and thus occurred more frequently the shorter the time the beam lasted, the more regular the maintenance, the less that had to be done on each occasion.

[2] The work-loads of nearly all tasks—both variable and constant—also varied with the sort, colour, and yarn count, but those variations, being no more than could be accounted for as random variations, were ignored—though it was accepted that working with coloured yarn of fine counts at high reeds was more difficult than for sorts requiring only low counts of grey yarn at low reeds.

[3] The workers agreed to these being fitted experimentally on being guaranteed piece-work earnings irrespective of quantity produced.

[4] Apart from changes in practice which were expected to be made experimentally and which would therefore make the too elaborate study of current practice irrelevant, the intention to determine work-loads by experience also avoided the difficult question of the general validity of time studies as major determinants for work-load allocation.

[5] The detailed figures from the first studies are given in *Table 3*, Appendix 2.

ber required for twenty-four looms at a warp-breakage rate of four. The part-skilled weaving tasks of shuttling and of fault prevention required respectively 2·0 and 0·8 workers; the fully skilled weaving tasks of warp-mending and smash-tenting 2·4 and 0·8; all the minimally skilled tasks, taken together, only 0·6, and the highly skilled tasks of gating and maintaining only 0·4 between them.[1]

Observations suggested, first, that shuttling, fault prevention, and warp-mending could be separated from each other; next, that the skills required for gating and maintaining were such that a worker performing both would be the natural group leader; lastly, that the tasks requiring minimal skill could be so separated in time that, if they were performed by one worker, the inconsistency in condition would not affect efficient working. These considerations made the idea of a small work-group seem quite possible. The theoretical model is shown in *Table 2*, which gives the

Table 2. OCCUPATIONAL ROLES, NUMBERS, AND TASKS FOR AN EXPERIMENTAL GROUP OF 24 LOOMS

Occupational Roles	*Theoretical Number*	*Rounded Number*	*Tasks*
Group Leader	0·4	1	Leading group, gating, maintaining, and helping other group members
Full-Skill Loom Workers	2·4	2	Warp-mending
Part-Skill Loom Workers	0·8	1	Fault-prevention and helping with warp-mending
	2·0	2	Shuttling
Helper	0·6	1	Oiling, warp-mounting, weft-distributing, and general help with other tasks
Totals	7·0	8	

occupational roles together with the theoretical and rounded numbers required for each task. The rounded number is one more than the theoretical number. The investigation of regression in the automatic shed had shown that to the theoretical numbers required in a group there should be added some allowance for the task of leading the group.

Twenty-four looms did not give an ideal balance between the work-load of the different tasks, but since no more were immediately available,

[1] The detailed figures are given in *Table 4*, Appendix 2.

it was decided to bring the experimental shed into being and to begin with two volunteer groups—one on each of the two shifts.

SOCIAL CONDITIONS FOR EXPERIMENT

The Managing System

The new venture could be run successfully only by men who, believing in its potentiality, were vested with full authority. The existing managing system could not provide this condition. The experimental shed was therefore set up outside the normal weaving departments, under the control of a senior supervisor reporting directly to the Works Manager.

The Senior Supervisor was given Shift Supervisors, each of whom might eventually be able to deal with seven or eight internally structured, autonomous work-groups. Since the main reason for setting up the experimental shed was to improve quality, responsibility for it was placed upon the Senior Supervisor.[1] Because cloth taken from a loom in any shift would be the product of all shifts, cloth inspection was made his direct responsibility. The actual organization of inspection was left to be discovered until after the experiment had started but it was agreed in principle that, once there were enough, the inspectors would also be organized as working groups with their own group leaders. The setting up of an inspection section within the experimental shed would, incidentally, eliminate the carrying of cloth outside the shed as a task for those engaged in production groups.

The occupational roles, tasks, and lines of responsibility of the intended managing system of the experimental shed are shown in *Table 3*.

The Measurement of Productivity and Wages

Management decided that, if necessary, all savings on direct labour costs made as a result of reorganization would be paid to the workers in the form of increased wages and bonus, provided efficiency was maintained and quality improved. This decision was made so that the wages offered could be sufficiently attractive to initiate the experiment. They were calculated on the basis that, provided no losses were made on the most difficult sort, savings would be made on other sorts. In view of the auto-

[1] Although, as yet, the level at which management controls should be located was unclear, the principle was accepted that the farther down the executive hierarchy responsibility for self-inspection and criticism could be placed the better.

Table 3. ROLES, TASKS, AND LINES OF RESPONSIBILITY OF MANAGING SYSTEM OF THE EXPERIMENTAL SHED

Occupational Role	*Tasks*	*Lines of Responsibility*
Senior Supervisor	Manage through subordinates all activities of the loom shed; obtain such services as are not available within the shed itself; coordinate raw material supplies and cloth deliveries with relevant departments. Responsible for quality and quantity of production and for maintenance	Responsible to Works Manager. Responsible directly for Shift Supervisors and Inspectors
Shift Supervisor	Manage through group leaders activities of one shift; provide services from within departments as required. Responsible for quality and quantity of shift production, for loom maintenance, and for records of output and quality for each group	Responsible to Senior Supervisor; has direct authority over group leaders and ancillary workers in the shed at any time
Inspector	Fold, inspect, measure, and record quantity and quality of output	Responsible to Senior Supervisor for work and method of doing it

matic shed experience, it was decided to pay minimum wages irrespective of performance. The grades, occupational roles, and minimum wages agreed for the experimental groups are shown in *Table 4*.

Table 4. GRADES AND WAGES FOR EXPERIMENTAL GROUPS

Grade	*Occupational Role*	*Basic Rates**
A	Group Leader	145
B+	Smash-Tenter and Deputy Group Leader	125
B	Full-skill Loom-worker (warp-mending)	115
C	Part-skill Loom-worker (shuttling and fault-prevention)	90
D	Helper	55

* These rates are exclusive of Dearness Allowance.

Bonus was to be paid for both quality and quantity. It would have been simpler to pay flat rates during an experimental period, but those who would be recruited for the experiment were used to receiving some form of bonus for their effort. As they were safeguarded by a guaranteed minimum, there was no reason why they should not make something extra. To pay such a bonus meant that quality and quantity had to be related to each other and this meant changing the basis of measuring both. Damage in the existing sheds was measured by calculating the number of damaged pieces (twenty to thirty yards) as a percentage of pieces woven. Since, however, weavers from different shifts shared in the weaving of the same piece, disciplinary action could only be taken for specific damage and not for the number of damaged pieces. It was decided to measure damage in terms of the number of damages occurring in 1,000 yards of cloth. Since cloth lengths vary in different manufacturing processes, it was also decided that quantity bonus as in the automatic shed should be based not upon yards but upon efficiency, as measured by the number of picks inserted, expressed as a percentage of the numbers possible. Consideration of the standards of work in the other loom sheds led to the following awards:

a. Quantity bonus—1½ per cent of basic wages for every 1 per cent increase in efficiency over 70 per cent.
b. Quality bonus—1½ per cent of basic wages for every damage less than 12 damages per 1,000 yards.

Since the emphasis was on an improvement of quality, no quantity bonus was to be paid unless the quality bonus was also earned, but a shortfall in quantity could be offset by quality bonus.[1]

Hours of Work

No significant work had been done in India on optimum periods of work. I felt that the existing hours, requiring two four-hour work spells with only half an hour break between, demanded too much under Indian conditions. The need for other breaks was accepted, but one of the difficulties of the existing arrangements was that breaks were organized on an individual basis and were neither coordinated nor controlled. Further, since in the existing system looms were not fitted with warp-stop motions, and since bonus for quantity exceeded any possible fine for bad quality, there was no incentive on the part of a worker, when left to look after his neighbour's looms, to do other than keep the looms running irrespective of the quality of the cloth woven.

[1] For example, a group weaving cloth with four damages per 1,000 yards would earn 12 per cent bonus for quality. If it only produced at 68 per cent efficiency the bonus paid would be 12%—3%= 9%. On the other hand a group which gave 80 per cent efficiency but 13 damages per 1,000 yards would receive no bonus.

Several possible shift arrangements were discussed, and it was decided to experiment with three shifts each of seven hours in an eight-hour spreadover. This allowed for three organized breaks, two of fifteen minutes and one of thirty minutes. Factory legislation regarding third-shift working made it unlikely that complete shift rotation would be possible. A start would be made, therefore, with two rotating shifts of seven hours, a permanent third shift being added once a method of working had been successfully established. Entry to the shed would then be through the third shift, i.e. any vacancies in the first or second would be filled from the third.

Permanent and Temporary Workers

The custom in India is to divide the workers of any employing institution into two categories, *permanent* and *badli*. Permanent workers are those who are guaranteed employment on any day on which they present themselves. Badli workers are those who only obtain employment if it is available because of absent permanent workers.[1] They present themselves at the mill every morning, and those not obtaining work return home.

Management agreed that no worker, permanent or badli, would be unemployed as a result of setting up an experimental shed or of any spreading of the new system if it proved successful. All workers engaged in the experimental shed would be given permanent passes, and such a number of permanent passes in excess of the number required would be issued as would take care of normal absenteeism. On those occasions on which there were fewer absentees than usual, work would be found for the surplus.

MAKING A START

The Communication of Intention

The discussions of the intention to test the proposed reorganization experimentally had been held between the Managing Agent, the Mill Manager, the Works Manager, the head of the Production Study department and myself. So far all we had was a theoretical exercise. The first step in implementation was made by the Works Manager when he seconded the Top Supervisor of the automatic loom shed, who by now

[1] Recent amendments to industrial legislation require that *badli* workers with more than 240 days continuous work must also be found work or be given compensation.

was used to experimental situations, to become Senior Supervisor of the new experimental shed. The Senior Supervisor, in consultation with the Works Manager, chose two Shift Supervisors who, after hearing about the proposed experiment, accepted their appointments with tempered enthusiasm.

The problem of communication to so large a number as those employed in the mills, when the exercise was as yet so theoretical and the outcome so uncertain, was formidable. If an attempt were made to discuss the experiment with all the workers (with different languages and many unable to read), the process of communication would itself need such elaborate experimentation and would take so long that the real experiment would be inordinately delayed. Yet, if the experiment were conducted in isolation (as for example by taking over a closed mill elsewhere in Ahmedabad) rumours would so distort the picture that the eventual introduction of the new working methods into the Calico Mills would probably be more strongly resisted. The experimental location selected was, therefore, an empty shed which had for a long time been used as a main thoroughfare through the mill. Though its use as a thoroughfare would be inconvenient, it would allow any workers in the mill to see for themselves what was going on.

It was decided to inform the trade union of what was being done, and, after the experimental shed had been in existence for a short time, to extend to all union officials an open invitation to visit it. Meanwhile applications for the experimental shed were invited from workers in other loom sheds, and detailed discussions were held with all applicants about what was proposed and the outcome expected.

The Start of the Experiment

The empty shed was painted and the humidification plant overhauled. The first twenty-four looms became available on 1st January 1954. They were erected, gated, tuned, and got running by 15th January.

It had been observed, during the work-load studies, that weavers had been reluctant to do fault prevention at the backs of looms, so much of their other work being at the front. Looms were therefore arranged in lines all facing in the same direction, instead of in the traditional way of alternate lines facing each other. This arrangement would by its strangeness draw attention to the importance of back work.

Enough interest had been aroused for the first announcement to bring a large number of applicants, of whom eighteen were chosen, two to provide spares. Whatever their expectations, their experiences of the experimental shed for the first two days were of confusion and chaos. Disturbance to the looms in dismantling and re-erecting, inexperience in the preparation of beams for looms fitted with warp-stop motions, and difficulties with the humidification of a shed long empty, made stoppage rates far higher than expected. On some looms they were as high as twelve per loom per hour, and on the best more than six. Also there was an abnormally high number of smashes. On one day there were fourteen in one shift, four taking more than four hours each to repair. As both supervisors and workers were unfamiliar with the new method of working, there were too few to deal with such high breakage rates. Extra help was given at once but with little result. The one idea of the new methods which had been assimilated was that the members of the group should help each other. They vied with each other in giving up their own jobs to help somebody else in trouble.

The experimental shed attracted large numbers of visitors from other parts of the mill. Apart from concern felt about neglect of work in their own departments, the visitors were welcomed even though they caused new difficulties by joining in what was going on. On the third day of the experiment I counted more than twice as many workers as were provided by the experiment working on the group of looms; the additions were all visitors giving a hand because of the high stoppage rates. It was not easy to make them understand that the more they joined in, the harder would it be to get any valid experimental results. But if this influx made the confusion of the first few days even more chaotic, as a method of communication to the rest of the mill it could scarcely have been bettered. It was also reassuring in that it demonstrated, as in the automatic shed, a spontaneous wish to make a success of the experiment. The visitors got nothing for their participation. Indeed, because of the neglect of their own tasks, they lost by it. Yet something made them want to help.

Change of Work Organization

Although the working of the first few days was most inefficient, the experience gained led in discussion with the workers to three modifications.

1. When a loom stopped, it was impossible without close inspection to tell whether it was for want of shuttling or for another cause. In

spite of rushing all over the group of looms, the shuttlers could not avoid looms standing idle for want of new weft. Even with mechanical or electrical signals to show the cause, stoppage rates would have had to be less than 1·0 per loom hour before shuttling and warp-mending could be efficiently carried out by different workers. It was decided to experiment with the differentiation of shuttling, warp-mending, and fault prevention into 'front work' and 'back work'. Within the scope of front work would be included shuttling and some warp-mending; within back work, fault prevention, and such warp-mending as could be reached from the back. When this was tried, an immediate improvement resulted both in efficiency and in comfort.

2. It was decided to reduce loom speeds. Looms had been running at the same speed as in other sheds. Experiments in the control of breakage rates by a reduction in speed were started on 12th February. By attention to preparation and by control of loom speeds a standard stoppage rate of $3\cdot0\pm0\cdot5$ per loom hour seemed attainable.
3. Examination showed that the shed could most conveniently hold 120 looms in twelve rows of ten. Since it was hoped that more looms would soon become available, the loom groups were fixed at forty, arranged in four rows of ten. Since back work and front work were now differentiated the looms were arranged in the conventional face-to-face pattern but with wider spaces between rows than in other sheds. This was to allow room for two workers to pass each other and for easy access for warp-mounting and gating.

When the change in work organization was first made, the front and back workers worked as a pair on one line of looms. After their initial experiences the workers themselves discovered the final form of organization—quartets of front and back workers for two lines of looms. The theoretical numbers required for forty looms were calculated, but not until the end of March was there a block of forty looms to work on. By this time sufficient experience had been gained to agree variations in numbers required for variations in warp-breakage rates.

The occupational roles, theoretical and actual numbers, tasks, and lines of responsibility for internally structured work groups operating forty looms at standard warp-breakage rates of $3\cdot0\pm0\cdot5$ per loom per hour are given in *Table 5*. The positioning of looms and the ambits of the

Table 5. OCCUPATIONAL ROLES, NUMBERS, TASKS, AND LINES OF RESPONSIBILITY OF EXPERIMENTAL GROUPS OF 40 LOOMS AT LOOM STOPPAGE RATES OF 3·0±0·5 PER LOOM PER HOUR

Occupational Roles	*Numbers* *Theoretical*	*Actual*	*Tasks*	*Lines of Responsibility*
Group Leader	0·7	1	Gating and Maintaining Group-Leading	Responsible to Shift Supervisor; responsible for work of group
Smash-Tenter (Deputy Group Leader)	1·0	1	Smash-Tenting	Responsible to group leader
Front Worker	7·4	4	Shuttling, Front-Warp-Mending	Two front workers and two back workers work as a quartet on 20 looms. Jointly responsible to group leader
Back Worker		4	Fault Prevention, Back-Warp-Mending	
Helper	0·9	1	Oiling (gating) Warp-Mounting Oiling (routine) Weft-Distributing Cloth-Removing	Acts as assistant to group leader
Totals	10·0	11		

workers concerned with loom-running are shown in *Figure 1*.[1]

By the end of March, an internally structured group of eleven had replaced what would have been on the conventional system an aggregate of twenty-two consisting of a line-jobber, twenty isolated weavers, and one isolated ancillary worker. Already the workers had shown a capacity to settle the main lines of their own internal organization, and a determination to make a success of the experiment.

[1] The detailed figures of variations in numbers for varying warp-breakage rates are given in *Tables 5* and *6*, Appendix 2.

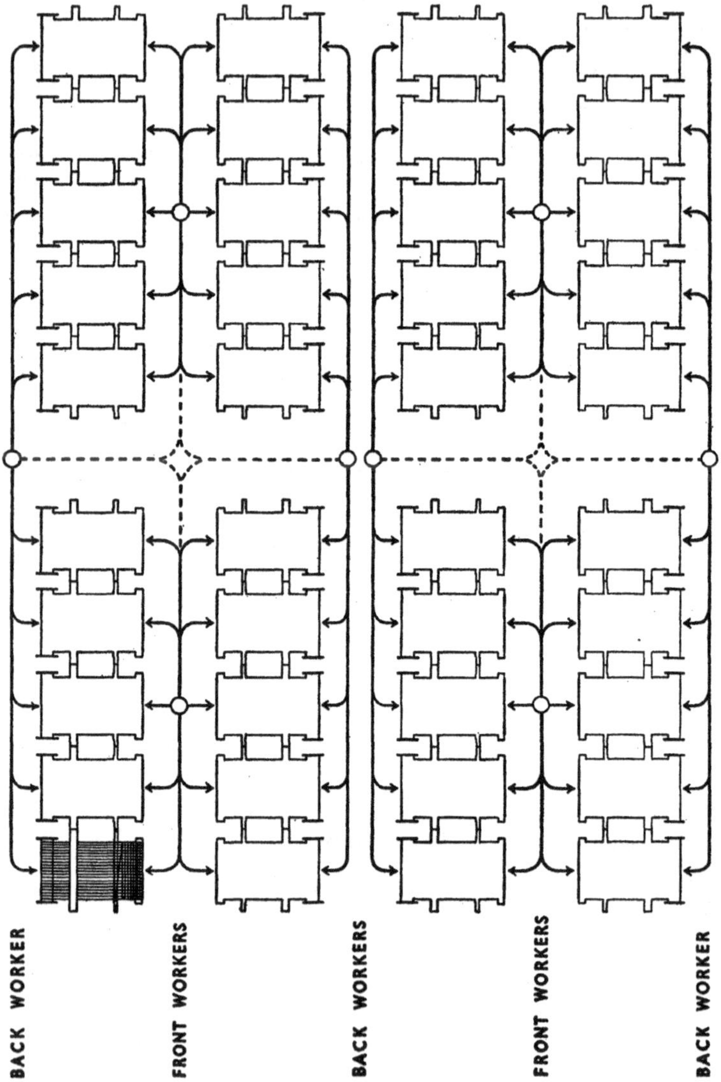

FIGURE I POSITION OF LOOMS AND AMBITS OF FRONT AND BACK WORKERS IN A BLOCK OF 40 LOOMS

CHAPTER 14

The Outcome of Reorganization

EVENTS AND PRODUCTIVITY JANUARY TO NOVEMBER 1954

Nine Phases of the Experimental Period

During the first phase when twenty-four looms were working the conditions, as already described, were chaotic. A conference of all those in the shed was held to find a solution. The beginning of the second phase was marked by the differentiation into front and back work. A second conference discussed the results, more looms were erected, and experiments were started in controlling warp-breakage rates by changing loom speeds. By the beginning of the third phase thirty-six more looms had been erected and the decision taken to lay out the loom shed in three blocks of forty looms each. Stoppages were standardized at $3\cdot0\pm0\cdot5$ per loom hour.

During the fourth phase sixty-four looms were working and others being erected. On the one completed block of forty the final form of work organization was started with quartets of front and back workers.

The national campaign against rationalization flared up. Though without much noticeable effect in the experimental shed, this intensified in the fifth phase, during which four groups worked on two blocks of forty looms on two shifts. In the sixth phase a third shift was started, and the campaign against rationalization in Ahmedabad centred on the experimental shed. Workers in the shed were hooted at as they walked through the mill and workers from other mills picketed the gates in an attempt to stop the third shift. The beginning of the seventh phase saw twenty more looms working on three shifts, but because of the campaign against rationalization further erection was halted. The law was changed to include experimental changes among those requiring either agreement with the recognized trade union or a court award. After negotiations, an enabling agreement was signed with the Textile Labour Association.

The eighth phase saw a return to normal, though the campaign did not die down until the end of the phase. Workers in the experimental shed were once more accepted in the mill, but the erection of looms was not restarted. The last and longest phase was a period of steady working. The erection of looms to complete the shed complement of one hundred and twenty was restarted. The phase ended when the experimental shed was formally accepted by the Weaving department as a manufacturing unit.

As the erection of the final group of looms was not completed during the experimental period, their results are ignored in the subsequent analysis. The experimental changes and the course of events during the nine phases are shown in their chronological order in *Table 1*. In the columns headed 'Experimental Groups' blocks of looms are indicated by capital letters and shifts by Roman numerals. Work-groups are therefore indicated by letter and numeral, thus CI & CII–24 means that twenty-four looms were working with two groups of workers, one on the first and one on the second shift.

Efficiency, Damage, and Cost

The mean percentage efficiencies of C and A groups are shown in fortnightly periods in *Figure 1*.[1] The equivalent efficiencies of similar looms on the same sort in other sheds during the same period are also shown. The change in work organization at the end of the first phase coincides with an immediate rise in efficiency which continued during the third phase until the starting of the A groups, when consequent transfers and re-erection of looms resulted in a temporary drop. The improvement was resumed in the fourth and fifth phases but was halted during the difficult days of the sixth and seventh. In the eighth it was resumed, and in the long ninth efficiency was maintained at a rather higher level than in other loom sheds, except for one brief lapse in the A groups.

The mean numbers of damages per thousand yards for the experimental groups are shown in *Figure 2*.[2] They vary inversely with efficiencies. The general pattern of steady improvement in the first five phases, the setbacks in the sixth and seventh, and the subsequent improvement in the eighth and ninth phases are reflected. It is difficult to compare the damage from the experimental shed with that from the other sheds with accuracy. The

[1] The detailed figures for each group are given in *Table 7*, Appendix 2.

[2] The detailed figures for each group are given in *Table 8*, Appendix 2.

Table 1. COURSE OF EVENTS IN THE NINE PHASES OF THE EXPERIMENTAL PERIOD 15TH JANUARY 1954–14TH NOVEMBER 1954

Phase	*Period*	*Working Weeks*	*Experimental Groups*	*Looms Working*	*Organizational and Technological Change*	*Internal Events*	*External Events*
1	Jan. 15–Jan. 29	2½	CI & CII	24	Differentiation of shuttling from warp-mending and fault-prevention. Extra help given for high stoppage rates	First conference Jan. 21. Discussion of working methods	
2	Jan. 30–Feb. 20	3	CI & CII	24	Differentiation of front and back work. Experiments in control of loom stoppages by variations in speed	Second conference Feb. 10. Discussion of working methods and bonus payments	
3	Feb. 21–Mar. 24	4½	CI & CII AI & AII	36 24	Pairs of front and back workers; loom stoppage rates standardized at $3{\cdot}0 \pm 0{\cdot}5$ per loom per hour	Third conference Mar. 10. Group bonus payment decided by first shift	
4	Mar. 25–Apr. 13	3	CI & CII AI & AII	40 24	Final form of work organization started in CI and CII—quartets of front and back workers	Group bonus payment asked for by second shift	Flare-up of national campaign against automatic looms and other forms of rationalization
5	Apr. 14–May 3	3	CI & CII AI & AII	40 40	AI and AII groups started final form of work organization	Workers stop staggering of break on appearance of General Manager. 'R' passes issued	Increasing force in campaign against rationalization. Daily press articles and speeches
6	May 4–May 14	1½	CI, CII, CIII AI, AII, AIII	40 40	Third shift started	Fourth conference May 12. Discussion of campaign against rationalization. Experimental workers hooted in Mill	Mill gates picketed by workers from other mills in attempt to stop third shift
7	May 15–June 11	4	CI, CII, CIII AI, AII, AIII BI, BII, BIII	40 40 20	Increase in loom stoppage rates	Enabling agreement signed between Trade Union and Mill—June 11. Hooting in the Mill continues	Meetings at gates, picketing of workers' houses. Muslim Holiday stoppage June 3 and 4
8	June 12–July 10	4	CI, CII, CIII AI, AII, AIII BI, BII, BIII	40 40 20	Erection of more looms for B group halted	Experimental shed workers accepted in Mill	All-India Communist leaders flock into Ahmedabad. Collapse of campaign so far as Mill is concerned
9	July 11–Nov. 13	18	CI, CII, CIII AI, AII, AIII BI, BII, BIII	40 40 20	Erection of remaining 20 looms for B group restarted. Change of shift hours	Experimental shed taken over by Manufacturing division as production unit. Fifth conference Nov. 13. Conditions for future working accepted by workers	

FIGURE I EFFICIENCY: C AND A GROUPS COMPARED WITH OTHER LOOM SHEDS

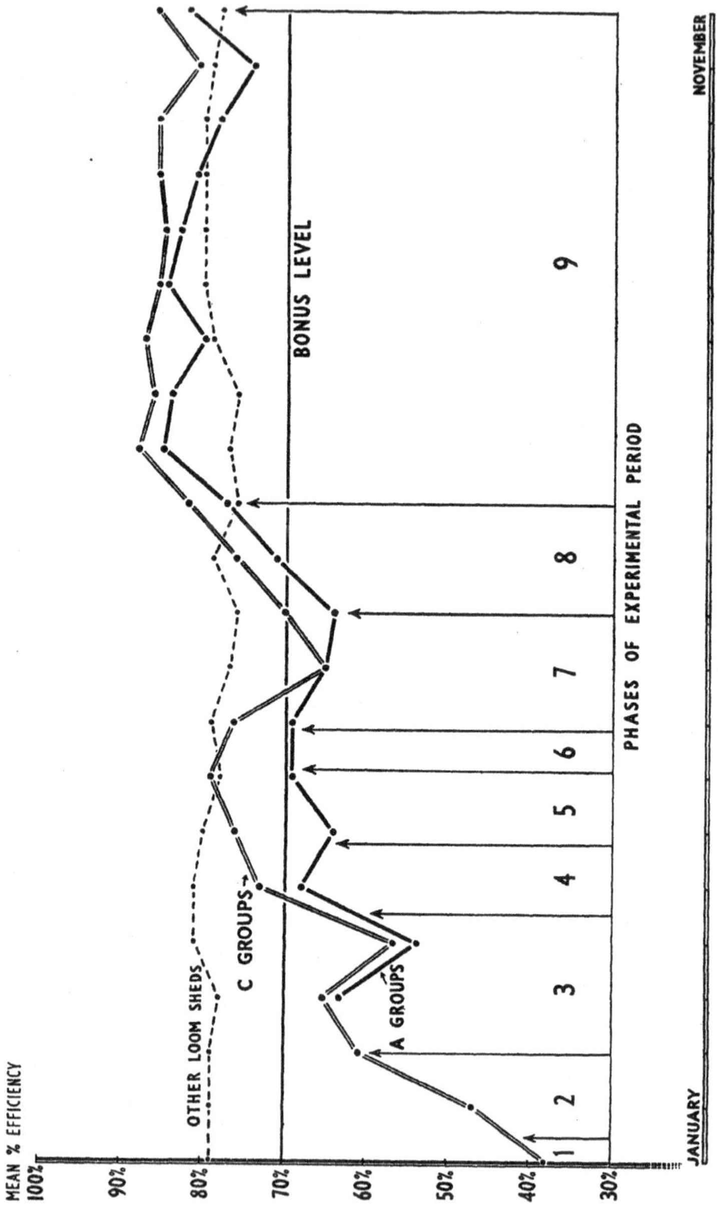

FIGURE 2 DAMAGE: C AND A GROUPS COMPARED WITH OTHER LOOM SHEDS

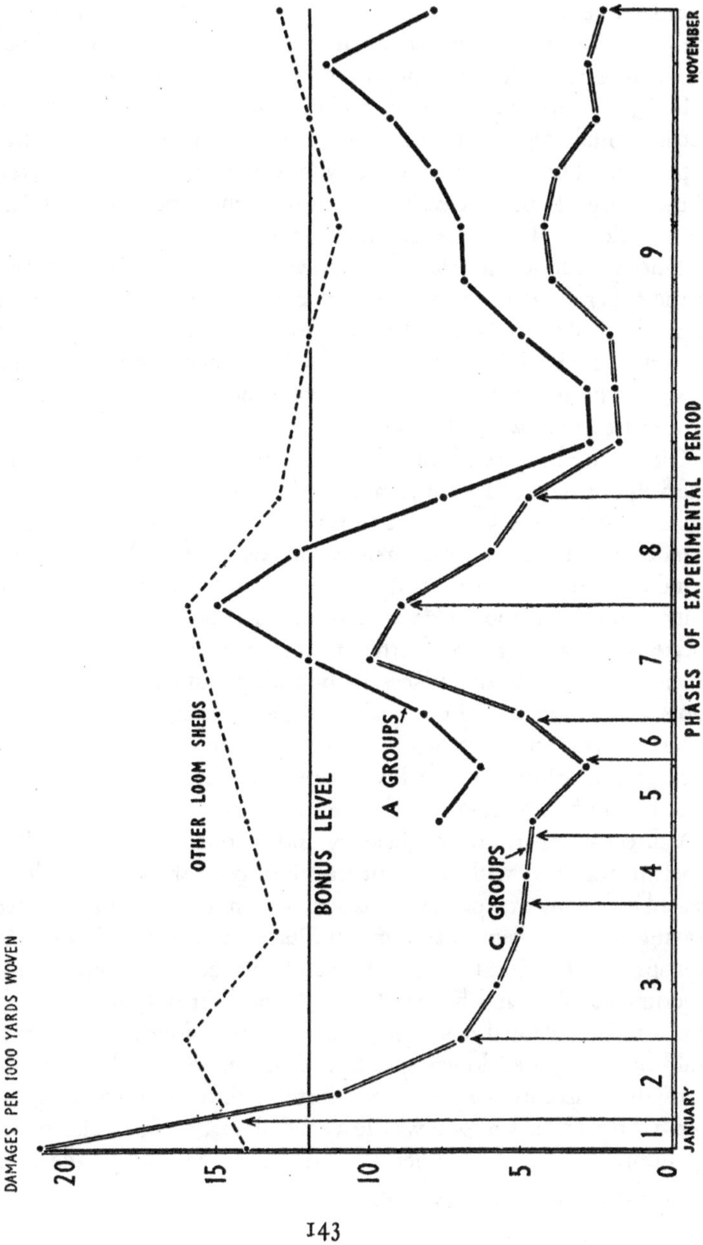

comparative test inspections made from time to time were so subject to the prejudices of the inspectors that limited reliance only could be placed on them. The results were, however, in the right direction.

In *Figure 2* the damage rates for other loom sheds are taken from the departmental records of normal inspections, where attitudes towards the experimental shed could not directly influence the findings. The standards of these inspections were easier than those of the experimental shed, so that the superiority of the latter is not exaggerated.

Among all concerned there was general agreement that the cloth woven in the experimental shed was of better quality than that woven in other loom sheds. As early as April an important export order for high-quality cloth was sent into the mill by the Sales department with the request that it be woven in the experimental shed. Other sheds, however, did not yet use looms fitted with warp-stop motions.

The mean numbers of warp-breakages per loom hour were sampled at intervals during the experimental period. In every sample there were more breakages on the A groups than on the C, and there was a direct correspondence between warp-breakages and damage, and an inverse correspondence between warp-breakages and efficiencies.[1] This correspondence cannot be pressed too far since increased attention to back work also reduced warp-breakages and other factors were known to have affected them—for example differences in humidity caused by the positions of doors and windows and the quality of loom-tuning. The differences between the performances of the C and A groups could not therefore be ascribed just to different quality beams. By the end of the experimental period there had been no conclusive explanation.

A direct comparison of efficiency and labour cost of one shift in the experimental shed with one shift in other loom sheds shows that an increased efficiency of 4 per cent was achieved in the experimental shed with a saving of 22 per cent in labour cost. Such a comparison is, however, inappropriate since it takes no account of the reduced loom speed in the experimental shed and hence of lower total shift output. Because of the profits to be obtained from loom running, it is doubtful if management could have tolerated lower speeds without increase in loom utilization. With the conventional two-loom system, third-shift working had not been worthwhile. Output was low and damage high. The new work organization of the experimental shed had made possible the profitable

[1] Detailed figures are given in *Table 9*, Appendix 2.

working of a third shift. The appropriate comparison therefore is between the results of total systems—the conventional two-shift two-loom system of existing sheds and the three-shift group system of the experimental shed. This comparison is given in *Table 2*, in which since, for security reasons, some figures have to be given as indices, all have been cast in the same form.

Table 2. PRODUCTION AND COST INDICES FOR EXISTING AND EXPERIMENTAL SHEDS DURING THE NINTH PHASE OF THE EXPERIMENTAL PERIOD

Indices	*Existing Two-Shift Two-Loom System*	*Experimental Three-Shift Group System*
Loom speed	100	89
Loom utilization	100	131
Efficiency	100	104
Output per man hour	100	187
Total system output	100	121
Damages	100	41
Total system costs	100	113

In this table the calculations of cost include all earnings,[1] and for the experimental shed, the extra overheads of third-shift working and the additional costs of inspection and preparation (cost of warp-stop motions plus cost of inserting drop wires for each beam). Estimated savings on capital investment by increased machine utilization have not been taken into account.

The average bonus earned in the experimental shed was 28 per cent, made up of a mean efficiency bonus of 18 per cent and a quality bonus of 10 per cent. On average, the workers in the experimental shed earned 55 per cent more than their equivalent grades in the other loom sheds. In other words, on the most difficult sort output was 21 per cent higher,

[1] The basic wages and bonus offered to the first experimental groups had been based on the policy of equating earnings with those in the automatic shed by returning savings on direct labour costs to the workers, the Company's advantage coming from extra savings on simpler sorts, and from increased returns on better quality. When the original cost calculations were made, the dearness allowance paid to each worker was standing at Rs 78 per month. Each reduction of one in the number of workers required for a given number of looms therefore saved Rs 78. During the experimental period the dearness allowance fell. The lowest figure reached was Rs 62, so that the saving made by the reduction of the number of workers was less than had been expected. In the calculations for *Table 2*, dearness allowance was taken at Rs 62 for the whole phase.

individual earnings 55 per cent higher, and damages 59 per cent less than in other loom sheds, for an additional total cost of 13 per cent.[1]

The quality of cloth woven, the improvement of which had been the foremost practical aim of the experiment, was such that the experimental shed was invariably chosen whenever high quality was paramount. In spite of the difficulties of measuring quality, there was sufficient practical agreement among all those concerned to lead to executive action.

RELATED SOCIAL AND PSYCHOLOGICAL EVENTS

The Development of Permissive and Collaborative Relationships

Although the behaviour of the first workers in the experimental shed and of the early visitors indicated a determination to make a success of the new system, no one believed that management would pay such high minimum rates without immediate results. The concept of 'experiment' had little meaning, and management's statements of its intentions had not carried conviction.

It had been announced that whenever necessary the looms would be stopped in order to hold discussions. The first time this happened the workers were surprised. Even the supervisors had misgivings about whether they were correctly interpreting management's intentions. While they accepted it as reasonable that success in solving the problems set by the experiment was more important than production, such meetings had never been held before. Nevertheless the stopping of looms, the calling of meetings during working hours, and the serious attention paid to what was said provided direct behavioural evidence that higher management meant what it said. This did more than verbal assurance could have done to convince the workers and supervisors.

The first informal meetings were supplemented by more formal conferences, also held during working hours. At these, changes, found necessary as the experiment proceeded, were discussed. The first conference met in two sessions, one for each shift. It was taken by the Senior Supervisor and attended by the Works Manager. At the second conference the head of the Production Study department responsible for the original work-load studies was present. This was the first time since his appointment some years before that he had been brought face to face with a

[1] Detailed figures of earnings are given in *Table 10*, Appendix 2.

group of workers in an atmosphere where free discussion was possible. When asked how he arrived at his results, his spontaneous explanation and acknowledgment of his department's limitations were well received, a lively but friendly discussion following. At this conference, the first shift stayed on and joined in the second shift's meeting, as they wanted to hear their views. Subsequent conferences, generally lasting two hours or more, were held partly in the first and partly in the second shift, and attended throughout by members of both, on a voluntary basis so far as their own time was concerned. When a third shift started, its members preferred to come to the conference of the first and second shifts rather than to have one for themselves. They too wanted to hear others' views. The third, fourth, and fifth conferences were attended by the Managing Agent and Mill Manager, and the fourth and fifth by the Weaving Master who was to take over the shed as a production unit. These attendances demonstrated management's concern, as did the Managing Agent's personal acceptance of the difficulty of some of the problems. Management in turn experienced the constructive contributions of the workers. Slowly but steadily both sides became convinced of each other's sincerity and willingness to collaborate.

In all, five conferences were held at which everything bearing on the experiment was discussed—more and more freely as time went on. All cost figures were disclosed. By the second conference, both management and workers began to feel secure enough in each other's company to disagree among themselves. By the fourth, newcomers' questions were more often answered by workers than by management.

The building of permissive and collaborative relationships released a flood of suggestions from the workers about beam mountings, new positions for warp-stop motions, and other technological changes. The supervisors, too, felt free to make experiments and take decisions that they would previously have referred to higher authority. Bad beams, which it had been intended to cut out and replace, were retained in order to provide controls for technological experiments. Innovations in methods of separating warp threads abounded. Indeed, at one time, so many such experiments were taking place that it appeared that everything was being tried except the experiment originally intended—that of finding out the productive capacity of internally structured small work-groups working under standard conditions. The enthusiasm and spontaneity were felt to be so valuable that nothing was done to check them.

The Growth of Work-Group Cohesion and of Stability in Management-Worker Relationships

The formal conferences provided evidence of the gradual growth of work-group cohesion as management and workers learned what to expect of each other. At the first conference on 21st January, during a discussion about methods of payment and group membership, workers expressed attitudes and feelings more consistent with individual working than with group working. 'I am all for groups but not if I can get 2 pies more by working on my own',[1] drew a big laugh but appeared to sum up the general feeling. At the third conference on 10th March the workers of the second shift were emphatic that they wanted pairs of front and back workers to be paid bonus on the performance of their own looms only, and not on the performance of the whole group. They were surprised and derisive when the men of the first shift preferred that all should be paid on the performance of the total group irrespective of differences between pairs. The second shift shouted that the first would regret such a decision. The arguments and differences were so loud and the exchanges so lively that my interpreter could not keep up with what was being said. The meeting resembled a rough, but good-natured, free-for-all. By this time workers felt able to disagree publicly. Management, with a sophistication too infrequent on such occasions, took little part in the discussion and agreed to pay each shift as it wanted. In the fourth phase the workers of the second shift unanimously asked that their method of payment be changed to that of the first shift.

At a second conference on 10th February the quantity and quality bonuses were discussed and workers expressed the view that the standards for the quality bonus were too tight. After the conference, the Senior Supervisor, Supervisors, and Group Leaders jointly inspected several hundred yards of cloth. There was complete agreement about the results of the inspection, i.e. about the number of damages that would be counted; but only the actual payment of bonus in the fourth phase finally dispelled the group leaders' and workers' amused disbelief in management's intention to pay it.

At the first conference there were many complaints of tiredness caused by so much extra walking. By the second, there were reluctant admissions by some workers that they were getting used to it. By the third, they

[1] 2 pies=less than one farthing.

showed a preference for the new methods of work. At all conferences they said that they worked much harder than in the other sheds. 'I work three times as hard—and only get paid twice as much' was always good for a laugh. It was as though they acknowledged that the amount of work done in the other loom sheds was too little and that now a fair balance had been struck. They found the change from traditional methods exceedingly hard, but by the fourth conference, called primarily to discuss the difficulties caused by agitation against rationalization, the majority were surprised at the distaste they felt at the thought of going back to their old sheds.

In the fifth phase, two other incidents, unimportant in themselves, provided further evidence not only of the growth of work-group cohesion but also of the lingering mutual doubts and suspicions existing between management and workers.

With the completion of both *c* and *a* groups of forty looms, an experiment was tried of staggering the midshift break so that some looms could be kept running throughout the break. This proposal was discussed by the Senior Supervisor with the Shift Supervisors, the Shift Supervisors with the Group Leaders, and the Group Leaders with the workers, and accepted by all. Group Leaders and workers were told that any resulting increase in production would increase their bonus since breaks would still be excluded from time worked for the calculation of efficiency. When staggering had been in operation for two days, the Mill Manager visited the shed at the time the break was due in order to observe its effect for himself. He was surprised to see all the workers stop work at the beginning of the break. When an inquiry was made, it was found that the workers had feared that the arrangement, by which, according to their view, they would receive extra pay for no extra work, could not possibly have been approved by higher management. In their wish to protect their own supervisors they had, without any overt, observable communication, spontaneously reverted to their earlier practice on seeing the Mill Manager. They were surprised and reassured to discover that the arrangement had his full approval.

The second incident is concerned with the issue of permanent passes to those who had previously been badli workers in other sheds and who by new management policy were entitled to permanent passes in the experimental shed. Since any worker in the experimental shed could, if he wished, return to his former job and status, a permanent pass for the experimental shed issued to a former badli worker had to be distinguished in a way that would show that his former status was badli and that his permanent pass only applied to the experimental shed. The new permanent passes were distinguished by the overprint of a letter 'R', and the passes were known as 'R' passes. It was found that the 'R' stood for my name. While this distinction was intended as a compliment, it also represented a lingering disbelief among middle management, who had to issue the passes, in either the seriousness or the rectitude of higher management in making them permanent. The unusual issue of permanent passes to more workers than there were jobs was identified, therefore, not as a management policy but as my policy. By virtue of my consultant role, I had no authority to issue passes, and, as a bird of passage, my influence was not permanent, and my curious ideas could be forgotten when I left.

These incidents, together with others of a similar kind, constituted a series of mutual test-outs, in which both management and workers tested each other's sincerity and integrity. Verbal assurances carried little conviction. Only when behaviour was experienced continuously over a long period as consistent with expressed intention were the workers' suspicion of management's motives allayed and management's doubt of the workers' capacity to collaborate dissipated.

The Active Campaign against Rationalization

Resistance to 'rationalization' is a problem of special importance in India at the present time. In the fourth phase of the experimental period it flared up and crystallized into a national campaign against the introduction of automatic looms in any mill in India. The Calico Mills were known to have been waiting for a long time for the endorsement of a licence to import automatic looms to replace old non-automatics. In Ahmedabad the agitation took the form of meetings of protest against the application for this endorsement. The meetings, which were not supported by the Textile Labour Association, were sometimes attended by a few hundreds, sometimes by many thousands, and were frequently held outside the mill gates. Processions of workers carrying banners and shouting slogans were a daily occurrence. Although the experimental shed was non-automatic, the workers in it were identified as supporters of 'rationalization' and therefore of automatics. They were subject to threats, whistles, catcalls, and boos whenever they walked through the mill, and the gates were picketed by workers from other mills in an attempt to stop them entering.

In May, during the seventh phase, their families were threatened that unless they stopped their husbands and sons from working in the experimental shed, they would be beaten up. One worker was stoned as he left the mill, but actual incidents of violence were few and nobody was seriously injured. More workers than usual exercised their right to return to their previous departments during this period, yet at no time did it appear likely that the experimental shed would be unable to continue. Indeed, one of the effects of the overt hostility was, as might have been expected, to increase the sense of group solidarity. At the fourth conference, held on 14th May, the workers' difficulties were discussed. As soon as management had accepted responsibility for looking after those who might be injured, either workers or their families, the worry about the agitation decreased to such an extent that the conference settled down, without further reference to it, to a serious discussion of the social and technological problems of the shed itself.

In view of the resistance to 'rationalization' and the failure to implement the four-loom system, difficulties had been expected in obtaining applicants for the new shed, in spite of increased rates and permanent passes. Over one hundred applications were, however, received for the first eighteen posts, the majority from existing permanent passholders. Whatever the response for the first two shifts, it was thought unlikely that there would be many applicants for the third shift in spite of the promise to fill vacancies in the first and second shifts from the third. Yet when the first eleven vacancies were announced there were over one hundred and fifty applications, nearly all from permanent weavers with established rights in their own shed on the first and second shifts. At the height of the disturbances there were fewer applicants, but even then there were always more than the posts available.[1]

The 3rd and 4th of June were Muslim holidays. The whole mill was closed for the holiday on 3rd June, but was open for Hindu workers on 4th June. In the past such religious holidays have frequently provided the occasion for demonstrations, and in the times of the Hindu-Muslim disturbances Muslims would always try to stop Hindus from working on the second day of a Muslim holiday. On 4th June very few Hindu workers presented themselves for work in the ordinary weaving sheds of the Mill but in the experimental shed not only the Hindus but all the Muslims of

[1] The numbers entering the experimental shed and returning to their previous departments during the experimental period are given in *Table 1*, Appendix 2.

the first shift and more than half of those of the second shift came to work. That they should come to work at all on a religious holiday was unusual; that they should come on a day on which their co-religionists were seeking to prevent even Hindus from working was quite exceptional.

On 11th June an agreement was signed between the Textile Labour Association and the Calico Mills to permit the continuation of the experiment. The agreement permitted the spread of the experimental results to other parts of the mill provided that no worker was unemployed, and that reduction be accomplished only by normal retirement and wastage. By the middle of June, leaders of the Communist party from all over India had assembled in Ahmedabad and had taken charge of the agitation against rationalization. But from 12th June to the end of the campaign early in July, conditions in the mill returned steadily to normal.

SUBSEQUENT EVENTS

Conditions for Future Entrants

A suspicion frequently expressed by those protesting against 'rationalization' was that as soon as the experiment had succeeded management would start changing the conditions of work.

At the conference on 14th November management announced its policy for spreading the results of the experiment. In this announcement the hours of work of the first and second shifts were increased to seven and a half, and those of the third reduced to six. Management did not believe that it would be practical to recruit only through the third shift if this worked permanently one hour longer than in other parts of the mill, when with extension of the system opportunities for transfer to the first and second shifts became fewer. If the workers who were already in the shed at the date of the announcement would accept the change in hours they would be compensated for the extra half-hour on the first and second shifts and no reduction in basic pay would be made for the existing third shift or for future entrants to it. Management left the problem to the workers but asked them to accept the revised hours since having different hours for one set of workers would be administratively cumbersome when the shed was no longer experimental. Management feared that such an alteration, by confirming the workers' suspicions, would lead to a deterioration of the newly built relationships, but felt sufficiently secure, by this time, to state their case. The workers accepted the change without exception.

Spread of Group System

Shortly after the experimental shed was accepted as a production unit, similar methods of working were started on the third shift in the Jubilee Mill, with volunteers from the first and second shifts. By the end of 1955, a shift of 476 looms was working.

The looms were not all the same size and did not all weave the same sort, but all were on medium counts of undyed yarn so that the sorts were simpler than that in the experimental shed. Because the first and second shifts continued to work as before, the looms could not be repositioned, which meant that the spaces between rows were too narrow for easy working of the new system. Two people could not pass each other at the backs or fronts, and the gating of new beams was awkward and difficult. Also because the first and second shifts continued to work as before, loom speeds could not be changed. Despite these disadvantages a group of nine workers managed blocks of forty-eight non-automatic looms.

Table 3. PRODUCTION AND COST INDICES FOR THE TWO-SHIFT TWO-LOOM AND THREE-SHIFT GROUP SYSTEMS OF THE JUBILEE MILLS

Indices of	*Two-Shift Two-Loom System*	*Three-Shift Group System*
Loom speed	100	100
Loom utilization	100	131
Efficiency	100	104
Output per man hour	100	300
Total system output	100	136
Damages	No figures available	
Total System Costs	100	79

The efficiency for the first four months of 1956 showed an increase of 4 per cent, and total costs a decrease of 47 per cent as compared with the first and second shifts of the same loom shed. Since the group system was working only on the third shift, no actual comparison of a three-shift group system with the conventional two-shift two-loom system was possible. But when the three-shift group system comes into being in the Jubilee Mill there is no reason to suppose that the performance of the first and second shifts will be worse than that of the present third—with re-positioning of looms it will certainly be better. On the assumption of an identical performance on all three shifts the indices given in *Table 3* have been constructed.[1]

During the same four months of 1956 the original experimental shed, now working 120 looms in three groups on three shifts—nine groups in all—continued to average 82 per cent efficiency and 6 damages per 1,000 yards over all groups.

Other Consequences

Because all sizes of looms weaving different sorts were mixed up in all sheds of the Calico Mill it would not have been possible to spread the three-shift group system immediately, even had all managers and workers been willing to cooperate. But in the year following the acceptance of the experimental shed as a production unit, a new attitude to weaving, stemming from the experimental shed, was observable throughout the Mill.

Warp-stop motions were installed on many looms without protest from the workers and without loss of efficiency. By the beginning of 1956 they had been ordered for all looms.

Once all badli workers had been absorbed, both volunteers for the experimental shed and absentees in all other sheds were replaced by the weavers left behind consenting to work the four-loom system. When towards the middle of 1955 a third shift was started with volunteers from the first and second shifts, they too were replaced by a further extension of the four-loom system. By the beginning of 1956 full third shifts were in operation in all sheds and only a minority of looms on the first and second shifts remained on the two-loom system.[2]

The inspection function for grey cloth is now located in the managing system of the Weaving department and will, as accommodation is made

[1] While the book was in proof, information was received that the group system has now started operating on all three shifts in the Jubilee Mill. The system has also started to spread beyond the experimental shed in the Calico Mill.

[2] Because all sheds had varying numbers of looms on two- and four-loom systems no accurate comparison is possible between production and cost indices of a three-shift four-loom system and a three-shift group system. Estimates indicate that they are approximately equal for both systems for the sort woven in the experimental shed. For simpler sorts, however, while the production indices remain approximately equal, the cost index of the group system is 25 per cent less than that of the four-loom system.

available, be located, as in the experimental and automatic sheds, in the managing system of each loom shed. Other loom sheds, though not yet working by the same system as the experimental shed, have been reorganized so that a Senior Supervisor is in charge of not more than four hundred looms, with a Shift Supervisor in charge of each shift and a supervisor in charge of major overhauls and repairs. The office of head jobber has been discontinued; the former holders of this office have become either supervisors or supervisors in charge of maintenance. Shift Supervisors now have only line jobbers reporting to them and each line jobber in charge of a group of weavers has an ancillary worker attached to him for such tasks as beam-carrying, oiling, and weft-distributing.

CHAPTER 15

Interpretation and Conclusions

In contrast to the automatic loom shed, where the system had already been grossly disturbed by the introduction of automatics, non-automatic weaving had remained the same since the Calico Mills were founded seventy-five years ago. Moreover the system had been imported, with the looms, from Lancashire where it had remained virtually unchanged for many years before that. The experimental reorganization has therefore been introduced into a system not only traditional in India but in the United Kingdom and elsewhere where non-automatic looms are still in use. Generations of weavers and weaving masters have subscribed not only to its technology but to its social organization.

While there was not, in the experimental shed, the same rapid implementation of the new system as there had been in the automatic shed, there was nevertheless much evidence of its spontaneous acceptance and of a determination to make it work—a marked contrast to the resistance to the four-loom system. In the early meetings and conferences the workers may have complained of feeling tired, expressed attitudes more appropriate to individual than to group working, and made pointed, if joking, remarks about the organization. Even as late as the fourth conference, they could express surprise over their distaste at the thought of returning to the old system. Yet throughout this time their behaviour belied their statements. In the first days of confusion and chaos there were the visitors who neglected their own work to try to help to put things right. Neither visitors nor members ever gave up trying in spite of impossible conditions, nor did members ever blame the new system for the difficulties they encountered. Had it not represented something of real value to them, they would surely have blamed those responsible for starting it.

Their acceptance of it was further evidenced by the flood of technological suggestions released as permissive and collaborative relationships were established. Although members of higher management and I, myself, were still concerned about the kind of work organization we had introduced, the supervisors and workers appeared to be far more concerned with detailed technological improvements. It was as though any question about the value of the system itself had already been answered.

Again, when the whole city was disturbed about 'rationalization' and workers not only from the Calico Mills but from most other mills were attacking the members of the experimental shed, the conference called to discuss the violence and the threats spent the greater part of its time on the internal problems of the shed and dealt very briskly with the possible consequences of the campaign against themselves. While it is common experience that hostility directed towards a group from outside will frequently increase feelings of belongingness among group members, the workers of the experimental shed must have felt that they had something worthwhile to preserve to enable them to tolerate with such assurance the jibes and threats of their fellow-workers. There was a still more dramatic demonstration of feelings about the new system on the occasion of the Muslim holiday. That the Muslims of the experimental shed should come to work on the day both of a religious holiday and of an attempt by their co-religionists to stop even Hindus working was unheard of. The only possible conclusion is that they felt that what they were doing in the experimental shed was more important to them than either the stoppage or the observance of a religious holiday.

It would have been tempting to interpret the dying down of the campaign against the workers in the experimental shed following the stoppage as an acceptance by the attackers of what the experiment was trying to do, or at least of the rights of the members of the experimental shed to do it. The situation, however, was complicated by the effect of the influx of communist leaders from other parts of India and their ardent support for the campaign. It may well have been that dislike of communist support was greater than dislike of the experimental shed; alternatively, that the issue had become too large for such a small experiment to be considered any longer important. Yet some outside support was certainly gained. Otherwise the Textile Labour Association would never have accepted the experiment under the new law or agreed to the spreading of the system to other loom sheds in the mill.

It was not possible fully to answer the questions of how far the increased wages alone would have attracted volunteers to the experimental shed or how far those who did volunteer were in any way distinguishable from those who did not. That increased wages alone would not have provided sufficient attraction in the first place is suggested by the resistance to the four-loom system in which wages for weavers comparable with those of the experimental shed had been offered without success.[1] That the wages by themselves would have been insufficient to hold those first attracted is suggested by the increased number who returned to their own sheds when trouble broke out in May and June. In most respects, those who came as applicants were an ordinary cross-section of the members of other sheds not biased in favour of Hindus or Muslims, older or younger employees or, more remarkably, permanent or badli passholders. Management was continually surprised at the proportion of permanent passholders, almost the same as in the mill as a whole, who applied for work in the experimental shed, particularly when entrance became possible only through the third shift. Naturally, with more applicants than vacancies, the supervisors, and later the group leaders, chose those whom they considered the better workers. Only in this sense could it be said that the members of the experimental shed were not a representative sample, but any differences brought about in this way arose from what would be ordinary industrial practice in such a situation.

In the conclusions about the experimental reorganization of automatic loom weaving it was suggested that the new system satisfied strong but latent needs for the security and protection derived from membership of small, stable, work groups, the opportunities for which had been lost by industrialization and urbanization, precipitated and exacerbated by job-breakdown. In sheds using non-automatic looms there had been no job-breakdown to confuse relationships and to focus attention on the social aspects of the production system. However, the spontaneous acceptance of the new system and the determination to make it work suggest, nevertheless, that the existing traditional system had left unsatisfied needs which the new system was intuitively perceived as satisfying. These needs had apparently been latent and unsatisfied for generations.

In view of the assumption about work-group size, it is noteworthy that the final form of work organization chosen by the workers should have included quartets of back and front workers—an arrangement which, in

[1] Minimum rates in the experimental shed gave B grade workers 9 per cent more and C grade workers 6 per cent less than four-loom weavers. Only when bonus was earned in the experimental shed did the members of the experimental shed earn more.

terms of the assumption, would not provide the most satisfying relationships for an independent group. The choice of this form of organization coincided with a remarkable change in attitude towards group payment by the second-shift workers. With pairs of back and front workers, they had asked for, and been given, separate payment for each pair, and had ridiculed the first shift's request for group payment. With the change in sub-grouping they asked for group payment themselves. Was this a recognition that quartets could not provide a sufficiently stable pattern of relationships as compared with either pairs, or groups of eleven? When back and front workers had been organized in pairs, the whole group, including the three who were not members of pairs, had acquiesced in the discrimination between pairs, but when, in their view, effective performance of the group tasks demanded quartets, discrimination between quartets was perceived as disruptive, and there was insistence that the whole group should share the same bonus rates.[1]

My own view is that the organization chosen by the workers is not, in reality, perhaps the most effective possible. It has, however, the overriding merit of being a structure that they have worked out for themselves, in a situation in which they were beginning to learn for the first time that social organization could be their own, as well as management's, business. I did not feel that my own need to discover what was the optimum organization should allow me to interfere, particularly since with simpler sorts or with beams of better quality different numbers of workers would be required and different forms of intra-group organization would inevitably be tried.

In India, as in the United Kingdom, there is a conventional distinction between management and workers as the 'two sides' in industry. At the same time, it sometimes appears, also as in the United Kingdom, that concentration on the differences between management and workers takes attention away from the equally serious differences that exist between one kind of manager and another and between one set of workers and another. In India the supervisor's position is perhaps less difficult than in the United Kingdom, in that there are fewer doubts about his management status. This arises in large part because the great majority of the supervisors is drawn from the literate, educated classes, frequently from those who have university degrees or who have at least matriculated, whereas a large number of the workers are illiterate. In the experimental shed the growth

[1] Cf. Bion, W. R., 'Experiences in Groups III', *Human Relations*, Vol. III, Nov. 1949.

of permissive and collaborative relationships led to a blurring of the conventional distinctions and to different kinds of identification. The creation of internally structured small work-groups gave the workers sufficient sense of security to enable them to lower some of their defensive exclusiveness and to identify themselves first with the supervisors of the experimental shed and finally with all those, up to the Managing Agent, who were concerned in its establishment.

Their identification with their own supervisors was shown most dramatically when the Mill Manager visited the shed shortly after the staggering of the mid-shift break. The workers' reversion to the previous practice of shutting down was spontaneous and unanimous. It showed an identification with their own shift and shed management so complete that they did not need to communicate overtly with each other before taking action. That the workers were prepared to back them so completely gave the supervisors considerable security both in their dealings with workers and with higher management. They took responsibility for decisions which they would previously have referred upwards. The change was also seen when it became necessary to appoint another supervisor because of the starting of the third shift. Quite unusually, he was chosen not from the ranks of English-speaking graduates but from the ranks of the workers.

The Senior Supervisor was at first very worried about taking the responsibility for inspection. While he acknowledged that the location of the function outside the shed might be construed as a vote of no confidence in himself, he also realized that its location within his own control was a challenge to his capacity to take full personal responsibility for the shed—such full responsibility was not at the time taken by anybody else in charge of a weaving department. The increasing support from both above and below so reassured him, however, that he was finally able to set up and maintain standards of inspection generally acknowledged to be tighter than anywhere else in the mill.

Members of higher management, too, learned during the experiment that workers would not always necessarily react in the conventional and defensive manner towards any changes suggested. If management had been sure that it could always give increased help to a hard-pressed group, it had been much less certain that when conditions improved it would be able to take it away again. Only the actual experience during the difficult early days of the experiment convinced members of management that workers too could, and would, take a realistic, task-centred attitude to such situations. That this attitude was not easily learned without such evidence was shown by the incident of the 'R' passes which were issued by an administrative department not directly involved in the experiment.

That changes were not confined to the experimental shed and that a new attitude to weaving was subsequently perceptible in the rest of the mill has already been stated. It might, however, be thought that the acceptance of the four-loom system in other sheds showed that the earlier resistance to it had been due to difficulties of relationship between management and workers rather than to any intrinsic imperfections of the system itself, and that better understanding within management and between management and workers would have led to its earlier adoption without the experience of the experimental shed. This view cannot be disproved and is indeed still held by some members of management. But management's relations with its workers had been good for many years, and the acceptance of the four-loom system was based upon a known policy of eventual conversion to the system of the experimental shed. Moreover, in the experimental shed new norms of productivity and wages had been established. While, in view of the long tradition of the two-loom system, it would have been unreasonable to have expected all managers and workers immediately to accept the new system, it is equally unreasonable not to have expected them to be affected by the achievement of new norms. Managers were challenged by the improved productivity; workers by the increased earnings. The extension of the four-loom system, with the continuation of pockets of the two-shift two-loom system, can therefore be interpreted as the resultant of opposing forces—those directed towards implementation of the experimental system and those directed towards preservation of the conventional. Change to the four-loom system became possible, with the experimental shed as a catalyst, because a more extreme change to the new system was still avoided.

The immediate practical result of the experiment has been to demonstrate that, given permissive and collaborative relationships, fewer workers, paid higher wages, could produce better cloth by the new system at no greater cost than by the old. A form of organization has been accepted flexible enough to take account of work-loads that vary with change of count, sort, colour, and conditions. The most difficult sort was chosen for the experiment. It has already been shown on the third shift of the Jubilee Mill that with simpler sorts, giving fewer loom stoppages, greater production than obtained in the experiment can immediately be reached by increasing loom speeds, and that costs can be reduced by reducing the number of workers in the group.

In the Jubilee Mill the building of a new loom shed and the installation of a new kind of machinery—automatic looms—had given management the opportunity to establish new norms of output and of reward. By offering wages greatly in excess of those earned in the non-automatic sheds they had set new standards for themselves as well as for the workers. But the full potentiality of the new technology had not been realized until a new social organization had been brought into being, which allowed the workers to recover something good which had been lost by job breakdown—the protection and security of small-group membership. In the experimental shed the looms were the same as those used in other non-automatic sheds, and the work organization was supported by years of tradition. Expectations of both wages and effort were comparable with general Indian standards. The payment of wages comparable with those of the automatic shed demanded new standards of productivity, both of output per man-hour and of quality. In effect it can be said that new norms have now been established for non-automatic weaving as a whole. To make this possible a new socio-technical system had to be brought into existence, in which realization of the advantages of job-breakdown depended upon finding a social organization that allowed the workers to create something good—internally structured work-groups—which did not exist in the conventional system of worker isolation with which the traditional norms were associated.

SUMMARY OF PART IV

1. The presenting problem was to improve the quality of cloth woven on non-automatic Lancashire looms. The workers had consistently resisted the installation of warp-stop motions because of the extra work involved. They were paid a bonus for quantity but, though fined for bad quality, the total fines that could be imposed were less than the bonus which could be earned by weaving damaged cloth.

2. On any one day forty main varieties with over three hundred sub-varieties were being woven. Varieties were put on looms without particular reference to the variety previously woven.

3. Studies of the existing production system showed that:

(*a*) Weavers, who each ran two looms, were, in their formal role-relationships, independent isolates. Informally they made supportive and mutually helpful relationships with each other, taking over each other's looms so that they could spend long periods outside the sheds.

(*b*) Weavers, who were responsible for the quality and quantity of cloth woven, were subject to the authorities of three departments: their own, the Preparatory department, and the Sales department. They had frequently to visit other parts of the mill to obtain weft yarn and to deliver woven cloth.

(*c*) In spite of multiple authorities and a wide range of movement, weavers performed an integrated 'whole' task—the conversion of yarn to cloth.

(*d*) Two supervisors of equal status were in charge of each shift of each loom shed. There was confusion about their responsibilities and authority. In addition, neither of them had any authority over some parts of the weaving process.

4. In the Indian textile industry there are three major barriers to change:

(*a*) No reduction is permitted in the number employed in any company without agreement with the recognized trade union.

(*b*) No change is permitted in working practices without agreement with the recognized trade union.
(*c*) No expansion of loom or spindle capacity is permitted in 'Surplus' zones—in one of which the Calico Mills is situated.

An enabling agreement between the mill owners and the trade union signed some months previously allowed a weaver to work up to four looms provided no one was unemployed thereby and the workers agreed.

5. An experimental shed was set up staffed by applicants from existing loom sheds. In the experimental shed:

(*a*) All looms were fitted with warp-stop motions.
(*b*) The tasks of weaving were differentiated as to task area, time period, skill, and condition.
(*c*) The tasks of loom-running were further differentiated into (i) front work—shuttling and warp-mending from the front of the loom, and (ii) back work—fault-prevention and warp-mending from the back.
(*d*) Small internally structured work-groups were constituted to perform all the tasks of weaving and maintenance on groups of forty looms, all of which wove the same kind of cloth continuously.
(*e*) The members of the work-groups performed interdependent tasks and formed interdependent relationships.

6. Minimum basic rates were fixed higher than had previously been paid. Four natural grades within a work-group were found: group leader, front loom worker, back loom worker, and helper. Bonus was paid both for quantity and for quality; fining for bad quality was stopped. The bonus was paid, at the workers' own request, for group rather than individual performance.

7. All tasks related to weaving, including inspection, were made the responsibility of the Senior Supervisor in charge of the loom shed. Standards of inspection were agreed after a joint inspection of some hundreds of yards of cloth by the Senior Supervisor, shift supervisors, inspectors, and group leaders. Self-inspection and self-criticism were accepted by management as imposing higher standards of inspection and better quality control than when inspection was a function of the Sales department.

8. The experimental period lasted ten months. The outcome during the first weeks was confused by the quality of the beams, difficulties with

humidification, and the inexperience of both workers and supervisors with the new methods. Improvements were made in the quality of the beams; the loom stoppage rates were partially controlled by variations in the speed of looms. Both management and workers 'tested out' each other's sincerity and willingness to cooperate. Gradually permissive and collaborative relationships based on mutual trust were built up.

9. The building of permissive and collaborative relationships between management and workers and the stabilizing of intra-group relationships were assisted by the institution of informal group meetings and of more formal conferences. The conferences were taken by the Supervisor in charge of the shed but were attended by the Managing Agent, the Mill Manager, the Works Manager, and later the Weaving Master, as well as by the supervisors, group leaders, and all workers in the shed—i.e. the whole executive chain responsible for production was present. At first separate conferences were held for the different shifts, but at the workers' request all shifts attended the same conferences, which were held partly in the first shift and partly in the second. When a third shift was started, the workers on this shift willingly came in, in their own time, to attend.

10. After the experimental shed had been running for approximately four months, a national campaign against 'rationalization', which had been simmering for some time, flared up all over India. In Ahmedabad meetings were held and processions shouting slogans marched to protest against an application for automatic looms by the Calico Mills. Although the experimental shed was not using automatic looms, its members were identified as supporters of rationalization: the mill gates were picketed in an attempt to stop them working; their families were threatened; they were hooted at as they walked through the mill and one worker was stoned. More members of the experimental shed than formerly exercised their right to return to their former jobs during this time, but there were always more applicants for work in the shed than there were vacancies. On the Muslim holidays of 4th June, no Hindu weaver appeared for work in the ordinary loom sheds, but all the Hindus and all the Muslims of the first shift and all the Hindus and more than half the Muslims of the second shift turned up for work in the experimental shed.

11. After a very slow start the efficiency of the shed climbed steadily, with a setback during the height of the campaign against rationalization,

until during the ninth and final phase of the experimental period it was somewhat higher than equivalent efficiencies in other loom sheds. The quality of the cloth woven in the experimental shed, after being worse than that woven in other sheds for the first phase, steadily improved, again with a setback during the anti-rationalization campaign, and finally settled down at a better standard than was achieved in other sheds.

12. The immediate practical result of the experiment has been to demonstrate that in the Calico Mills the breakdown of the 'whole' task of weaving into component operations, each performed by a different worker, and the reintegration of the workers into an internally structured work-group that performs the 'whole' task on a group of looms, can be accomplished in one process provided that permissive and collaborative relationships can be built up between all those concerned.

13. The workers earned an average bonus of 28 per cent during the ninth phase of the experimental period; the mean earnings of the group were 55 per cent higher than the equivalent mean earnings in other sheds on the two-loom system. The cost of the experimental shed was 13 per cent higher than the cost of an equivalent number of looms in other sheds. The output was 21 per cent higher and the number of damages 59 per cent less. These results were achieved on the most difficult sort regularly woven in the mills.

14. The system has since been spread to other sheds, where, on simpler sorts, similar earnings have been achieved, with a 4 per cent rise in output and a 47 per cent reduction in labour cost.

15. The experimental system has established new norms of performance and earnings for non-automatic weaving. The conclusion was reached that the acceptance of the new system and the determination to make it work were due to its providing more opportunities for effective task performance and for the building of stable and secure small work-group relationships than those existing in the conventional system with which the traditional norms of performance and wages were associated.

PART V

The Experimental Reorganization of Management

THE CREATION OF NEW MANAGING SYSTEMS

CHAPTER 16

The Background to Management Reorganization

In his first discussions at the Institute, the Managing Agent accepted, without reservation, that changes in the production system of the Calico Mills would require changes in management. He had no illusions about the possibility of changing workers' attitudes towards increased mechanization without some corresponding changes in management attitudes—'starting with my own'.

By 1953, the social changes described in Chapter 2 were making themselves felt with increasing force. The influence of the trade unions, exerted primarily through political action, had restricted the powers of management. The wartime and post-war booms had changed to competition. Technological development became imperative, but was seriously hampered by restrictions on changing methods and on installing new machinery. Managers were now required to manage in a situation which placed a premium on their ability to bring about change when their power to order change was being severely limited.

The introduction of such new processes as had been permitted had raised personnel problems as well as more obvious technological disruptions. The personnel problems, though as yet minor, nevertheless gave warning of what might be in store in the future. Because nobody in the Company had had practical experience of running a modern installation of automatic looms, a specialist with American training had had to be appointed. The development of new cloth processes and finishes had led to the appointment of chemists, chemical engineers, and research technologists in numbers far greater than previously. The new specialists were young men trained abroad and not brought up in the older industrial traditions in India. Fitting them into the existing organization had not been accomplished without difficulties over their status and authority.

For all these reasons, apart from the current changes occurring as a result of the project, a study of management was carried out in parallel with other work during the three years with which this account deals. The experimental reorganization of management was slower than other reorganizations, and, because of the interaction of events in all parts of the mill, more difficult to control. Successful experiments in work reorganization encouraged management to go ahead with its own examination, but failure to achieve attempted change raised doubts about the advisability of changing anything.

Just as changes in work organization had their effects on management, so also the slow but steady progress in the reorganization of management stimulated changes in other areas of mill activities. The experiments described in Parts III and IV represent those parts of the project that have reached the stage at which results have been sufficiently reliable to make them reportable and in which the effects of other events both inside and outside the mills could be assessed with some confidence. As the work has extended, cause and effect have become more difficult to disentangle. From the beginning the project was conceived as a collaboration between the Company and the Tavistock Institute. This collaboration has become more real as the members of the Company and myself have come to know each other better and have learned to work together with decreasing surprise at each other's preconceptions and prejudices. By now, I am a member of a group concerned with the identification and solution of any problem the Company faces. The project has begun to lose its discrete identity, and changes initiated, in the first place, as a part of it are now one with the changes initiated by members of the Company.

In this chapter, as an introduction to reorganization of management, some of the other changes that have taken place will be briefly described.

PROCESS LAYOUT: BLEACHING, DYEING, PRINTING, AND FINISHING

Once cloth has been woven it is 'unfinished'. If undyed yarn has been used in its weaving it is known as 'grey' cloth and, whether undyed or dyed, it is collected in the 'Grey Room' to be sorted and prepared for finishing. The first finishing process is to remove the loose threads and ends left on in weaving and then by chemical processes to remove the size put on the yarn during preparation for weaving. Thereafter the cloth goes through a variety of processes depending upon the purpose for which it is intended—bleaching, mercerizing (which gives it a lustre), dyeing for coloured piece goods, printing for patterned piece goods, backfilling, shining, waterproofing, stentering, and others. Finally, there is Sanforizing (a preshrinkage process) or calendering, which is large-scale ironing. Between each process the cloth has to be washed and mangled and often dried as well. All cloth goes through the first and last processes, and most through more than one intermediate process. A small proportion goes through them all.

The rapid development of new processes for cloth-finishing has been a remarkable feature of the post-war textile industry. In Europe and the United States the development has been fostered by competition from artificial fibres. In India, where few artificial fibres have yet had the success they have enjoyed in more temperate climates, the conflicting demands of standardization and diversification have encouraged mills to compete by offering a wider variety and a higher quality of 'finish'.

The introduction of new processes and the development of established ones had already overstretched the capacity of the existing buildings and had called into question plans for expansion. The trouble was that since finishing processes are both mechanical and chemical and the majority of the machines are large and heavy, rearrangement was difficult without severe interruption to production.

Moreover any improvement that meant more washing, mangling, and drying, severely strained not only the capacity but also the planning of the central department containing the washers, mangles, and driers, through which some lengths of cloth had to pass five or six times before they were finished. Although bigger and faster machines were becoming available, a re-examination of the total finishing process suggested the breakdown of this central department into a large number of smaller units. Accordingly it was proposed to attach a small washing, mangling, and drying unit to each of the other processes. The smoother throughput and greater flexibility so obtainable would more than offset the losses caused by having machines not always fully loaded and the larger capital investment involved.

A new layout was planned, which by eliminating central washing, mangling, and drying, allowed departments responsible for different processes to be better spaced, with room for expansion. Building of the new extension started in 1955.

KEY MILL LAYOUT

The Calico and the Jubilee Mills occupy the sites on which they were originally built, chosen to allow for expansion. Even so, with technological developments unforeseeable at the time, major building activities and alterations have had to be undertaken. The experience in the Processing Mill led to the drawing up of the 'Key Mill Layout'. This plan is an attempt to allow for the changes that may be required within the next twenty years. All likely changes could not, of course, be foreseen, but some, such as the need to replace certain machines within a given time, were known, and others could be anticipated. In making the plan it was assumed that

1. Material flow should be in a uniform direction. It should not have to turn back on itself. Nor should lines of flow cross each other without some arrangement for separating the traffic.
2. Where, in a manufacturing process, material has to pass through the same machine more than once, more than one machine should be provided.
3. Material should be transported between processes as little as possible, but where transport was found necessary, either continuous or bulk transport should be made available.
4. Roadways should provide for adequate circulation of traffic with one-way traffic systems wherever necessary. They should be permanently fixed and have all services concentrated in them.
5. Provision should be made for expansion with the minimum of machinery moving. Any steps taken now should be consistent with the Key Mill Layout, particularly in the erection of buildings, the laying of services, or the installation of heavy machinery.

While there was nothing novel about these assumptions, it was useful to have articulated them and to have gained their acceptance at a time when so much machinery was being installed and so many rearrangements being made.

PROCESS MANAGEMENT

The replanning of the process layout, and the consequent rearrangement of departments, necessitated re-examination of process management. The organization had been determined largely by historical growth. After weaving the first processes introduced were cropping, singeing, de-sizing, bleaching, and calendering. A Bleaching Master, ranking with the 'Masters' in charge of spinning and weaving, took charge. Next came preshrinking and stretching. As new processes were added, the Bleaching Master included them in his own department until his command embraced both bleaching and finishing. So far the new processes did not require new technological skills, but when printing was added it was so specialized that a Printing Master was appointed. Later, a Dyeing Master was added.

The number of processes were now so many and represented so large an investment that a new post was created to provide management for processing as a whole. The growth had been so gradual and the tradition so strong that the new post was entitled 'Bleaching Superintendent', and the command the 'Bleach House'. The better to distinguish him, the original Bleaching Master became known as the 'Bleaching and Finishing Master'.

The Bleaching and Finishing Master controlled the beginning and end processes as well as washing, mangling, and drying. He therefore controlled total throughput and 'import' and 'export' of the Printing and Dyeing departments. As against this he had no control over what happened in the Printing and Dyeing departments, so that his plans for total throughput were frequently upset. The splitting of the central washing, mangling, and drying department would remove some of his problems, but would still leave him with a command very much larger than the others and including both beginning and end processes. In these circumstances not only production planning but quality control would still be difficult. Attempts by the Finishing departments to trace the blame for faults either to Printing or to Dyeing would almost invariably be traced back to Bleaching.

The imbalance in the commands, the dominant position of the Bleaching and Finishing Master in production planning, with, however, the diffused control of throughput—the divergence of management and process organization—placed a premium on the relationships between the Bleaching Superintendent and his subordinates. That the regular throughput of over one hundred and ten miles of cloth each day was accomplished with little friction was a tribute to the quality of these relationships, but the system left too much to chance.

The organization was discussed with the Bleaching Superintendent and his three subordinates, the Bleaching and Finishing, Dyeing, and Printing Masters, and with their subordinates, the Supervisors. Reorganization was agreed. The Bleaching Superintendent became the Processing Mill Manager with six subordinates of comparable status. Four—Bleaching, Printing, Dyeing, and Finishing Masters—were responsible for four differentiated operating systems. Two—a Planning and Control Officer and an Engineer—were responsible for control and service functions in the Mill managing system.

EXPERIMENTAL WORK REORGANIZATIONS

Processing differs from spinning and weaving in that the great majority of the activities are chemical as well as mechanical. The kinds of control that can be maintained have a different quality, and the steps taken to rectify mistakes are of a different order. Once chemicals have been mixed and cloth fed into the machine, there is little to be done other than to keep watch and make adjustments to flow tension, temperature, and speed. So much is out of the immediate control of the workers that good quality and high efficiency become dependent on the constant watching of instruments and on skill in interpreting what they record. Excuses for poor results are easy to find and mistakes easy to hide.

In many processes chemicals once mixed cannot be left standing and interruptions involve cleaning out the machine before it can be restarted. Continuous running therefore throughout the twenty-four hours is even more important than in many purely mechanical processes. In mercerizing, for example, it is more efficient to run two machines for three shifts than three machines for two, and three machines for two shifts than six for one.

Because so much of the work in the Processing Mill consists of watching instruments and seeing that cloth is fed evenly and smoothly into machines, the workers spend a great deal of their time standing about. Conventional work-load studies were not helpful in suggesting economies or role interchanges. Their effect was rather to point to the need to invent automatic controls. Tests of the frequency with which adjustments had to be made, and calculations of the cost of not making those required, showed however that the time-lag between the detection of a fault and the beginning of disaster was longer for some checks than for others. In a few places the cost of a fault was less than the cost of constant vigilance.

Slight though it was, this flexibility provided some possibility of worker mobility. Machines requiring three or four workers could be linked togather so that they could be manned by work-groups of a size that would provide more satisfying personal relationships. In the Mercerizing department three machines were being run on two shifts. Each machine was separately manned and there was one labourer who performed general departmental duties. Internally structured small work-groups were first organized to run two machines on three shifts, and, as production expanded, three machines on three shifts. A work-group leader is responsible on each shift to the Shift Supervisor for all machines, and a work-group of ten (including the leader) is divided into those who maintain constant watch over certain parts of the process and those who form a mobile force patrolling all machines.

At the beginning of 1956 similar working groups were organized for the Dyeing department at the workers' request. They have been working smoothly, the supervisors finding it easier to make relationships with groups than with individuals, particularly in relation to third-shift working. More machine hours and, hence, greater production are being obtained. The proportional increase is greater than the addition of the machine hours that a third shift would account for.

One other experimental work reorganization is now being tried. In ring spinning—the final process in the conversion of raw cotton to yarn—it is common practice in the industry to differentiate two main tasks, *piecing*—the joining of the ends of broken yarn—and *doffing*—the removal of full bobbins on which yarn has been wound. Other tasks, maintenance, cleaning, oiling, and carrying are sometimes differentiated, particularly where 'redeployment' has taken place, and are sometimes left as part of the main tasks. Usually the *piecers* work as isolates, each to his or her own frames, while the *doffers* work as gangs over whole sections of the spinning room.

In the Spinning department of the Calico Mill, an internally structured small work-group, with interchangeable tasks, is experimentally running twelve ring frames as an integrated unit, taking responsibility as a group for all tasks. The results are promising and in line with those achieved in other departments. Fewer workers, paid higher wages, are able to produce efficiently at no greater cost than before reorganization. The experiment has not yet continued for sufficiently long to make the results reliable, nor have other workers in the Spinning department yet asked for permission to reorganize themselves in the same way.

THIRD-SHIFT WORKING

In the automatic and the experimental non-automatic sheds, third-shift working, contrary to earlier experience, had proved successful. Towards the end of 1954 a working party was set up to study the possibility of introducing it into all other departments of the mills. The working party, to which I acted as infrequent consultant only, was composed of the former Senior Supervisor of the experimental shed, the Supervisor responsible for setting up experimental reorganization in Mercerizing, the Spinning Master of the Jubilee Mill, and the head of the Production Study department. All were relieved of other duties while they made their investigation.

The working party considered all the conditions—technological, social, and economic—that would need to be satisfied if production was to be satisfactory and workers attracted to the third shift. By reorganizations of various kinds the working party was able to consider paying substantial wage-increases to those who would volunteer for the third shift and to those who, from the reduction in numbers on the first and second, would have more to do. The general change in attitude among both management and workers made it possible for management to offer the new wages and conditions, and for workers to accept them. Not that their anxiety about each other's motives was completely allayed. Each continued to test the other's sincerity, but the level of anxiety was below that which inhibits progressive action. The report initiated a series of changes that resulted one year later in both mills going over to three-shift working with scarcely any increase in numbers of workers over those previously employed on two shifts—under the industrial conditions of Ahmedabad, a remarkable performance.

In the past, supervision on the third shift had never been as good as on the other shifts. It had been unpopular with management as well as with workers. In consequence, the most junior supervisors had been posted to it. Not unnaturally the combination of least experienced workers and most junior supervisors had succeeded in proving correct those who believed that third shifts were not worth while. It would have been of little avail to try to improve this situation by the appointment of third-shift managers to whom all third-shift supervisors would report. Such an appointment would have made any third-shift supervisor subject to two authorities—the head of his own department and the third-shift manager.

The principle was accepted that the manager of any three-shift department should carry responsibility for his department throughout the twenty-four hours. The difficulty in the past was that so much of the administrative work had been carried out during day-time office hours, that visits by the head of the department to the third shift had tended to be a spare-time activity. In consequence they occurred only occasionally. By the provision of administrative assistance, particularly in production planning, heads of departments were freed to arrange their working hours so that they could attend all three shifts, spending the bulk of their time where they felt most needed. Such administrative arrangements would not by themselves ensure more senior managerial attention on the third shift. What was also required was a marked change in the attitude of higher management towards subordinates in charge of departments. The expectation that the head of a department would always be available whenever his superior felt like sending for him had to be modified. The superior had to tolerate absence during office hours to allow subordinates to put in time on the second and third shifts.

The form of organization for three-shift working depended primarily on the technological complexity and diversity of departmental processes. Where the technology was uniform, as in weaving, management could be organized on the basis of temporal priority, i.e. the immediate subordinates of the head of the department could be in charge of shifts, with their subordinates in charge of sections. Where the technology was diverse, as in spinning, management could be more appropriately organized on the basis of technological priority, i.e. the immediate subordinates of the head of the department should be in charge of technological processes with their subordinates in charge of shifts.

EXPANSION OF SALES OUTLETS

The demands of the market for lower prices and high quality, transmitted to the mills by the Sales department, were experienced by the manufacturing departments as exacting and, during slacker times, as capricious. Designs and qualities, which had previously sold readily, were no longer adequate, and merchants were reluctant to accept new designs. Production plans, especially in the Processing Mill, had frequently to be altered to satisfy important customers. At the same time the reorganizations that had led to manufacturing departments taking more responsibility had made it less easy for the Sales department to obtain ready acceptance of alterations in production plans. Meanwhile, the increased output coming from third shifts required the Sales department to move more cloth than before.

With the exception of a small percentage sold through a few retail shops, all cloth produced was distributed through certain large merchants who, in turn, distributed it to smaller merchants and wholesalers all over India. Increased output meant that the merchants were being called upon to take financial risks, large even for the biggest of them. In consequence they were cautious in their ordering of quantity and conservative in their acceptance of designs. A greater number of direct outlets was imperative. Marketing consultants made a field survey. Within less than a year, the Company extended the number of outlets from twenty to over three thousand, located in all important centres of population throughout India. In this expansion the number of links between Mill and consumer was reduced from four to two.

SALES DEPARTMENT ORGANIZATION

The change in the number of outlets and the new arrangements with the merchants—who now acted as agents working on commission—entailed reorganization within the Sales department itself. The existing department was responsible for the inspection and storing of grey cloth, and for the inspection, folding, and packing of finished cloth. It also made out invoices, collected cash, and decided about customers' credit. It was more like a quasi-independent marketing organization than a department of the Mills. Its independence appeared to be limited only by being tied to one supplier. The same organization could, with little alteration and without this restriction, have acted as an independent merchant house. By the nature of his primary task, an independent merchant will identify himself with whichever side of the market has the greater power. In a seller's market he will identify with manufacturers, since almost any cloth is in short supply and is being sought by buyers. In a buyer's market he will identify with customers, since cloth is abundant and manufacturers are the supplicants. However understanding of manufacturing difficulties he may be, he cannot help, in a buyer's market, but be biased in favour of his own needs to satisfy powerful, captious, and fickle customers. When mistakes are made in sales-forecasting or manufacturing he will try to correct them where least resistance is likely. In a buyer's market, this is manufacturing. The existing Sales department appeared to manufacturing departments as their only, highly privileged, and frequently difficult, customer.

By contrast, a sales department that is a part of an integrated manufacturing and selling organization is required to sell what the manufacturing departments produce. It may complain—and frequently does— that what is produced is difficult to sell; but it does not make an independent assessment of quality. It has to accept and sell a company standard. It must believe in what it sells, and identify itself with manufacturer rather than buyer, irrespective of market conditions. Its selling plan must be an integral part of an overall production plan and it must share responsibility for the consequences of any change.

Parallel with the expansion of sales outlets, changes were made in the organization of the Sales department. The inspection function, part of which had already been experimentally included in the managing systems of the automatic and experimental non-automatic sheds, was taken away completely, and all invoicing and cash collection were transferred to a new finance division. Organizationally, Sales was streamlined for selling.

ATTEMPTED REORGANIZATION IN WINDING AND WARPING

In Winding and Warping, yarn from Spinning is rewound to provide warp beams and weft bobbins for Weaving. By rewinding under tension and by passing the yarn through carefully graded slots, weak places are eliminated and loose fluff is removed. The Calico Mills had obtained permission to install new machinery for winding and warping which, by performing automatically some of the operations formerly carried out manually, would ensure higher production and less variation in quality. Delivery of the new machines would not be made for more than a year. It was proposed to attempt social reorganization to prepare the way for the impending technological disturbance.

Analysis of activities, tasks, and occupational roles was made as for the weaving sheds. Discussions were held with management, supervisors, and workers. In some sections, discussions were held with small groups; in others whole sections of fifty or sixty were seen together. The discussions, which frequently involved the simultaneous use of five languages, were not easy, although it was not difficult to establish a rapport. The findings were, however, depressingly similar from all groups. The workers felt too insecure in their relations with other departments and with management to consider any changes other than those they would have to deal with once the new machines arrived. They would talk of little except the alleged evils of Spinning that provided poor yarn, or of Weaving that demanded impossible standards.

'Only Spinning and Weaving matter; nobody bothers about us, we just don't count';

'It's no use talking to us about quality, it's the Spinning departments you have to go to'; and,

'We don't want to change, we're all right, just leave us alone.'

The nature of the existing machinery and the impending installation of new precluded the setting up of a comparatively inexpensive experimental unit for which volunteers could have been invited. In spite of the general insecurity it appeared more than likely that sufficient volunteers would have come forward had such a unit been established, and that a demonstration of this kind would have served as a more general change-producing agent. Without this possibility many more discussions would have been necessary before the workers could have dealt with their discontent sufficiently to allow them even to discuss anything else. The urgency of other work that gave greater promise of earlier results, the relatively short time available before the installation of new machines, and the generally agreed policy that no change should be imposed, suggested that, apart from drawing up recommendations of steps to be taken once the new machines did arrive, no further action should be taken.

THE NEED FOR CHANGE

The impact of all these changes, and others, such as the need for integrated accounts and more rigid stock control, fell with particular severity upon the Managing Agent. To him, as the head of a concern still organized as a family business, most decisions of any importance had to be referred. So much of his time was being taken up with comparatively minor matters that he could not give sufficient time to overall company policy.

In a family business the Managing Agent carries so much responsibility and wields so much authority that the power of others, however senior, is dwarfed by comparison. The Company was already large, yet it was still managed on a personal and informal basis. The combination of size and rapid change required more specialized knowledge and experience than were available, and more delegation to executive managers than current practice allowed. Nevertheless informal and personal management had succeeded for many years and was valued by those who worked in the Company. They feared that greater formality would be more impersonal and less comfortable—a feeling shared by the Managing Agent. The need for change was accepted with varying degrees of reluctance. It was generally agreed, however, that if changes had to be made, they would be better made as planned and controlled changes than as expedient modifications or, still worse, as sudden upheavals. The next four chapters describe the reorganization of management over a period of three years.

CHAPTER 17

Management in 1953

On my first visit to Ahmedabad, early in 1953, my discussions with the Managing Agent and other senior managers about management organization were general and allowed me to get some appreciation of the extent to which the need for change was accepted. On my second and subsequent visits, more specific problems were discussed. I attended a large number of meetings between the Managing Agent and other managers. I saw all senior managers, some of them many times, both individually and in groups, reported back my tentative proposals, and wrote memoranda that were discussed with all those concerned. The first task was to get a picture of the existing organization, of the reasons for its development, and of how it worked. Thereafter the overall socio-technical system of the mills was analysed and appropriate managing systems evolved, discussed, modified, and finally established and manned.

Apart from discussions about management organization and fact-finding interviews, I was available to any manager who wished to talk to me about his own command and, if he wished, about the consequences for himself of any proposed reorganization. Such individual discussions were held under professional conditions. None of the information so gained was communicated to anybody else except with the permission of the informant. Even when information was given, the comments were about roles rather than about individuals. Inevitably, communication about roles frequently implied comments on those who had been taking them, or were about to do so. As far as was possible these implications were also discussed and clarified before anything was said.

The reorganization is not completed, and there are many repercussions whose effects cannot yet be estimated. The aim was not so much to provide a new organization as to explore an approach to the problem of the adaptation of management to change such as would produce a system sufficiently stable to deal with current changes and yet sufficiently flexible to make future adaptation possible.

THE INFORMAL EXECUTIVE RELATIONSHIPS

The executive structure in 1953 was made up of a series of informal personal relationships between the Managing Agent and other managers. This series of relationships was complemented by close family ties between the Managing Agent and other members of Karamchand Premchand Ltd. There was no organization chart with formal lines of communication between managers. Although there was a recognized and accepted order of seniority among managers, direct contact between the Managing Agent and managers of all levels was both expected and accepted. Other members of Karamchand Premchand Ltd. could communicate directly with managers in the mills without violating any rules of procedure or contravening accepted practice. The Managing Agent 'looked after' the Calico Mills on behalf of, and in consultation with, other members of Karamchand Premchand Ltd. As his 'assistants' he had a number of managers of differing status and seniority, many of whom had been in the business longer than he had.

The pattern was not dissimilar to that of the management of family businesses in other countries than India; but in India, more than in the West, it was supported by the traditional joint family system which is still characteristic of the social life of the country. The traditional Indian household comprises the sons of any given pair of parents, together with their wives, children, unmarried sisters, widows, and dependants. The eldest male, if mentally and physically competent, succeeds as head of the family and has considerable authority over all other members. He carries a correspondingly heavy responsibility for their welfare. All members of the family, whatever their particular relationships, look to the head of the family for care and accept his authority. Authority and responsibility among the other members of the family are diffuse, informal, and personal. Any adult will always accept responsibility for his or her juniors whoever the parents may be. A child is not disciplined by any one adult or by any pair of adults but is a member of a group in which anyone older than himself has some authority over him, and is also someone upon whom he can rely for help and protection. When a son marries, an arrangement usually made by the parents of the bride and bridegroom, the wife becomes a member of her husband's family, and minor domestic adjustments are made in the household to accommodate the new couple.

In the Calico Mills, the Managing Agent had direct contact with, and overriding authority over, all managers. Although junior managers were subordinate to particular senior managers, the latter had general authority over all those junior to them. New appointments at all levels were made, or at least approved, by the Managing Agent. The tendency in higher management was to find jobs for people rather than to find people for jobs. The qualifications and needs of employees, particularly of senior managers, were given greater weight than is customary in modern Western industrial organizations. It may be added, however, that in the West the diffusion and confusion of the lines of executive communication, which occur far more frequently than is admitted, are not supported, as in India, by a strong joint family tradition that makes the inevitable by-passing not only acceptable but desirable.

An analysis of Calico Mills management in terms of American or European theories of management would be not only inappropriate but misleading. Against this, the technology of the Calico Mills was Western in character and changing as mechanization increased and new processes were developed. However successful management had been in bringing development to its present stage, recent changes had raised questions about its capacity to exploit the advancing technology.

So far as there was a recognized structure, the Managing Agent had two chief subordinates of equal status, both of whom carried the title of 'Manager' and shared the major functions of management between them. One was broadly responsible for purchasing and finance, the other for production and sales. In addition, the Manager responsible for purchasing and finance was also responsible for the chemical operations of the company. The allocation of their duties was agreed between them and the Managing Agent. It was the policy of the Company 'to exchange allocations between the two Managers every three years or so in order to enable each Manager to tackle matters which tend to become routinized, with a fresh outlook'.[1]

The Manager (Production and Sales) had as his chief subordinates a Works Manager responsible for spinning and weaving in both the Calico and the Jubilee Mills, a Bleaching Superintendent responsible for all processing operations, two Engineers, one mechanical and electrical and one civil, two 'Salesmen' (equivalent to area sales managers in British terms)

[1] The full lists of allocations of duties are given in Appendix 3.

and a Personnel Manager responsible for engaging and dismissing mill workers and for 'Training within Industry'. The Spinning and Weaving departments of the Calico and Jubilee Mills were headed by a Spinning or Weaving Master and the Bleaching Superintendent had Bleaching and Finishing, Dyeing, and Printing Masters under him.

The Cloth department, where finished cloth was inspected, folded, packed, and stored pending delivery, was under the charge of one of the Salesmen. Cloth was also inspected at the grey stage and this inspection was also included in the Sales Department. Some of the consequences have already been discussed in Parts III and IV.

The Manager (Purchasing and Finance) had as his chief subordinates an Administrative Assistant, who was responsible for the purchasing of supplies and stores and for office management (including the engagement and dismissal of all clerical staff), and a Company Secretary, who with a staff of accountants was responsible for all financial accounts, relations with shareholders, reports to the board, and all the work necessary to comply with company law.

Apart from daily meetings between the Managing Agent and the Managers and frequent contacts between the Managing Agent and other managers, two executive meetings were held regularly—a fortnightly production meeting, and a weekly Bleach House meeting. The production meeting was attended by the Managing Agent, the Manager (Production and Sales), the Works Manager (Spinning and Weaving), the Personnel Manager, and the Spinning and Weaving Masters of both Calico and Jubilee Mills. Various other managers attended if required. The purpose was to review the production records of the Spinning and Weaving departments of the preceding fortnight. The meeting had before it the efficiency figures of all departments, together with the results of such investigations as had been made into any falls below standard.

The Bleach House meeting was attended by the members of the production meeting, plus the Bleaching Superintendent, the Bleaching and Finishing, Dyeing, and Printing Masters, the 'Salesmen' and the head of the Cloth department. The purpose was to review the quality of the cloth produced over the preceding fortnight and to enable those responsible for production to hear at first hand the latest market intelligence. The meeting had before it various examples of cloth—some that had not passed inspection or were the subject of complaints from customers; others that were the products of a change in manufacturing method, or the result of some specific action following previous meetings. The cloth brought out was chosen by the Cloth department.

The picture of informal executive relationships would be incomplete without mention of the Managing Agent's younger sister who is a member of, and is paid by, Karamchand Premchand Ltd. By profession she is an architect and designer. She is the only other member of the family at present taking a regularly active part in the work of the Calico Mills and acted as a personal assistant to her brother in the design of cloth and of new buildings. She also manages a museum in the grounds of the Calico Mills —famous for its collection of rare handwoven textiles. The relationships between her design studio and the artist's department responsible for routine designs were, like other relationships, informal, while her authority in relation to the Civil Engineer's department nominally responsible for building remained undefined. There was less doubt about her power and prestige.

RESEARCH AND DEVELOPMENT

The task of planning for expansion was allocated to the Manager (Purchasing and Finance). He had neither office nor staff for this and there was no differentiated research or development function. Both research and development were actively carried out in all parts of the mills. From time to time managers of the company travelled abroad—to Europe, America, and the Far East—to inspect new processes and machinery and to meet foreign technicians. Every year at least one manager, sometimes several, made trips lasting some months for these purposes. The Managing Agent himself spent not less than six weeks of each year abroad, during which he took every opportunity to visit mills and machinery manufacturers. Various experiments, particularly in finishing processes, were initiated and carried out in the mills themselves.

On their return all those who had been abroad discussed what they had seen with the Managing Agent. Since the implementation of new ideas usually involved capital investment and reallocation of space, frequent and often long-drawn-out discussions were necessary both before and during implementation. It was as though most managers carried two roles, one as manager and the other as technical staff officer to the Managing Agent.

The Managing Agent as a young man had worked in various departments of the mill for two years, but neither he nor the Managers were textile technicians with formal qualifications. One Manager was a Chartered Accountant, the other had been a mathematician of distinction. They and the Managing Agent had by years of experience acquired an immense knowledge of the industry. Yet all of them were dependent for technological judgments on those managers who were specialists, with scientific as well as practical qualifications in textile technology. The possibility of applying techniques and practices seen abroad depended in the last resort on the capacity of Indian technicians and workers to do in India what foreign technicians and workers were able to do under more temperate conditions. Only technologists with relevant experience both in India and abroad could advise with authority. The Managing Agent and the Managers were therefore dependent not only in the ordinary sense in which every executive is dependent upon his subordinates for the carrying out of his orders but also for judgment about the advisability of giving the order at all.

Executively, managers were responsible for the output of over one hundred miles of cloth per day. They were also responsible for developments initiated either in the mill itself or as the result of experience abroad. The experimental stages of such developments required technical concentration at a time when results, in terms of output, were small. There was conflict between short-term, day-to-day production and long-term development. As advisers, managers reported on what they had seen abroad. Where implementation did not match foreign performance, they had, as executives, to account for the short-fall. This was most easily rendered by reference to Indian climatic conditions and the lower norms of performance, wages, and expectation common throughout India.

When the Managing Agent himself had examined some technological improvement abroad and failed to get it put into practice in his own mill, he was frequently left with the feeling that it ought to be possible, even though his advisers had advised against it, and his executives had proved him wrong.

THE DIFFICULTIES OF DELEGATION

In the changing situation the informal management relationships, and the diffusion of research and development, had begun to lead to difficulties in defining and delegating responsibility and authority. Because of the double roles carried by managers, there could be no distinction between executive and advisory functions. If as the result of a discussion between the Managing Agent and the Works Manager the Managing Agent decided on action, that decision was thereby communicated directly to the Works Manager. In a formal sense, the Manager (Production and Sales) had been by-passed and could not accept full personal responsibility for the action decided. Attempts to cope with these difficulties by including the Manager (Production and Sales) in any meeting between the Managing Agent and the Works Manager had not been successful. Apart from the times when he was absent abroad, unless he attended every meeting and read all memoranda and reports, he could not make adequate contributions to the discussion. On the other hand, if he did attend every meeting and read all necessary papers, his other work suffered. That meticulous care was taken to inform him of any executive decisions did not avoid the difficulty. If the Manager had views to express that might modify the decision, it meant that the decision had first to be rescinded. By then it was sometimes too late. Not unnaturally too, decisions were often minor and implicit rather than explicit. It was only after some time that a large number of minor and implicit decisions accumulated into what was recognizable as a communicable decision.

Difficulties over the delegation of responsibility and authority were also in evidence at the executive meetings. When all the managers were in Ahmedabad, both the production and Bleach House meetings were attended by what in formal terms would be considered as four levels of management. While such meetings brought together all those directly responsible for whatever the meeting might be about, thus saving a great deal of time, their structure was such that the Managing Agent could hardly avoid giving orders to those who were, in formal terms, his subordinate's subordinates' subordinates. It is true that he did this in the presence of his subordinate and of his subordinate's subordinates; but when they disagreed with him, it was not easy for them to disagree so publicly, particularly in view of his paramount position. Even when they agreed, it was only natural that they should not feel the same sense of personal responsibility as if they themselves had given the orders.

The Managing Agent and his senior managers were very aware of their difficulties. But they valued their informal contacts and tolerant relationships. Managers also valued the position of the Managing Agent, to whom they could always refer any difficult decisions even if, at the same time, they wanted more responsibility and authority for themselves. The Managing Agent himself wanted to spread responsibility and delegate authority. In a changing situation so much was being referred to him that he either neglected longer-term planning or became a bottleneck in decision-making. But he too was apprehensive about changing a management organization which, though out of touch with future needs, had worked well enough for so long.

The informal and traditional nature of existing management was based upon a series of very personal relationships. Roles, as distinct from those who took them, and role relationships, as distinct from personal relationships, were of minor importance. The task of the company in the changing conditions required more formal management. Formalization of this kind meant that the structure of the managing system and its manning should be considered to be as important as individual personality and preference. Attention was therefore turned to the primary task of the managing system—the management of the textile operations of the Company.

CHAPTER 18

Analysis of Textile Operations

FIRST-ORDER SYSTEMS

The Company is a public company whose primary task is to make a profit by the investment of shareholders' capital in textile and chemical operations. The owners are the shareholders; and 'government' is vested in a board of directors whom they elect. Import is capital; conversion the making of profit by investing the capital in the Calico Mills; exports are dividends paid to shareholders and surplus profits that are reinvested.

The raising and investment of capital and the payment of dividends are under the supervision of the Board, which delegates the operations of conversion to the Managing Agency, Karamchand Premchand Ltd., who in their turn delegate them to the Managing Agent. Import and export are carried out in one operating system directly controlled by the Board.

The administrative work of this system—transfer of shares, payment of dividend warrants, keeping of accounts, and filing of all records required by Company law—was carried out by the Finance department of the Calico Mills. The operations of conversion were differentiated into two discrete systems, one for textiles and one for chemicals. With the Company as the frame of reference there were therefore three first-order operating systems:

1. Financial Operations (Import and Export)—the raising of capital, investment, and the allocation of profits.
2. Textile Operations (Conversion)—the making of profit by the manufacture and sale of finished cloth.
3. Chemical Operations (Conversion)—the making of profit by the manufacture and sale of industrial chemicals.

The first-order managing system consisted of the Board of Directors, the

Managing Agency, and the Managing Agent as chief executive of the textile and chemical operations. The first-order systems are shown in *Figure 1*. Since the work to be described was concerned with the textile component only, the first-order systems in which the financial and chemical operations were carried out will be considered only so far as they affect textile operations.

As analysis proceeded proposals for reorganization began to be formulated, but the point at which analysis became proposal was not easy to determine. By the time a proposal was sufficiently advanced to be formulated explicitly, it had usually been implicit for some time. The second-order operating systems into which the first-order system of textile operations was differentiated, and the major functions of its managing system, came to be known as *divisions:* and those in charge of them as *divisional managers*. For convenience these terms will be used throughout.

SECOND-ORDER OPERATING SYSTEMS

The primary task of the first-order textile operating system is to make a profit by the manufacture and sale of cloth. Import is raw cotton; conversion, the manufacture of finished cloth from raw cotton; and export, the delivering of finished cloth to customers. Examination of the existing organization showed that import, conversion, and export were already carried out in a number of separate departments:

Import— Cotton-purchasing department, under the control of the Manager (Purchasing and Finance).

Conversion—Spinning and Weaving departments in both the Calico and Jubilee Mills, and Bleaching, Mercerizing, Dyeing, Printing, and Finishing departments in the Calico Mills, under the control of the Manager (Production and Sales).

Export— Sales department, also under the control of the Manager (Production and Sales).

The tasks of import, conversion, and export were examined in turn. In spite of the different numbers involved and the skills required they could be regarded as three second-order systems, each making comparable contributions to, and carrying comparable responsibility for, the primary task.

Purchasing raw cotton represents an investment of working capital equal to more than one half the cost of making and selling cloth. It requires

FIGURE 1 *THE FIRST-ORDER SYSTEMS OF THE AHMEDABAD MANUFACTURING AND CALICO PRINTING COMPANY*

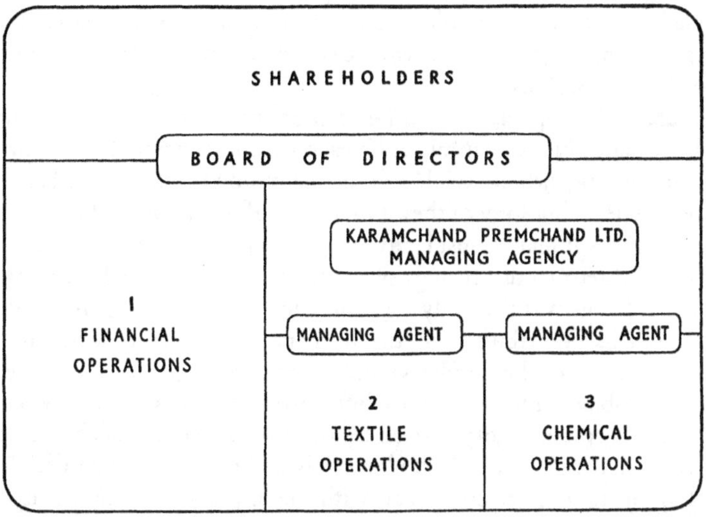

specialized knowledge of cotton fibres and experience of the world's cotton markets. The supply of cotton varies from year to year with crops in various parts of the world. For this reason stocks have to be kept, the amount depending upon judgments about the future movement of prices. If prices of some cottons in regular use are low and believed about to rise, large quantities are bought and stored. Manufacturing and selling plans are examined to discover if more of the cloth requiring the low-priced cottons can be profitably manufactured and sold. If prices are high, stocks are cut down, only the minimum being bought to keep the mills running, while other mixtures of cotton are tried to manufacture the same cloths. The work of cotton-purchasing requires few people, but the responsibility is heavy. Opportunities are almost unlimited for improving the profit position by good purchasing or for affecting it disastrously by bad judgments about the time and price at which to buy. There was no doubt that purchasing should be carried out in a discrete operating system of the second order, and that whoever was in charge should have the status of a divisional manager.

The manufacture of finished cloth from raw cotton uses the greater part of the working capital not absorbed by purchasing. It requires machinery, equipment, and buildings representing almost the whole of the fixed capital invested in the textile operating system. It demands specialized knowledge of textile technology and of both mechanical and chemical processes. Its management involves the coordination and control of a wide range of specialist skills.

Manufacturing operations can be divided into spinning and weaving, which are basically mechanical, and bleaching, mercerizing, dyeing, printing, and finishing, which, while still carried out on machines, are basically chemical. The technology of these two classes of operations is different and the skills are dissimilar. Consideration was given to the possibility of creating two or three manufacturing divisions, but the intuitive judgment of the Managing Agent was that only by containing manufacturing in one division would its contribution to the primary task compare with that of cotton-purchasing. The numbers employed were far greater and the management problems more complex but once capital has been invested in equipment, a responsibility carried by the Board, the risk taken was of a different order and mistakes were less costly and more easily rectified.

Selling operations are concerned with the disposal of output. Through them working capital is replaced and profit margins assured. Successful selling requires a wide knowledge and experience of markets in all parts of India and abroad and the ability to interpret future trends and forecast future sales. Apart from the diversity of the export market, the Indian market is itself large and heterogeneous. It is affected by a wide range of climatic conditions as between north and south, hills and plains; also by a variety of customs and traditions about dress, which mean that colours and designs that sell well in one part of India have little or no sale in other parts. Different states have different selling regulations and different taxation policies and the many different languages present difficult problems of advertising and branding. The Managing Agent had no doubt that the selling operations should be carried out in a discrete second-order operating system, nor that if one manager were responsible for selling he should rank as a divisional manager.

SECOND-ORDER MANAGING SYSTEM

The possible differentiation of the first-order textile operating system into three second-order operating systems—divisions—required a second-order managing system to control and service them. Examination of the existing control and service functions showed that apart from the function of general management which was exercised by the Managing Agent as head of the textile operating system two others were already located in top management: finance, one of the functions of the Manager (Purchasing and Finance), and development and research, carried out on a part-time basis by a number of managers who reported directly as technical staff officers to the Managing Agent. In addition to these control and service functions, other functions—the purchasing of equipment and supplies, personnel management, planning, inspection, maintenance, and power supply, civil engineering, design, and transport—were located at various levels in the organization. To determine their correct location, each was examined in turn.

Financial Control

The existing Finance department prepared the accounts of the textile operations—a second-order control function—and carried out the administrative work of financial operations at company level—a staff function of a first-order operating system. The kind of accounts required for the two systems were different, and concerned with different time scales. Examination of the Finance department showed that it was designed primarily to produce the records and accounts required by the Board. It was not designed to provide a control instrument for textile operating management. It was for this reason that costing had not been included in the Finance department. It was with the Manager (Production and Sales) and because of its separation from Finance it had only limited information at its disposal.

Two consequences followed. First, the information provided by the Finance department was largely historical, and of such distant history as to be of doubtful use as guidance for immediate action. Second, the information provided by costing was so limited as to be misleading. An adequate second-order control function must provide continuous contemporary information that integrates accounts and costs. For example, on those frequent occasions when the prices of different qualities of cotton were moving in different directions, up-to-date information was imperative. Only by balancing manufacturing costs, current and estimated future cotton prices, and cloth-market forecasts against each other could the worst gambling risks be avoided. During 1954 the prices of some high-quality cottons, which, in normal circumstances, would have been twenty per cent higher, fell below those of the medium qualities. Strong competition in the cloth market made Sales and Manufacturing demand better quality raw cotton. A fall in the price of high-quality cotton lent force to their demands, but any change of mixture required modifications throughout manufacturing departments, which for a time reduced efficiency and added to costs. Provided the changed mixture could be continued long enough, the additional costs could be recovered from the better prices obtainable. The degree of continuation feasible, however, was dependent on assessing a large number of variables impossible to deal with under the existing financial and costing arrangements.

A finance department designed to control textile operations was essential. Only such a function could provide the controls required by general management. The administrative work of the first-order financial operating system directly controlled by the Board was so different in character that it would be more efficiently carried out in a separate department designed for the task. Some of the reasons for the existing organization became clearer when it was recognized that the accountancy qualifications of the Manager (Production and Sales) had to some extent obscured the most appropriate location of the costing function. A contemporary and authoritative second-order financial control function would, it was postulated, require such skills and such a degree of responsibility to be taken that the manager in charge of it should rank with the divisional managers of purchasing, manufacturing, and sales.

Research and Development

While a certain amount of research and development had always been carried out, the function had been dispersed and mixed up with operations. Research and development activities had sometimes taken place at the expense of operations, or had been held up because of the pressure of operational work. A separate organization was essential. Not that research and development can take place in isolation. The identification of problems, the working out of solutions, and the implementation of results all require the active collaboration of operational divisions, but separation provides greater opportunities for thinking and experiment.

The location of research and development as a unified function of the second-order managing system followed naturally from its service to all divisions, its common use of certain skills and equipment, and from the

Managing Agent's demonstration of its importance by his having already taken direct responsibility for it. Its scope was seen as ranging from fact-finding through the running of experiments to the operation of pilot schemes.

An examination of the work currently being carried out suggested the following sections:

1. Spinning and weaving—technological and mechanical developments, the blending of different kinds of cotton, and the use of artificial fibres.
2. Cloth-processing—bleaching, mercerizing, dyeing, printing, and finishing—the invention of new finishing processes and the development of existing ones.
3. Design—colour, form, and quality related to raw cotton, artificial fibres, manufacturing needs, and marketing possibilities.
4. Engineering—new kinds of machinery, process layout and services, buildings, roadways, and ancillary equipment.
5. Marketing—the exploitation of different kinds of outlet and methods of selling, and advertising.
6. Organization Development—the analysis and organization of the work and social systems in all parts and at all levels of the company.
7. Statistics—as a service to all other sections.

Such a division would offer scope for two kinds of appointment:

1. Senior and junior posts for those who by temperament and qualification were better suited to research and development than production.
2. Junior posts for those who, by reason of their technical qualifications, could make a contribution to development or research, and for whom a tour of duty in such work would provide additional experience of value to them, and to the company, when they returned to operating management.

The inclusion of all these activities in one division would ensure that the results of research and development would be introduced into the operating systems as coordinated wholes, and that their impact on all dimensions of the socio-technical system of textile operations would be felt. The manager of such a division would need to be able to appreciate overall system policy as well as to coordinate a programme of diverse activities.

Purchasing of Machinery, Equipment, Chemicals, and other Supplies

The purchasing of machinery, equipment, chemicals, and other supplies was largely a service to manufacturing but was also to a lesser extent a service to cotton-purchasing, sales, and finance. A research and development function would also require service, particularly in relation to the possible suppliers and the prices of new equipment and machinery. The purchasing of machinery, equipment, chemicals, and other supplies requires specialized knowledge and experience of a large number of different markets, and an administrative machinery to check prices, quantities, usage, and stocks, to follow up deliveries, and to authorize payments—a machinery similar to, but more complex than, that required for the purchasing of raw cotton. In addition, a great variety of articles has to be stored.

There appeared to be three possible locations for this function:

1. As a centralized service in the second-order managing system, serving all other divisions, but also controlling the issue of supplies.
2. As decentralized functions within each division and coming under the control of each divisional manager.
3. As a part function of Cotton-Purchasing—machinery, equipment, chemicals, and other supplies being considered as part of the total imports into the textile operating system.

Although a knowledge of diverse markets and a complex administrative organization were required the manager in charge would not have either responsibility or authority comparable with other members of the second-order system. The specialized knowledge and experience and the common use of some supplies by all divisions suggested that it would be uneconomic to have separate purchasing functions within each division. The most practical location, from both economic and administrative points of view, was within the Cotton-Purchasing division. Such a location would add to the responsibilities of the Divisional Manager (Cotton-Purchasing), but not to such an extent as to overweight his command in relation to other divisional managers.

Personnel Management

So far as the function of personnel management had to provide services and control for all divisions, it would be appropriately located in the second-order managing system. So far as it provided services and control only for the Manufacturing division, and other divisions serviced and controlled themselves, it would be more appropriately located in the Manufacturing division.

The personnel department was in the command of the Manager (Production and Sales). The Personnel Manager was responsible for the engagement and dismissal of all mill workers and of those members of the Sales department employed in the Cloth department. He was responsible for employment services in the mills and for T.W.I. training courses throughout the company. The Administrative Assistant to the Manager (Purchasing and Finance) was responsible for all clerical workers not employed in the mills. The personnel function, as carried out by the existing Personnel department, was therefore a function of the second-order managing system only for T.W.I. Otherwise it was within the Manufacturing division, except for its service to the Cloth department of the Sales Division.

Recent industrial legislation, with its provisions for written agreements whenever working methods were changed, and for appeals to specially constituted industrial courts in cases of disciplinary action, had increased the legal work of the Personnel department. It was now so preoccupied with the interpretation of law and with ensuring that the mill complied with the constantly amended official regulations that many tasks that it would normally have undertaken had been no more than started. Joint consultation was embryonic. The selection and training of new workers, supervisors, and managers had been confined to the running of T.W.I. courses. The development of a 'professional' component in work with personal and group relationships had been hampered and embarrassed by the involvement in disciplinary action. The difficulties of taking disciplinary action had led executive managers to refer so frequently to the Personnel department that it had taken over an executive function.

The Personnel Manager, like other managers, acted as adviser to the Managing Agent about company personnel policy; but negotiations with the recognized trade union had been carried out by the Managing Agent, the Managers, or the Works Manager (Spinning and Weaving).

To become a full function in the second-order managing system the scope of the work would have to be modified and expanded. Alternatively special arrangements would have to be made about T.W.I. and either the Cloth department would have to become a part of the Manufacturing division, or the Sales division would have to take over responsibility for its own personnel function. The decision depended on future company policy on the relative responsibilities of executive management and the Personnel department for disciplinary action, and on the social and organizational developments, undertaken by a Research and Development division. Policy was not yet clear enough to allow a decision to be made, though the increasing incidence of employment problems suggested that personnel would eventually need to be a function of the second-order managing system. Temporarily, it was put with the Divisional Manager (Manufacturing). Personnel problems at second-order level were left as an undifferentiated function of general management.

The location of welfare services—the hospitals, schools, library, housing, sports facilities, crèche, and canteens—would depend to some extent on the decision about personnel. Should personnel be located in the second-order managing system, welfare services could become part of it. If, on the other hand, it was located in each division, welfare services would need special consideration. The location of welfare services was therefore also left in abeyance.

Planning

So far as planning was concerned with matching manufacturing and sales, and purchasing with manufacturing, it was a function of the second-order managing system. Under stable manufacturing and trading conditions, the fitting together of operational plans from all divisions and the consequent building up of an overall plan might well remain an undifferentiated function of general management. When conditions were subject to frequent change, a specialized planning function became more necessary.

The only department with separate planning was Sales, which issued manufacturing plans based on orders received and expected. This meant that long-term manufacturing plans had little chance in competition with short-term changes in sales demand. The purchasing of raw cotton, on the other hand, by its very nature had to be planned as a long-term operation. Under difficult market conditions manufacturing was thus caught between the long-term plans of purchasing and the short-term variations in sales plans.

At this stage of the development of management, however, planning could not be seen as a differentiated control function with divisional status. There remained two possible locations: as an undifferentiated function of general management, for which the Managing Agent would require staff assistance; or as a part of another second-order control function. The introduction of budgetary control into a new Finance division suggested that this would provide a first basis for planning and that financial control might be extended to include operational planning, becoming a commercial rather than a purely financial function. Decisions about planning were therefore left in abeyance pending the development of the new finance function. For the time being it continued as an undifferentiated part of general management, but steps were taken to break down overall plans into divisional and departmental plans to avoid the uncoordinated alteration of plans in different parts of the total system.

FIGURE 2 *SECOND-ORDER SYSTEMS OF TEXTILE OPERATIONS*

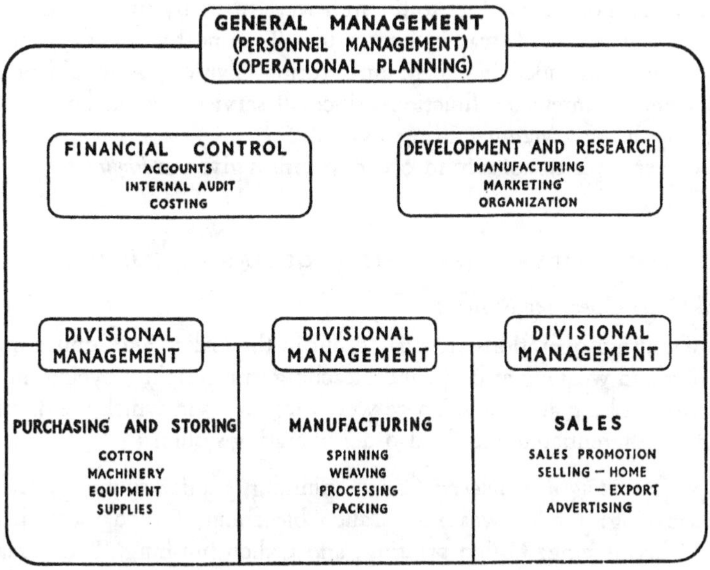

Inspection

Inspection did not require to be located in the second-order managing system, since its function was to decide how well the Manufacturing division had performed its primary task. Its inclusion anywhere but within Manufacturing would be a vote of no confidence in the Divisional Manager. Its present inclusion in the command of the Mill Manager (Production and Sales), but within the Sales department, was an anomaly.

Since it had been provisionally accepted that the existing quasi-independent Sales department should become a Sales division, the location of inspection in the Manufacturing division followed automatically. The transfer of inspection also meant that the Cloth department could be transferred, thus including in Manufacturing all processes concerned with the conversion of raw cotton into finished cloth.

Other Functions

Examination of the remaining control and service functions showed that civil engineering and design, so far as they related to new projects, were already provisionally located as sections of a proposed Research and Development division, and that transport was concerned almost entirely with internal transport. Deliveries to the mill were made by suppliers and finished cloth was carried away by contractors. Transport would therefore be appropriately included in the Manufacturing division; as would power supply and maintenance functions, since all services would now be required by the new Manufacturing division.

The overall picture of second-order systems is given in *Figure 2*.

THE THIRD-ORDER SYSTEMS OF MANUFACTURING

Third-Order Operating Systems

Manufacturing operations are carried out in the Calico and Jubilee mills, spinning and weaving at both, and bleaching, mercerizing, dyeing, printing, and finishing at Calico. There were three ways in which the division could be differentiated into third-order operating systems:

1. *As operating departments:* Calico spinning; Jubilee spinning; Calico weaving; Jubilee weaving; Calico bleaching; Calico mercerizing, Calico dyeing; Calico printing; and Calico finishing. Traditionally the heads of all such departments are designated 'Master'. There might also be some advantage in separating preparation from weaving—in some parts of the world Preparation Masters are common. Even without this separation and with the possible combination of bleaching and mercerizing into one department, this form of organization (with the addition of control and service functions) would give the Divisional Manager a very large number of direct subordinates.

2. *As process units:* Calico and Jubilee spinning; Calico and Jubilee weaving; Calico and Jubilee preparation; and Calico processing. This structure would have the advantage of reducing the number of direct subordinates of the Divisional Manager and of making the commands technologically uniform. Except for the processing unit, each unit manager would however have a command split into two parts, with subordinate managers each at opposite ends of the city.
3. *As separate mills:* Calico spinning, preparation, and weaving; Jubilee spinning, preparation, and weaving; and Calico processing. This structure would also reduce the number of direct subordinates. Though it would again introduce an extra level in management it would make third-order operating systems spatially coherent.

After full discussion it was decided to organize the Manufacturing division into three mills: Jubilee, Calico, and Processing.

Third-Order Managing System

With the decision to differentiate the Manufacturing division into three third-order operating systems, personnel management and transport could be located in the third-order managing system.

On the other hand, the arguments that had led to the exclusion of inspection from the second-order managing system applied with equal force to its location in the third, i.e. within the command of the Divisional Manager. Such a location would imply a vote of no confidence in the Mill Managers. That some level would be reached at which the implied vote would need to become explicit was accepted. But it was also accepted, as in the experimental shed, that the farther down the executive chain the responsibility for self-inspection could be placed, the more effective was criticism likely to be. Tentatively, it was proposed to locate inspection within the commands of the Mill Managers, with the possibility that it would ultimately be delegated to departments within the mills.

The location of maintenance was more difficult in that technology was changing continuously. The equipment and machinery used in spinning and weaving do not require specialized engineering skills for their overhaul and maintenance, which can be carried out by members of the departments; by contrast, processing equipment does. On the face of it there was a case for delegating maintenance to each mill. Against this, increased mechanization and the development of automatic devices demanded greater specialization. The outputs of certain new machines were so high that one or two could carry out an essential operation for a whole mill. This was introducing the 'fire brigade' atmosphere into maintenance work, the cost of a breakdown being so great that it was necessary to have specialized help, largely unused, but always ready 'just in case'. Centralization would therefore be more economic.

Maintenance was left in the third-order managing system, in the command of the Divisional Manager, with the proviso that each mill should have its own attached unit, using the centralized department only for specialized services. The third-order systems of manufacturing are shown in *Figure 3*.

FIGURE 3 *THIRD-ORDER SYSTEM OF MANUFACTURING*

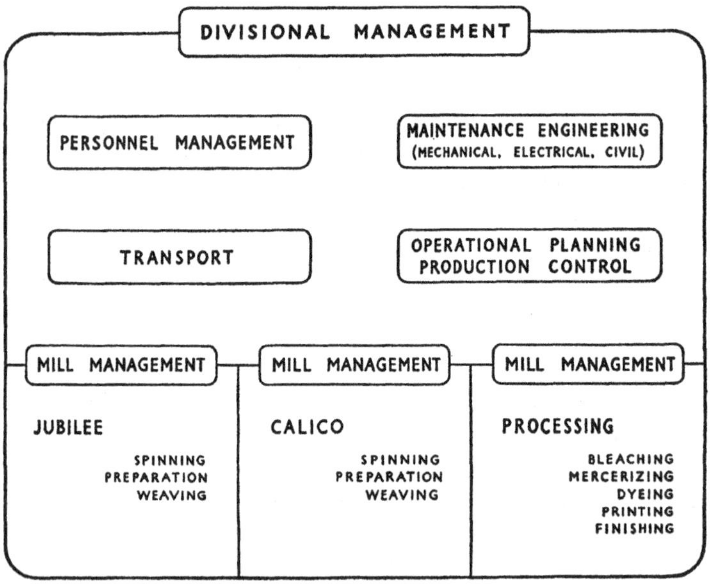

The Existing Executive

The existing informal structure whereby the Managing Agent had contacts with a number of managers at different levels was not only a cultural extension of the Indian family system but also a consequence of changing conditions. These did not permit general management to be carried out through only two subordinates. A larger group had come into existence. The bringing of it into existence in the traditional pattern, without formal structuring, had, however, led to difficulties in the delegation of responsibility and authority. The seniority of two members of this larger group, the Managers (Purchasing and Finance, and Production and Sales), and their nominal sharing of the major managerial functions between them had obscured the need for the development of the more specialized roles.

The nominal top-management group of three, the Managing Agent and the two Managers, was an awkward group, since one Manager was responsible for two operating systems, manufacturing and sales, while the other was responsible for an operating system (purchasing) and a control function (finance) which controlled all three operating systems. The Manager (Production and Sales) was not only dependent upon the Manager (Purchasing and Finance) for his raw materials, equipment, and supplies, but was also subject to the control exercised by the Finance department. The premium on their maintaining good personal relationships was formidably high—a premium to which other members of management, by their more junior status, could not easily subscribe.

The effective performance of the primary task of the textile operating system required a top-management group to which the Managing Agent could delegate responsibility and authority for the management of specialized operating systems and specialized control and service functions. It needed to be a group of a sufficient size, with members of such comparability of status that they could obtain satisfaction alike from their membership and from their contributions to the performance of the task of general management. The existing informal executive did not provide these conditions. To change the existing pattern might disturb relationships and demand changes in habits and behaviour. It was accepted, however, that the need to make a change, having been openly displayed and discussed, could not be ignored. It was decided therefore to use the analysis as a basis for reorganization, and to test its effectiveness in practice.

CHAPTER 19

Establishing the New System

THE COURSE OF EVENTS

During my first visit to the Calico Mills there were some preliminary discussions about management problems, but no changes were made. The period between my first and second visits was used by the Managing Agent and other managers to accustom themselves to the idea that reorganization had become necessary. A Board decision to expand chemical operations by building a new factory in Bombay lent force to the idea, and the course of events in the automatic shed encouraged the belief that reorganization need not be a catastrophic experience. Between my visits the Managing Agent also made one of his periodic trips to Europe. He and I met in London, and management organization was among the many topics we discussed. In these discussions, held a long way from Ahmedabad, it was easier to go further with general appreciation and analysis than would have been possible amid the worry and urgency of immediate day-to-day management affairs.

On my return in October 1953, I began to take up specific management problems, attending executive meetings and holding discussions with all those whose roles and positions were likely to be affected by any reorganization. The Managing Agent stated that he would not expect results from any proposals until his own role had been clarified.

The general analysis of the management organization was worked out, in the first place, with the Managing Agent. As different parts of the organization became clearer, first the Manager (Production and Sales), with the Manager (Purchasing and Finance), and subsequently, as they became affected, other managers, were drawn in. The creation of a new role frequently suggested the name of somebody to take it. As soon as this happened, the person concerned was told. Anybody likely to be personally affected was given the opportunity to select or to reject himself as well as to be selected or rejected. He was allowed to work out his disappointment or his elation in private rather than to be surprised by public or semi-public announcement.

As the general picture became clearer and the proposed reorganization agreed, the problem of communicating to those not directly affected had to be considered. Discussions went on for four months and rumours of impending changes began to spread. Those not directly affected, and therefore not previously consulted, began anxiously and resentfully to speculate about why they were being left out of what was becoming a large-scale managerial activity. Before the speculation could cause too much disquiet, a series of meetings that brought in all members of management was held, at which the proposed changes and the reasons for them were announced and discussed.

All the various nominees accepted the posts offered to them. Were they persuaded to fit into the new organization by their loyalty to the Managing Agent, or by their fear of the consequences of not doing so? How far was there real choice? During the course of the reorganization, and for some weeks afterwards, the majority of the managers saw me privately to discuss their qualifications for the jobs they had been offered and their feelings about the changes. My experience of these interviews was that while feelings of loyalty were obviously involved—and some fear—their decisions were, on the whole, based on reality.[1]

THE SIX PHASES OF THE REORGANIZATION PROCESS

The process of implementing the reorganization can be divided into six phases in which it moved at different rates in different areas of mill activities. The first phase—a long one lasting a year—covered the preliminary discussions, the theoretical analysis, and ended with the issue of a working memorandum setting out the basis of the reorganization. A Joint General Manager to act as a deputy in the Managing Agent's absence was appointed. During this phase the regression in the automatic shed, and the investigation and recovery, while encouraging persistence with attempts to reorganize, also demonstrated that decisions to implement experimental change were not by themselves enough. Hard work and follow-up were required if change was to last.

[1] Their appointments are detailed in Chapter 20.

The second phase, from February to June 1954, saw the implementation of much that had been previously decided. The provisional conclusions reached during the previous four months and the tentative decisions about appointments were confirmed. The agitation against rationalization came to a head and the new structure faced a severe test before it had had a chance fully to realize itself. Yet at the height of the difficulties the Managing Agent did not find it necessary to postpone his departure for London. planned some months previously.

The third phase was a period of consolidation. The Managing Agent visited London again and we were able to consider what had happened and what remained to be done, away from the worries of the immediate situation.

The fourth phase, which coincided with my third visit to the mills, was characterized by the institution of formal executive meetings and of management conferences. The effect of the changes already made could be seen in the setting up of the working party about the general introduction of a third shift, and in the articulation of management policy about controls and discipline. The experimental shed was taken over as a going concern and the Development and Research division started to make a positive contribution to the working life of the mill. The fourth phase ended with the appointment of Acting Managers of both the Purchasing and the Development and Research divisions. This enlarged the top management group to six, and changed its character.

The fifth phase saw the start of budgetary control, the beginning of third-shift working with volunteers from the first and second shifts, the implementation of plans in the weaving sheds for the installation of warp-stop motions, the spread of the four-loom system, and the reorganization of selling methods. The methods of work of the experimental shed were also accepted and put into practice for all non-automatic looms on the third shift in the Jubilee Mill.

By the beginning of the sixth phase, which coincided with my fourth visit, third-shift working, with virtually no increase in the number employed, was general throughout the mills. The phase was characterized by an intensive follow-up of previous work and by the pushing forward of reorganization to the fourth- and fifth-order systems of the Manufacturing division. Experimental work systems, based on the same assumptions as those used in the experimental shed, were started on the third shift in the Spinning department under the control of the Manufacturing division, and the methods of marking and packing finished cloth were completely reorganized by the Development and Research division.

The six phases can be seen as a process in which a period of getting used to the idea of reorganization was followed by one of intensive study, analysis, and first implementation. First implementation was followed by consolidation which, in its turn, was followed by a second period of intensive activity in which much of what had previously been left undone was completed. During the last fifteen months the pattern was repeated, except that consolidation and relative inactivity in management reorganization coincided with a period of activity and application in other parts of the mills. The main events are given in *Table 1*.

EXECUTIVE MEETINGS

With the management reorganization accepted, and the first posts filled, regular weekly meetings of the members of the second-order managing system were instituted. These were attended by the Managing Agent, the Joint General Manager, and the divisional managers. Their purpose was to make policy for the textile operating system in accordance with overall company policy. The results of purchasing, manufacturing, and sales were reviewed, and reports from the Finance and the Development and Research divisions were discussed. The meetings were executive. Although the Managing Agent asked for opinions from others present, the responsibility for the decisions taken at them was his. After being called first 'Divisional Managers' then 'Top Management' meetings, they finally became known as General Management meetings.

Meetings between divisions for the discussion of work and relationships were also instituted. The managers of the Manufacturing and of the Development and Research divisions and their immediate subordinates held some meetings to discuss difficulties of relationships between the members of their two divisions. Similarly the Financial Controller and his subordinates met all the other divisions in turn to discuss problems of the implementation of budgetary control.

Meetings of third- and fourth-order systems were also started.

None of these meetings was peaceful. Opinions were expressed that there had never been so much trouble before reorganization. The difficulties had existed, however, but in the informal multi-level meetings pre-

Table 1. EVENTS IN THE PROCESS OF MANAGEMENT REORGANIZATION

Phase	*Period*	*Months*	*Events of the Change Process*	*Events Directly related to the Change Process*	*Events Indirectly related to the Change Process*
1	March 1953 to February 1954	12	1. Acceptance of new management structure by those concerned 2. Issue of Working Memorandum I 3. Joint General Manager appointed	1. Preliminary Survey and verbal report on management. 2. Managing Agent visits London 3. Inquiry into specific problems, study of executive meetings, analysis of management working, discussion with all involved	1. Automatic Loom Shed Experiment started successfully, followed by regression, investigation and recovery 2. Start of Non-Automatic Loom Shed experiment 3. Difficult trade conditions 4. Policy of expansion of Chemical operations decided
2	February to June 1954	4	1. Development and Research division set up 2. Manager, Manufacturing division, appointed 3. Financial Controller appointed 4. Manager, Processing Mill, appointed 5. Manager, Jubilee Mill, appointed 6. Issue of Working Memorandum II	Reorganization of Processing Mill Management (fourth-order system)	1. Trouble about rationalization all over India 2. Disturbances in Ahmedabad and in mills 3. Moslem holiday stoppage
3	June to October 1954	4	Issue of Working Memorandum III	Managing Agent's visit to London	Trouble about rationalization dies down

Table 1 (continued)

Phase	*Period*	*Months*	*Events of the Change Process*	*Events Directly related to the Change Process*	*Events Indirectly related to the Change Process*
4	October 1954 to February 1955	4	1. Formal weekly executive meetings instituted 2. Acting Manager, Purchasing division, appointed 3. Manager, Development and Research division, appointed 4. Issue of Working Memorandum IV	Four executive conferences held	1. Working party for third shift set up 2. Definitive policy about budgetary control and discipline announced 3. Experimental loom shed accepted as production unit
5	February 1955 to February 1956	12	Manager, Calico Mill, appointed	Three executive conferences held	1. Spread of four loom system 2. Warp-stop motions installed 3. Marketing reorganized 4. General third shifts started with volunteers from first and second shifts 5. Extension of group system of working to whole third shift Jubilee Mills Weaving Shed
6	February 1956 to April 1956	3	1. Manager, Sales division, appointed. 2. Reorganization of fourth and fifth order systems Manufacturing division 3. Issue of Working Memoranda V, VI and VII	Follow up of reorganization of second and third order managing systems	1. Experimental group working in Spinning department 2. Cloth department reorganized 3. Full third shifts general throughout mills

viously held they had been dispersed and hidden. Now, if there was more discomfort and worry, rather more problems got dealt with.

MANAGEMENT CONFERENCES

As the executive meetings and the interdivisional meetings got into their stride and intra-divisional meetings were started, the question of the rapid communication of new policies and of reactions to them within other management ranks became important. Management conferences were therefore established. All members of management of the appropriate level for the particular purpose attended them. Their model was taken from the conferences held in the experimental shed. These conferences were not executive; no orders were issued, but the discussions helped to mould future policy.

Direct connections between changes in policy and discussions at conferences were not easy to observe, particularly with so much happening; nor was it easy always to discover where the initiative for change arose. One effect of the new executive structure and the consequent meetings and conferences was, however, certain: whereas previously most change processes started with the Managing Agent, they were now not only initiated by others, but were followed up more thoroughly.

At a conference in October 1954, the slow spreading of the methods of work in the experimental shed was discussed. Arising from this the continued resistance to the installation of warp-stop motions in other non-automatic sheds was raised. The workers' resistance was based on what they said was the drastic reduction in their bonus-earning capacity. Work studies of the consequences of fitting warp-stop motions showed that some compensation was required; but it was far less than limited experience had suggested—provided that the workers spent the majority of their time in the department and not outside. This led to a long discussion of the rules about being outside the department, and this in turn to questions of timekeeping and general disciplinary procedures. Recent industrial legislation had made disciplinary action against workers subject to review by industrial courts, which had the power to reinstate those dismissed. Appeal to the industrial courts had become inevitable, and the procedure was long-drawn-out. Disciplinary action was, in consequence, taken only when a worker had deliberately broken a rule approved by the trade unions and already recognized by the courts. The first reaction to the discussion was to attempt to tighten the rules and regulations and to add to them. Subsequently, however, rules came to be considered in relation to the task of the system for which they were being made. Whether a rule was or was not being broken was less important than the effect on the work being done. Even if the breaking of a rule by one worker did not lead to deterioration in his own work, but disaffected others, it was the effect on the work of the whole group or department that was important, rather than the breaking of the rule. Not having so many rules would increase the need for good management, but having rules could not serve as a substitute.

As a result of these discussions the Managing Agent ultimately announced a change in the policy on the maintenance of discipline. Action would be taken only when task performance was affected; the observance of rules, as such, would no longer be a standard of judgment. In practice this meant that when a manager saw a worker breaking a rule, he would not necessarily act about the behaviour itself, but about the ineffectiveness of task performance. It also meant that whether a rule was being broken or not, a manager was expected to act if a task was inadequately performed. He would not necessarily take disciplinary action. It might be training or re-training that was required. But he was no longer absolved from responsibility because no rule was being broken.

The first worker to be dealt with under this new policy did not appeal against the action taken—an unheard-of occurrence. The only thing that surprised him, he said, was that management had taken so long to find out what an indifferent worker he was.

TURNOVER AND PROFIT

The primary task of the textile operating system is to make a profit by investment in the purchasing of cotton and the manufacture and sale of finished cloth. How well that task has been performed can be judged, to some extent, by examination of the balance sheet; but so many factors contribute to the final results that it would be improper to assume that the effect of any particular cause can be accurately assessed.

For the sake of completeness the Company results in recent years are given in *Tables 2* and *3*. They include the results of both textile and chemical operations, which are not separated in the published balance sheet. In *Table 2* the figures are given to the nearest lac of rupees. (1 lac Rupees = Rs 100,000 = £7,576 or $21,000 U.S. approx.) In *Table 3* the results are given in the same form as for those of the leading mills in Chapter 2, that is, turnover and gross profits have been equated to the figures of the year 1948 at 100. Direct comparison between *Table 3* and the corresponding table in Chapter 2 is not appropriate since it depends upon relative performances in 1948—the base year—which could only be made by choosing some other, equally arbitrary, year as base.[1]

Table 2. CALICO TURNOVER AND GROSS PROFIT, 1948–1955, IN LACS OF RUPEES

Year	*Turnover*	*Gross Profit*
1948	614	134
1949	574	59
1950	587	76
1951	811	127
1952	639	62
1953	624	91
1954	649	82
1955*	675	137
1956†	853	186

Table 3. CALICO TURNOVER AND GROSS PROFIT INDICES, 1948–1955

Year	*Turnover*	*Gross Profit*
1948	100	100
1949	93	44
1950	96	57
1951	132	95
1952	104	46
1953	102	68
1954	106	61
1955*	107	102
1956†	139	139

* During 1955, the end of the accounting year was changed from December to March. The published figures for 1955 therefore cover fifteen months. The published figures have accordingly been reduced to 4/5 for the purposes of this Table.

† The figures for year ended March 1957 became available while this volume was in proof.

[1] During 1954 the Calico Mills shares were quoted on the Ahmedabad stock market at Rs 322. The quotation in September 1956 was Rs 668. In September 1956 an increased excise duty and other legislation affecting the textile industry brought all mill share prices tumbling down; the Calico Mill dropped to Rs 500. The latest quotation (May 1957) is Rs 570. In the meantime there has been a one-for-ten bonus issue, and application has been made for permission to make another free bonus issue of one for two. Since 1954 the dividend has been raised from Rs 18 to Rs 30 per share per annum.

A graph of the increase in cloth production from 1953 to 1956–57, published in the annual report for the year ending March 1957, is reproduced in *Figure 1*.

FIGURE 1 *CLOTH PRODUCTION*

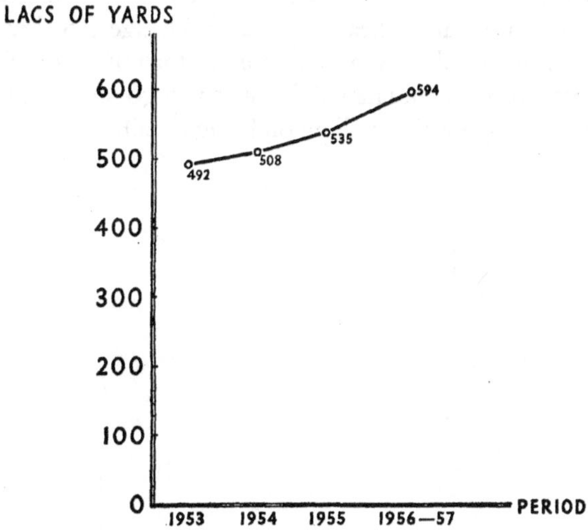

The changes brought about have had the effect of matching the different orders of managing system more closely to the tasks that have to be performed. The earlier pattern had been consistent with the informal and personal systems traditional in Indian culture. They had been appropriate to the successful growth of a substantial business at a time when the most important requirement for growth had been the personal ability and credit of the members of one family. The rapid changes in technological, social, and economic conditions of the last decade have demanded greater delegation of authority and responsibility to trained specialists than could be accomplished under the traditional system. The work of the project demonstrated that the difficulties encountered in adapting to change were not due just to the personal characteristics and qualifications of the members of management but stemmed from a misfit in the social, technological, and economic dimensions of the existing system. This demonstration allayed anxiety about change to a point where alternative systems could be considered, and practical steps taken to reorganize.

The acceptance of difficulty, the taking of time to work out the problems involved, and the continual measuring of any proposal against the demands of the primary task of the operating or managing system in question became an established practice. This encourages the hope that the changes eventually made will not only be satisfactory in themselves, but will serve as a preparation and rehearsal for future change. The learning of a new approach to the problem is more important than simply achieving a structure; for new problems and new difficulties will go on being encountered, and further reorganization will go on being required.

CHAPTER 20

Manning The New Structure

DEVELOPMENT AND RESEARCH DIVISION

The first step in the implementation of reorganization was the setting up of the Development and Research division. Since the Managing Agent had always played a leading part in development and research, the new division was put under his control. That he would be taking two roles, one as Managing Agent and a second as Manager, Development and Research division, and that any specialists appointed to the division would be reporting to him in his second role, was made explicit. Seven possible sections were required concerned with spinning, weaving, processing, design, engineering, marketing, and organization. In addition a statistical section was required to serve all sections, as well as to investigate record-keeping problems in the mills. One section was already in existence—the experimental design studio. A second—weaving—was in embryo, in that the experimental non-automatic shed had been established. It was possible to set up two other sections immediately, since the work of both the Bleaching Superintendent and the Chief Engineer was, at the time, far more concerned with experimental work than with production. The Production Controller, from the Works Manager's office, was appointed to take charge of the statistics section, though he could not, like the others, move over so quickly. The work on which I was engaged was also seen as forming the basis of the section dealing with organizational problems.

It is not to be supposed that this first modest step in reorganization was accomplished without much misgiving on the part of those appointed, who, with the exception of the Managing Agent's sister, were not unreasonably anxious about giving up their more orthodox roles. Temporary absorption in experimental work had not required them to relinquish their own posts. Acceptance of appointments in the untried Development and

Research division meant that their former posts would be filled. Nor could the Works Manager view with equanimity his loss of control of the development and research work for which he had reported directly to the Managing Agent.

The setting up of a Development and Research division inevitably involved its members in relationship problems with members of operating divisions and departments. In particular, the implementation of any change arising from the work of the new division would involve them in relationships at all levels of executive management. These relationships would not be made easier by the explicit or implicit criticism of executive management, arising from the need to propose change. To avoid the danger that members of the division would be seen at best as having mainly nuisance value, or at worst as exercising a secret police function, a definite code of behaviour had to be worked out. It was recognized that rules of behaviour are statements of ideal rather than of practical expectation, but their formulation and publication helped to deal with the conflicts and hostilities consequent on the setting up of the new division. Three rules were laid down:

1. Members of the division would report only about work not about individuals.
2. When members of the division felt that they were meeting with obstruction with which they could not deal themselves, they would offer to report to the Managing Agent jointly with the person obstructing.
3. Where a joint report was impossible, they would inform those concerned before they made a report.

There was a further condition for anyone appointed as Organization Development Officer: that he would not be required to advise on reorganization either within his own division or within any second-order systems. This was to allow him some protection from conflicts within his own group, or among those immediately reporting to the Managing Agent.

A beginning was made in the setting up of the division in April 1954, and from then until February 1955 the Managing Agent acted as manager. The experience of these ten months was encouraging in the amount of technical work accomplished; less encouraging in the quality of the relationships with other divisions. Whatever misgivings members of the division had about accepting their appointments, their release from day-to-day manufacturing had a marked effect on their productivity in development and research work. The dual roles taken by the Managing Agent were however found to deprive them of an effective leader. Because of his preoccupation with his role as Managing Agent, particularly at a time when so many changes were taking place, members of the division were left without any very clear directive on policy. More unfortunately, they were left to make their own relationships with those with whom they worked, not as a stable and coherent group, but as individuals with no real backing. They found it more difficult to call on the Managing Agent for advice and support than they would have done on a different superior.

By January 1955 it had become essential to separate the roles of Managing Agent and Divisional Manager. Various members of the division had qualifications for the manager's position. With such little experience, however, of the way in which the division would eventually fit into the framework of the company, it was difficult to make a decision with any certainty that it would not be a source of future embarrassment. In this dilemma I drew attention to the Managing Agent's sister. She was the head of a section of the division in her own right and, as a member of the Managing Agency and a sister of the Managing Agent, she had considerable power and prestige. This had always embarrassed her; she frequently expressed the view that her work did not warrant the deference with which she was heard. Yet, while she worked in the mill her relationships with other managers would be coloured by her membership of the Managing Agency and by her relationship with the Managing Agent.

After much discussion both at top management and in the division, it was decided to make her the Divisional Manager. Reluctantly she accepted a temporary appointment.

The effect was immediate. The division became a coherent whole instead of an aggregate of individuals. Its members felt that they were supported by the group to which they belonged and that they could work to a known and defined policy. The division now spoke with a separate voice in management. The fact that, as his sister, the divisional manager had a special relationship with the Managing Agent, was offset by her being able to disagree with him in a way not always easy for other members of the company.

DIVISIONAL MANAGEMENT

The granting of Government licences for the building of the new chemical factory in Bombay in the early part of 1954 made it necessary for the Manager (Purchasing and Finance) either to relinquish his duties in textiles, or to withdraw from chemicals. It was decided that he should take over active direction of chemical operations, including the expansion programme, and that, while this and other projects were getting under way, he would train a replacement for himself in cotton-purchasing. In the meantime, cotton-purchasing would remain as an undifferentiated part of the responsibility of the Managing Agent, in which he would be assisted by the former Manager (Purchasing and Finance).

Difficulties over delegation had been increased by the frequent trips abroad of the Managing Agent and other managers. The informal relationships that existed had made it easy for the duties of anyone absent to be taken over by others; but the very ease with which this could be done increased still further the diffusion of responsibility and authority. A more formal structure meant that handing over during absence should also be more formal. It was decided that each member of top management including the Managing Agent should have a deputy. With so many functions left undifferentiated in general management, an appropriate appointment would be that of a Joint General Manager who would act as a full-time deputy to the Managing Agent, taking over from him in his absence.

The Manager (Production and Sales) was appointed Joint General Manager. This appointment created vacancies for managers of the Manufacturing and Sales divisions. The post of manager of the Manufacturing division was offered to the Works' Manager (Spinning and Weaving), who accepted only after anxious consideration of the implications of his having to take responsibility for the Processing Mill, in which he had had no technical experience. His acceptance was made easier by his having handled for some years most of the organizational problems of the Cloth department and the trade union relationships for both the Processing Mill and the Cloth department. These duties had not appeared in any list of his responsibilities but had been part of the informal arrangements. He had undertaken them because in the handling of production problems he was so much more experienced than the members of the Sales department in whose charge the Cloth department had been, and because it had been easier to channel all trade union questions through one person. The Works

Manager and the trade union officials had over the years built up a relationship based on mutual respect and liking.

Pending the reorganization of the methods of selling, the vacancy in the Sales division was not filled; the newly appointed Joint General Manager devoted almost his whole attention to Sales management. With the help of the survey made by marketing consultants, he carried out the whole reorganization described in an earlier chapter. During this time the Managing Agent did all the work of general management together with the undifferentiated functions of personnel management, operational planning, and—assisted by the former Manager (Purchasing and Finance) —cotton-purchasing.

The vacancy for a Financial Controller was advertised and, after a selection procedure in which I acted as adviser, an appointment was made in May 1954. The new Controller took up his appointment in October 1954, and has since reorganized the entire accounts system, introduced and implemented budgetary control, taken over all invoicing and cash collection from the Sales division, and reorganized and moved all the relevant offices. Much training and retraining has been involved as well as the making of adequate relationships both within his own division and between his division and others.

At the end of 1954 the former Administrative Assistant to the Manager (Purchasing and Finance) was appointed Acting Manager, Purchasing division. He immediately started reorganization of the purchasing of equipment and supplies and of stores methods. Before, however, he had sufficiently rearranged this side of his work and trained subordinates for it so that he could start his own training for cotton-purchasing, he became the Manager of the reorganized Sales division. The transfer took place at the end of May 1956, and the head of one of the sections of the Finance division was promoted to train as the prospective Manager, Purchasing division.

MANUFACTURING MANAGEMENT

In the Manufacturing division the former Personnel Manager was first appointed as Manager of the Jubilee Mills and later transferred to Calico, a new appointment being made to Jubilee. The Assistant Personnel Manager was appointed Labour Officer in the Manufacturing division. The appointment of a new manager for the Processing Mill, consequent upon the transfer of the Bleach House Superintendent to the Development and Research division, was accompanied by the reorganization of the Processing Mill already described—the first fourth-order system to be tackled. Early in 1956 the reorganization of fourth-order systems in the other two mills was complete with the weaving command split into preparation and weaving, both headed by 'Masters'.[1]

The Production Officer of the Development and Research division, who had been in charge successively of both the automatic and the experimental non-automatic sheds, had, on the retirement of the existing Weaving Master, been appointed Weaving Master of the Jubilee Mill. He took over his appointment at the end of April 1956, starting a process that had been envisaged when the Research and Development division was established.

As soon as the reorganization of the fourth-order systems had been agreed, working parties of appropriate executives were set up to consider fifth- and sixth-order systems. In the meantime the third-shift working party had presented its report and the Divisional Manager (Manufacturing) was involved in the organization of third shifts with all the managerial and supervisory problems involved. The reorganization of fifth- and sixth-order systems, and the starting of third shifts, required the finding of large numbers of heads of sections and shift supervisors. It became company policy to find the majority of these from among present employees including the group leaders, line jobbers, and workers in the mills. Previously supervisors had been drawn from those with a University or Technical College training in textiles. This practice had barred the workers, many of whom were illiterate, from supervisory posts. Minimum standards of literacy, sufficient to read instructions and keep records in Gujarati, were now accepted as academic qualifications, with the emphasis placed on experience and capacity to manage.

All divisional mill and departmental managers were new in the sense that the posts they filled were newly defined and their relationships with each other changed. Only one divisional manager and two mill managers were new to the Company. In the year following, all of them were involved in major reorganizations of one kind or another, and were affected also by what was happening elsewhere in the Company. Simultaneously they had to deal with the day-to-day managerial problems of a textile

[1] The Spinning departments have since been split into preparation and spinning, both headed also by 'Masters'.

operating system buying large quantities of raw cotton and other supplies and manufacturing and selling over thirty-six thousand miles of cloth per year.

SOME CONSEQUENCES OF THE CHANGES

Between January 1954 and May 1956 twenty-one new senior posts were created in the second-, third-, and fourth-order operating and managing systems (divisional, mill, and departmental management). These took the number of senior management posts in textile operations from twenty-nine to fifty. During the same period five posts fell vacant. Four were due to transfers either to the financial operating system at Company level or to the newly enlarged chemical operating system. One was caused by retirement. Of the total of twenty-six vacancies, ten were filled by external recruitment, sixteen being filled by internal promotion and transfer.

Out of the original twenty-nine posts, the duties and responsibilities of seventeen underwent major modification. Only twelve remained as they had been before reorganization and even these were affected by the changed role relationships consequent on the creation of new, and the modification of existing, roles. In all only six members of senior management remained in posts that had existed previously. The dimensions of the reshuffle are shown in *Table 1*.

Table 1. RESHUFFLE OF SENIOR MANAGERS DURING REORGANIZATION JANUARY 1954 TO MAY 1956

	Appointments made by				
Classification of Posts	*Internal Transfer*	*External Recruitment*	*Still Vacant*	*No Change*	*Total*
Newly created	12	6	3	–	21
Duties and responsibilities modified	14	2	1	–	17
Previously existing	4	2	–	6	12
Totals	30	10	4	6	50

Similar data for heads of sections and shift supervisors (fifth- and sixth-order systems) are not available. The starting of third shifts alone necessitated finding more than thirty new supervisors of whom more than two-thirds were found in the mills.

That structure, culture, and personality are interdependent variables was accepted by all those concerned in the reorganization, as was the need for new attitudes and new ways of behaving. The earlier managing system, being consistent with a traditional cultural pattern, had satisfied many of the basic psychological needs of those taking roles in it. Whether the same needs would be as well satisfied by the new structure was uncertain.

The extent to which the loss of traditional satisfactions will be replaced by the satisfactions of membership in a new kind of organization, more directly related to the primary tasks of the company, cannot yet be assessed. It seems reasonable to predict that existing cultural mechanisms, both conscious and unconscious, will modify the new system, and that the new system will lead to the growth of new cultural mechanisms; but it is likely to be a long time before the interactions can be gauged.

The reorganization has already caused stress both to former members of management and to newcomers. They have found themselves called upon to make a great many personal adjustments, not all of which have been easy. The stress and the need to make these adjustments will continue for a long time.

The way in which the effect of the changes was perceived in the Company itself may be illustrated by part of a letter I received from the Managing Agent before I left England for my fourth visit.

5th November 1955

'Everyone is working under great pressure. Plans have been made to get third shifts working throughout all mills by December 1st. The financial control system is doing a good job but is in some arrears. Damages are still high and there are more instances of overt non-cooperation between the operating and managing systems. As expected, with the solution of old problems, new problems appear. These are being recognized and tackled. In the meantime the mill is doing very well.'

SUMMARY OF PART V

1. The management in 1953 was made up of a series of informal personal relationships between the Managing Agent and other managers. The Managing Agent managed with the assistance of a number of managers of different status and seniority. The pattern was consistent with the traditional Indian joint family system.

2. Rapid changes in social, technological, and economic conditions made necessary more delegation of authority and responsibility for management functions to specialist managers than was possible in the informal and personal managing system.

3. Development and research were carried out actively in all parts of the mill, but were dispersed among operational departments and were sometimes in conflict with operational needs.

4. The textile operating system of the mills was examined. Three operating divisions of the second order were established—Purchasing, Manufacturing, and Sales—with three control and service functions of the second-order managing system—General Management, Finance, and Development and Research.

5. The Manufacturing division was differentiated into three third-order operating mills, Calico, Jubilee, and Processing, and appropriate controls and services were located in the third-order managing system. Reorganization of fourth-order systems was completed and that of fifth- and sixth-orders started.

6. New appointments to newly created commands changed a top-management group of three into a group of six, with one still to be added as soon as possible. Two more control and service functions were adumbrated in the second-order managing system but left in abeyance for the time being. New appointments were made in the third-, fourth-, and fifth-order systems of the Manufacturing division and a large number of posts created in the sixth-order system.

7. Policy about promotion and about the maintenance of discipline was modified and the modifications implemented.

8. Twenty-one new posts were created in the second-, third-, and fourth-order systems. These, together with five other vacancies were filled by sixteen internal promotions and ten external recruits. The majority of fifth- and sixth- order posts were filled from within.

9. Every divisional manager was involved in a major reorganization of his division, and in all divisions new techniques were introduced.

10. Results could not be adequately related to their causes, but the new management was able to exploit changing conditions more ably than had the old.

PART VI

Social and Technical Change

CHAPTER 21

Tasks and their Organization

In the Introduction it was suggested that although the work described in this book was carried out in an Indian textile mill the findings might have some generality. The concepts and assumptions on which the work has been based are not specific to Indian industry, but arise from experience in many different social and technological environments. This chapter and the next will discuss these concepts and assumptions more generally.

THE PRIMARY TASK

One of the striking facts about the project was the response to the new organizations. In both the automatic and non-automatic sheds the workers' capacity for cooperation in the performance of the primary tasks was remarkable. There appeared to be few problems of defining or accepting the primary task. Once a new organization that satisfied their social and psychological needs had been established, those concerned became determined to make it succeed. In other situations, either because of the complexity of the system itself or because of social, political, and economic conditions, the definition of primary tasks may prove more elusive. In consequence the capacity for cooperation in their performance may be more difficult to achieve.

The larger and more complex a production system, the more likely is it to contain systems of different orders and a number of components of the same order. Every succeeding differentiation increases the possibility that agreement about the primary tasks of components may fail to add up to acceptance of the primary task of the whole. The employees of a factory may accept its primary task. They may be prepared to cooperate enthusiastically in its performance. But this does not mean that they necessarily accept that the primary task of the Company, of which the factory is a part, is to make profits.

Decisions taken within one component system which are consistent with its primary task may appear irrelevant or even harmful in a system of a different order. Even within a factory, acceptance of the primary tasks of different operating systems may lead to decisions that appear inconsistent to the members of other systems of the same order. Decisions about purchasing taken for sound reasons about the supply and price of raw materials can appear to members of manufacturing departments as bad decisions because they interfere with the effective performance of the primary task of manufacturing. 'How can we be expected to make good window frames with this green wood?' was a frequent complaint of carpenters and joiners in the building industry in the immediate post-war years when timber was scarce. No amount of explanation, no intellectual conviction about difficulties of supply, could replace the loss of satisfaction arising from ineffective performance of their primary task. 'It's just not worth making a good job of them, they warp as soon as they are made.'

Even when there is acceptance of primary tasks in both total and component systems, changes in external conditions may still affect task performance. Economic conditions, particularly in an export market, are subject to rapid and unpredictable changes. It is no consolation for the workers in a factory to learn that, in spite of a superlative performance of their own primary task, market conditions have so changed that their products can no longer be sold.

Groups tend consciously or unconsciously to redefine their primary tasks. Not infrequently irrational refusal to accept obviously rational solutions may be described as failure to agree about the primary task. Workers, for example, may frequently oppose the introduction of a technological change that can be shown to result in higher productivity, lighter work, and better wages. The irrational opposition is seen to have a convincing logic only when it is recognized that the workers' definition of their primary task is to preserve a social system giving them satisfaction and security and is no longer the carrying out of the production process. Even the argument that, unless the technological change is introduced, the Company will no longer remain competitive may not in such circumstances convince them of the urgent need to accept change.

It has often surprised the administrators of wage structures that workers have not welcomed an opportunity to discard complex and incomprehensible methods of wage-fixing in favour of more simple ones by which the make-up of earnings can easily be calculated. But if the primary task of the workers, not necessarily disclosed or even consciously recognized, is to fight management, and the complex and incomprehensible wage structure is one of their weapons, then the introduction of a simplified structure can be seen as disarming rather than benefiting them. In a study of a wage negotiation in the Line Shop of the Glacier Metal Company[1] it was shown that, although the apparent task of a negotiating group was to settle a wage dispute, its primary task was to encapsulate a conflict between management and workers about a programme of expansion. This programme caused acute insecurity. The wage negotiation had to be kept alive while the expansion continued, and only when expansion had been completed could the negotiating group perform its apparent task and accept a rational solution of the wage dispute.

The definition of a primary task given here may be compared with the definition of a *sophisticated task* given by Bion.[2] Bion defined the sophisticated task as the specific task for which a *work-group* meets. He distinguished the work-group from the *basic group*, which is the same group acting on one of the basic assumptions—fight-flight, dependence, or pairing. He showed that the performance of the sophisticated task was made difficult by the effect of emotions associated with the basic assumptions. The more a group manages to maintain a sophisticated level of behaviour, the more it does so by using the emotions associated with one basic assumption to control those associated with the other two. Conflict is found between:

1. The basic group (the group behaving as if a basic assumption were operating) and the individual members who compose it.
2. The work-group (the group created to perform a sophisticated task) and the basic group.
3. The work-group suffused with the emotions associated with one basic assumption and the other basic assumptions.

However, Bion says, 'In my experience the psychological structure of the work group is very powerful, and it is noteworthy that it survives with a vitality which would suggest that fears that the work group will be

[1] Rice, A. K., 'The Use of Unrecognized Cultural Mechanism in an Expanding Machine-Shop' *Human Relations*, 1951, Vol. IV, No. 2.

[2] Bion, W. R., 'Experiences in Groups', I, II, III, IV, V, and VI. *Human Relations*, 1948, 1949, and 1950, Vols. I, II, and III.

swamped by the emotional states proper to the basic assumptions are quite out of proportion.'[1]

The primary task includes the sophisticated task; it may also include other tasks undertaken by a group, of which its members may or may not be completely aware.[2] Both the management and workers of an industrial organization may, therefore, seek to mobilize the emotions associated with the same basic assumption but for different tasks. Management may seek to mobilize the emotions associated with the fight-flight basic assumption to carry on a fight with competitors; they may succeed only to find that the emotions aroused are used by the workers to carry out an internal fight with management.

The primary task is the task that a production system or sub-system is created to perform, but its definition may not be the same for all members of the organization. Differences in definition, as between different members of an organization, may be neither explicit nor even conscious, and may be detectable only by examination of behaviour. The importance of the concept is that a latent capacity for cooperation may still be realizable if the conditions inhibiting its realization can be removed.

That this realization is less improbable than may appear is shown by much common experience. Even in the middle of a bitter dispute, managers and workers may both be heard defending the quality of their products against outside criticism. In spite of the difficulties about the introduction of improved technology, it is not unusual for all the members of an organization, including those who have suffered from the resulting social dislocation, to express pride in its effects. In a factory in which the introduction of mechanical handling had caused considerable difficulty, workers were heard within a few weeks of the disputes to boast that their factory provided more horsepower per worker than that of their chief American competitor. Whatever views they had expressed about the evils of mechanical handling, they had approved and encouraged the introduction with at least a part of themselves.

The problem for the technological and social development of industry is how to realize this latent capacity for cooperation in the performance of primary tasks. There is danger that its frustration will lead to discontent. Change processes are likely to be most successful when they are perceived as contributing to the effective performance of an agreed and accepted pri-

[1] Bion, W. R., 'Experiences in Groups, V', *Human Relations*, 1950, Vol. III, p. 6.
[2] Cf. Rice, A. K., *op. cit.*

mary task. Conversely, changes that are felt to hinder effective performance can be expected to meet with resistance.

For management there is no permanent escape from the difficulties attendant on the introduction of change in not taking advantage of technological developments. This is true even when ignoring them does not immediately jeopardize the Company's economic future. Effective performance entails the use of effective technology. The continued use of out-of-date equipment will itself lead to ineffective performance and hence to dissatisfaction. In the long run, therefore, management will not be excused even by those whose working lives are dislocated for failing to take advantage of improvements in technology.

A major cause of disruption in management-worker relations is the use by management of outside conditions to force through technological innovation that would otherwise have required social as well as technological reorganization. Highly dependent groups may expect management omnipotently to control external conditions, but no group is likely to forgive management for using difficult conditions to achieve what is management's own responsibility—so to manage that the benefits of technological change can be realized without social damage.

WORK-GROUP ORGANIZATION

Strong support is given to the assumptions about work-group organization by the rapid and spontaneous implementation of small work-groups in the automatic shed, the determination to make similar groups successful in the non-automatic shed, and the readiness with which a larger top-management group was accepted for textile operations. Whether individual or small or large work-group organization will give greatest satisfaction depends upon two main factors; first, individual personality, and second, the structure and culture of the society of which the individual is a member. Most societies provide their members with opportunities for individual and for small and large group activities. Members of different societies can satisfy their needs for isolation and for various kinds of group membership through a variety of institutions.

Where a society provides stable social institutions outside work for the satisfaction of needs derived from different kinds of group membership, individual 'whole' tasks may be appropriate. Where, on the other hand, a society provides fewer opportunities, work may become an important source of such satisfaction. The breakdown of institutions providing satisfactions derived from group membership—families, villages, guilds—was the social accompaniment of the industrial revolution in the United Kingdom. The industrialization of undeveloped countries is characterized by the same process today.

In India there has been a highly structured form of society for many centuries. The caste system—primarily a work-organization—is proving resistant to attack by social and legislative reforms. Even industrialization and the consequent movement from villages to towns and cities have not succeeded as yet in doing more than blur the divisions between castes. Whatever may be the faults and virtues of the caste system, it has in the past provided its members with a stable, if restricting, social organization in which they could find security. So far as reform and industrialization have succeeded in beginning the breakdown of established institutions, members of caste and village communities need to find other opportunities for the satisfactions derived from group membership. Since independence, legislation has been directed towards increasing the civil liberties of underprivileged groups. At the same time, industrial development is taking people away from traditional village occupations and family work-groups. In the more highly industrialized countries of the West specialization brought about by technological change has tended to decrease the opportunities for group activities and to increase social isolation. To the losses derived from industrial and urban development must therefore be added those arising from the reduction of the number of individual 'whole' tasks consequent on the increase of mechanization. Organizations that so arrange tasks that they can be performed by work-groups of such a size that their members can derive social and psychological satisfactions from their membership will be more acceptable than organizations which, by segregating individuals from each other, do nothing to compensate for isolation in other areas of life.

Not only the size but the kind of group most appropriate in a given production system will also depend upon the culture of the society in which it is situated. Some societies may provide expectations of larger groups than others; different societies will demand different kinds of behaviour from both leaders and group members. Because of current conditions in India, hierarchically structured groups with the possibility of restricted and defined intra-group mobility best fitted the expectations of group leaders and members. In some parts of the British coal-fields small egalitarian groups with free and informal role- and task-mobility have been found satisfactory. The leader of such a group, even where formally acknowledged, has no higher status in terms of rank or pay than any other member. In other parts of the industry there are larger groups with formal role interchange, but again no formal leadership. These also have been found to work well.[1]

Every society has its own patterns of leadership and followership and its own mechanisms for handling problems of authority relationships. These must be taken into account in creating work organizations. Once work organizations have been established, their own structure and culture need in turn to be examined in relation to changes in the society. They may become too deviate—on the one hand, because of too rapid changes at the behest of technological innovation or, on the other, because of 'cultural lag.' While the force of technological demand and satisfaction in effective task performance can make work-groups growing points of social change, they can also become backwaters of outworn tradition.

[1] Trist, E. L., 'Some observations on the Machine Face as a Socio-Technical System'. A Report to the Area General Manager, No. 1 Area, East Midlands Division, N.C.B., 1953.

CHAPTER 22

Systems and their Organization

OPERATING AND MANAGING SYSTEMS

When Trist first introduced the concept of a socio-technical production system it was to examine all the dimensions of a system and their interaction with each other. It was first used to describe what has here been called a primary production system. Subsequently, in examining the management of a total coal-getting operation, he added the concept of a system external to the production system which serviced and controlled the primary unit. When, later, he and I were trying to account for changes in the labour-turnover of the Glacier Metal Company we called this external system 'the governing system'.[1] We defined it as the system, external to the production unit, which controls, coordinates, and services its activities. A convenient illustration of our meaning was to be found in the 'governor' of the early forms of mechanization, and in the habit of referring to the owner of a business as the 'Governor'. In the work with the Calico Mills the concept has been further extended to facilitate the analysis of more complex systems. The terms 'operating' and 'managing' have been used to accord with the transition from comparatively small-scale industry with its personal and informal management, to larger and more complex organizations with their formal and professional management.

I have distinguished operating systems, which carry out a part of the primary task of a total production system, from a managing system, which controls and services more than one operating system. But every control or service function has its own primary task. It too may be regarded as a production system with its own import, conversion, and export. As in any

[1] Rice, A. K., and Trist, E. L., 'Institutional and Substitutional Determinants of Change in Labour Turnover', *Human Relations*, 1952, Vol. V, No. 4.

other production system, these operations may or may not be carried out in discrete systems. If the operations are so differentiated, then they too will require a managing system to service and control them.[1] For example, a financial control is a production system in which imports are records and reports from purchasing, manufacturing, sales, banks, creditors, and debtors; conversions are the accounting manipulations that reduce the various figures to common denominators and put them together; exports are the cost and financial statements used as services by other systems and as controls by management.

CONTROL, SERVICE, AND OPERATIONS

The task of a managing system is to control and service the operating systems which together make up the production system that is to be managed. Although control and service functions have been distinguished from the management of operating systems the operating systems are controlled and serviced by each other as well as by the control and service functions of the managing system. An operating system responsible, for example, for purchasing, both services the operating system responsible for manufacturing and, by providing or not providing what is asked for, controls it. Similarly manufacturing, by making goods, provides a service to sales and, by controlling the quantity and quality of the goods, also controls it. Sales in its turn, by selling or not selling goods, services and controls both manufacturing and purchasing.

There are characteristic differences, however, between the kind of control exercised by one operating system over another and that exercised by a control function of a managing system. An operating system carries out a part of the primary task of the total production system; by contrast, a control function of the managing system does not. The Financial Controller of the Calico Mills, discussing the relationships between his division and others, suggested that the difference was like that between the control exercised by a player and that by a spectator. The spectator may see more of the game but a player's attitude towards control will differ with the status of the controller. Criticism voiced by a colleague playing in the same team will not be regarded in the same way as criticism by a spectator—whether the spectator has or has not anything to do with team management.

[1] Cf. Jaques, Elliot, *The Changing Culture of a Factory*, p. 273, 'By this definition (of an executive system) everyone—the managing director, departmental managers, supervisors, specialists, operatives, and clerks alike—is in his executive role when carrying out his normal working duties.'

Difficulties of relationship between managers are frequently caused by confusion between control functions and operations. The inevitable conflicts between operating systems can be exacerbated if a manager responsible for an operating system is also responsible for a control function. The control function gives him the authority to criticize the working of other operating systems from a different point of view. The frequent combination of finance and purchasing in a manufacturing unit often gives the purchasing manager greater power than other managers, not because of the importance of purchasing, but because criticism of purchasing can lead to retaliation through financial control.

CONTROL AND SERVICE

Although control and service functions are different and distinguishable, both are managerial functions at different places on a continuum. A control, by providing checks and information, implies a service. A service, by variations in its quality and quantity, implies a control. The emphasis, or 'centre of gravity', of some functions, finance, for example, is in control of others in service. Both include control and service.

The possible conflict between the control and service aspects of any function can be seen in relation to the personnel function of management. The acceptability and status of personnel departments in the United Kingdom rest largely on the extent to which the two aspects of the function are exercised. As service functions, maintaining relations with recruiting agencies and administering welfare services, personnel departments are widely acceptable but have low status. As control functions concerned with the administration of discipline and the selection and training of managers, they have to earn their acceptance by their contribution to the effective performance of the primary task of the company to which they belong. Having earned their acceptance, their status is high.

The greater the contribution a control or service function makes to the primary task, the more readily will operating management accept it and give it high status. Where the primary task is adequately defined and accepted, the functions most readily differentiated from total system management are those most necessary to increase the effectiveness of system performance. In the change from a simple undifferentiated primary production system to a more complex system requiring both operating and managing systems, the control and service functions first differentiated can be directly related to the forces that have brought about the organizational change. If the growth of a small factory or workshop is dependent on finding new capital from external sources, the provision of such capital is frequently accompanied by the differentiation of financial control. Similarly the shortage of labour in the United Kingdom during the war led to a considerable increase in the number of personnel departments in British industry. It was no accident that in the Calico Mills, with such rapid economic and technological changes, the first to be differentiated as specialist functions were financial control and research and development. Nor was it accidental that in a reorganized automatic shed the first functions to be included in the managing system should be production-study and inspection.

GENERAL MANAGEMENT

Where all necessary control and service functions are differentiated and delegated to specialists, total system management becomes the management of managers, or for convenience 'general management'. The manager of the total system is then a general manager.[1] In practice, complete differentiation and delegation are an ideal limit, and general management invariably contains one or more partially or wholly undifferentiated components of control or of operating system management. When general management retains totally or partially undifferentiated functions the general manager must take two or more roles. In one he is responsible for the management of other managers; in the others he is their colleague and, formally speaking, has no direct executive authority over them. It is hardly possible for any general manager completely to separate his multiple roles or to avoid investing the undifferentiated function with his authority as a general manager. It is seldom possible for other managers not to regard him as a general manager, whatever role he is filling. In the first stage of reorganization of the management of the Calico Mills the Managing Agent took the roles of General Manager and of Manager, Development and Research division. Neither the members of his own division nor the managers of other divisions found it possible to look upon him as other than the Managing Agent.

The retention of partially undifferentiated functions in general manage-

[1] The function of general management may be exercised by more than one person, a committee, etc. The appropriate form is determined by the social, technological, and economic dimensions of the system.

ment is a frequent source of difficulty because of the resulting imbalance between the responsibilities of the general manager's subordinates. When, for example, a manager is appointed to a function that is only partially differentiated, either his actual responsibility is so much less than that of other managers that he carries little weight in relation to colleagues, or, because part of his function is suffused directly with the authority of the general manager, his power is inflated.

Just as it is rare in practice for the differentiation of all functions of a managing system to be complete, so is it unlikely that delegation will ever be equal. Because of the importance of a particular function, of the needs of the immediate situation, of the personal characteristics of those involved, or of the background and interests of the general manager, some functions will always receive from a general manager more attention than others.

When partial differentiation and unequal delegation are neither explicit nor fully recognized, the difficulties are increased. Problems of this kind are often encountered in the rapid expansion of small organizations. When the original owner has to move out of operating management into a managing system he is likely to retain an undisclosed and undifferentiated part of the management of one operating system in his own command. In the usual conflicts between manufacturing and sales, a general manager's personal interest in manufacturing, carried over from the days when he managed it, frequently leads the new manager of manufacturing to feel that his views are not listened to with the same respect as those of the Sales Manager. Alternatively, or even at the same time, the Sales Manager may feel that sales policy is invariably subordinated to manufacturing policy, to the detriment of company results.

Since differentiation can seldom be complete or delegation equal, the role relationships between a general manager and his subordinates must vary with the degrees of differentiation and delegation. All pair relationships, general manager-subordinate, will therefore differ each from one another. But because all are parts of the same system, concerned with the same primary task, they will also be dependent on each other. The relationship pattern of a general manager and his subordinates is therefore a series of interdependent pairs which, taken together, represent the whole of system management—differentiated and undifferentiated, delegated and retained. It follows that a managing system should contain all the functions necessary for effective performance and that their location outside the system, for whatever reason, decreases effectiveness. It may happen in practice that the loss of effectiveness in external location is less than the loss of providing them within the system. This may arise because the functions can be most economically centralized to serve more than one operating system, or because of inefficiency in the system in which they should be located. If external location is decided because of inefficiency in the system itself, the decision may be explicit or implicit, disclosed or concealed. Making the decision explicit may provoke anxiety and disclosing it may hurt. But leaving it implicit may seriously weaken management's capacity to define its own task, and concealing it may lead to such ambiguous relationships as to jeopardize security and stability.

CHAPTER 23

The Machine Culture

THE DEMANDS OF A MACHINE TECHNOLOGY

Where manufacturing processes have become mechanical the primary producers are power-driven machines. The tasks of those who operate them are to serve machines—by loading, unloading, correcting faults, making adjustments, and carrying out routine maintenance and periodic overhauls. The products of a machine technology are standardized. Variations in them are largely determined by mechanical tolerances. The tasks and the products of a mechanized industry may be contrasted with those of craft industries, in which the producers are men and women and the products are unstandardized. Variations are determined by individual skill and idiosyncrasy.

The transition from craft to mechanized industry—and much of modern industry is still transitional—has been accompanied by changes in work organization and by changes in the social structure of industrial institutions. For the most part, these changes have been the consequence of the changes in technology rather than the result of social planning. In India the majority of hand-spinning and hand-weaving is carried out by families working in villages. Even with the development of village cooperatives—as with the guilds of early European industry—the working unit is still the family, or is structured round the family. By contrast the mills that have been built in industrial centres are divorced from families and family structures. The new technology has been considered of such paramount importance that production systems have been designed as though they had only technological dimensions. Social organization has been a projection of technological demand. The social and psychological needs of the members of industrial work organizations have been so inadequately satisfied that resistance to technological innovation has been inevitable. But for the insistent demand for its products resistance would have halted mechanization long ago.

The effective employment and development of a machine technology demand an appropriate work organization. It should be appropriate not only to the technological equipment and layout but also to the satisfactions provided for those who take roles in it. Since satisfaction is dependent on effective performance, a work organization employing a machine technology must be staffed by those who believe in their machines and in the products of their machines. They must think of, and feel for, what the machine can do rather than what they can do themselves. They must behave in such a way that machine performance is maximized rather than their own. Trist has called this constellation of attitudes, beliefs, customs, and patterns of behaviour a 'machine culture'.[1]

A 'machine culture' must be appropriate to the level of mechanization reached. The persistence of a culture appropriate to one level will cause conflict and difficulty when the level changes. The title of 'weaver' was no longer appropriate for one who was concerned with the running of automatic looms. The work culture traditionally supporting the weaver, and resulting in his being held solely responsible for weaving efficiency, obscured a cardinal rule of the new system, namely that all workers, whatever they might be called, were concerned with the simultaneous performance of interdependent tasks directed towards continuous weaving on all looms.

Even in non-automatic weaving, the carry-over from the hand-weaving industry of having one man—the weaver—responsible for the whole task resulted in a work organization which not only failed to provide for social and psychological needs but was so inflexible that full advantage could not be taken of the level of mechanization reached.

A complete machine technology does not exist until the level of mechanization reached is such that quality is completely determined by the accuracy of machine-movement, and quantity by the speed and duration of machine-run. The tasks of operational managers and workers would then be wholly concerned with keeping the machines running at maximum speed. In textiles neither yarn nor cloth would be handled from raw material to finished product. While this level has not yet been reached, machines have already become dominant and demand the active development of an appropriate 'culture' where none exists. For example, successive interdependent operations mean that the whole tempo of work should be con-

[1] Trist, E. L., private unpublished memorandum.

sistent with machine speeds, and that machine operating and maintenance, which so largely determine machine utilization, should be accurate and efficient. High machine speeds and efficient servicing are incompatible with the informal work traditions associated with craft industries, in which hours and speed are subject to individual choice.

Indian industry has had a tradition of cheap labour. Labour costs have been such a small proportion of total costs that it has been easier to engage extra workers than to inquire into the behaviour patterns that have led to inefficient machine utilization. The rise in wages in recent years has drawn attention to the number of workers employed on various tasks as compared with more industrialized countries. The economic and political importance of 'rationalization' has tended to obscure the social and psychological consequences of the tradition and the attempts to change it. Even when wages were very low it would have been in the interests of efficient production and worker-satisfaction—I doubt if they can ever be separated—to tackle problems of 'rationalization', as a means of developing an appropriate machine culture.

The low-wage tradition is closely linked to hours of work. The custom in most Indian industry is to have long shifts, but because of climate, working and living conditions, and health standards to take the work at a leisurely pace. In the spontaneous work organization that has grown up workers are accustomed to absent themselves from their work-places for long periods during which colleagues look after their machines. This tradition has continued when hours of work have been shortened and working conditions greatly improved; but casual, uncontrolled time-out can never be compatible with the need for precise control of machine servicing. It has been demonstrated that this tradition can be changed in the Calico Mills.

COMPREHENSIVE MECHANIZATION

Mechanization is unlikely to occur at the same rate in all parts of a process, yet uneven mechanization may interfere with the development of appropriate attitudes, beliefs, customs, and patterns of behaviour. It is not uncommon in those countries with a cheap labour tradition for mechanical handling to cost more than the equivalent manual process. Where this occurs the cost of installing mechanical handling may have to be compared not with the equivalent cost of manual handling but with the cost of manual handling, plus the cost of slowing down the growth of a machine culture appropriate to the general technological level. In the long run, not having mechanical handling may cost more than the saving on manual handling.

In a recent account of coal-mining in the U.S.S.R.[1] the consistency of mechanization throughout all operations is referred to as 'comprehensive mechanization'.

> 'The experience of recent years has shown that the most effective use of machines and equipment may be achieved if the main as well as auxiliary operations are mechanized as a complete unit, i.e., all the links in the chain of mining processes fit into the mechanization scheme.'

Trist[2] has stated the principle more generally: 'a reduction in the efficiency of a technological system as a whole may be expected whenever there is inequality in the level of mechanization of its parts. Once technological change has occurred in one sub-system, strong forces are brought into existence inducing it in others. Only when the required changes have occurred throughout all parts of the system will a new equilibrium be established. Only then can a work system be expected to maintain "the steady state" under operational conditions.'

One of the difficulties of costing and comparing performance as between different industrial production systems is the wide variety of measures of efficiency commonly used. Even with similar equipment and layout, measures of efficiency fall into four main classes:

1. Actual production expressed as a proportion of possible production, taking as given the number of hours worked and the normal stoppages required for rest-breaks, loading, unloading, and other regular services;
2. Actual production expressed as a proportion of possible production, taking as given the number of hours worked, but ignoring other stoppages;
3. Actual production expressed as a proportion of the possible production in 168 hours per week of non-stop running at existing speeds;
4. Actual production expressed as a proportion of the possible production in 168 hours per week of non-stop running at maximum speeds.

Different measures may be required for different purposes. The first or second may be suitable for the calculation of piece-work bonus. But as

[1] Central Institute of Technical Information, Ministry of Coal Mining Industry, 'Coal Mining Industry of the U.S.S.R.' Translated in *Colliery Guardian*, 1956, Vol. 193, No. 4981.

[2] Trist, E. L. Private unpublished memorandum.

mechanization increases, productivity depends more than ever on the duration, speed, and accuracy of machine-run. The third and fourth measures now become appropriate. In an industry with high capital investment in plant and equipment it may be dangerous to accept anything but the last as the measure used to determine manufacturing and equipment-purchasing policy. In the Calico Mills, rough calculations showed that in terms of profitability twenty minutes extra running-time was approximately equivalent to one per cent increase in efficiency, as measured by the second criterion. The problems and cost of increasing efficiency beyond a certain limit were only too well known, and it was found less difficult to increase running-time in spite of the disadvantages of third-shift working.

SOCIAL RESTRICTIONS OF MECHANIZATION

Increasing mechanization restricts the choice of individual action, and hence the skills required for machine operating. It increases the skills required for machine design, machine maintenance and for what might be called 'machine supervision'—the controlling of processes by the interpretation of instrument readings. With full mechanization or, to give it its more fashionable name, automation, the need for machine operating, as distinct from machine supervision, ceases. In the transition to full mechanization, fewer and less skilled machine operators are required. At the same time the increased capital investment raises the cost of idle time or inefficient utilization placing a high premium on smooth running. Fewer workers are required to take more responsibility for continuous servicing and rapid maintenance.

Reliability and stability are in high demand as qualifications for those who work on operational processes in a mechanized industry, and specialized training and skills are required for machine supervision and maintenance. Both trends were already observable in the Calico Mills. The change to automatic weaving had reduced the scope of the 'weaver's' jobs while increasing the need for maintenance skills. In certain bleaching and finishing processes, 'machine supervisors', with qualifications in chemistry or engineering were already employed to control machine running where adjustments depended upon the interpretation of abstractions recorded on instruments.

Traditionally in the textile industry machine maintenance is carried out in operatinga deprtments by workers with all-round skills—jobbers, fixers, tenters, etc. Many of the machines have high tolerances. The introduction of automatic and electronic controls reduces tolerances. Machines, or parts of them, are already beginning to require more specialist attention than can be given by unspecialized jobbers, fixers, or tenters. The 'fire brigade' attitude towards breakdowns and the need for reorganization to accommodate the specialist members of such a brigade have already been discussed. Where the primary producer is a machine, maintenance work, like machine running, must be directed primarily towards the prevention of faults and breakdowns. When breakdowns do occur, it must minimize loss of machine time. Preventive maintenance and replacement engineering increase in importance with mechanization.

The growth of machine technology has also led to the grouping of similar machines, e.g. spinning frames or looms, in organizationally distinct operating systems. In India different departments tend to be staffed by different castes or sub-castes and by different ethnic groups. Two important consequences have followed. First, any difficulties, rivalries, or jealousies between different ethnic groups have been reflected in productivity. Second, worker mobility has been restricted still further. This problem is not confined to India. In Lancashire, where 'vertical' organization is less common than in India, there are 'spinning' and 'weaving' towns; in the Scottish jute industry, the relationships of spinners and weavers in the inter-war years were perpetuated in the social life of the community.[1]

Where tradition has determined relative status—as between weavers and spinners—there will be resistance to reorganization that changes the relative status. This resistance may sometimes express itself as resistance to the changes in technology and, in consequence, in the inadequate use of production potential. Some of the resistance to the rationalization of selection and training procedures that is frequently encountered may arise from the same causes.

Paradoxically, increasing mechanization requires more rather than less attention to the social dimensions of production systems. Social systems need to be devised which increase rather than reduce social mobility.

COMPREHENSIVE ORGANIZATION

Just as uneven mechanization may inhibit the development of an appro-

[1] Oeser, O. A., 'Methods and Assumptions of Fieldwork in Social Psychology'. *British Journal of Psychology*, 1937, Vol. 27.

priate machine culture in manufacturing, so inadequate technology in other operations of a production system, or uneven mechanisms in managing systems, may inhibit the adequate exploitation of improvements in manufacturing. It would be unthinkable for the offices attached to a highly mechanized factory to continue to write all their letters by hand and to take copies on old-fashioned presses—irrespective of the relative costs of handpresses and typewriters. A machine technology demands consistency in related systems. Peter Drucker, referring to the new principle of the mass production of standardized parts for the manufacture of diverse products, says: 'Obviously the application of the mass-production principle is not simple. It goes well beyond manufacturing and requires hard and extensive work on the part of the marketing people, engineers, financial people, personnel people, purchasing agents, and so forth. It carries risks as it must be based on a fairly long production cycle at a constant rate of machine utilization—three, six, in some cases eighteen months. It requires new accounting tools.'[1]

In the Calico Mills it has been shown how the need to deal with social, economic, and technological changes forced changes in marketing and greater specialization in management. Greater specialization in management led to the delegation of responsibility and authority and hence to management reorganization. In particular, financial control and development and research became so specialized that nothing less than their complete reorganization was appropriate.

In contrast to the primary work-groups of mechanized industry, the managing systems of India have preserved many of their family characteristics. The Managing Agency system has been absorbed into the traditional joint family. In a traditional managing agency, family membership and family relationships are of overriding importance. All members have equal rights of access to the head of the family, even though some may be senior to others, and each member of the family contributes to the common task according to his abilities. In the derived management organization the power of family members, irrespective of role, is greater than that of non-members. But the relationships within the organization are informal and are governed more by personal than by task considerations. In able families the system has led to the building up of large enterprises that have carried through the first stages of the transition from village crafts to urban mechanization. The changes in technological, economic, and social conditions

[1] Drucker, Peter F., *The Practice of Management*, London, Heinemann, 1955.

that have taken place in recent years, however, have called for such varying, specialized, and hence exclusive, knowledge and experience, that only those with specialized training have been able to undertake certain functions of management. Unless highly trained specialists happen to be available among the members of a family, greater responsibility and authority have to be delegated to others. This disturbs the traditional family relationships. It also means that relationships between different specialists have to be adjusted to task needs rather than to personal preference. Just as the machine has become the producer, and has limited the worker's freedom of action, so the demand for specific mechanisms of control and service has limited the manager's individual idiosyncrasy.

The problems of such changes are not confined to the managing agencies of India. They arise wherever management has to deal with changing technological, social, or economic conditions. Increasing size and complexity and the need to introduce new kinds of specialists are leading to equally acute problems in the West. But because of the longer industrial tradition the problems are neither so easily observable—nor so easily dealt with—as in India.

The introduction of a new kind of specialist into any organization implies failure on the part of those already there to cope with the problems for which the specialist has been introduced. Whether the failure is conscious or unconscious, the introduction can be expected to arouse a complex of feelings towards the specialist, ranging from profound relief to open hostility. In most situations there are elements both of acceptance and of rejection. Irrespective of the feelings aroused, the introduction occasions re-allocation of duties and re-arrangement of relationships. In consequence, it constitutes a threat to the status of existing members. In India the familiar, personal, and informal nature of management makes the need for change obvious and the change process inevitable, however painful. In the West the specialization and professionalization of management have already gone so far that not only may the need for change be less obvious, but the change process may be inhibited by vested interests in existing specialization.

CHAPTER 24

The Management of Change

The productivity of a craft industry with an associated work organization based on an individually organized social system is limited by the skill and working capacity of individuals. The first stage in mechanization, by which individuals are given power-driven assistance, has led to considerable increases in output. But productivity based on this level of mechanization is still confined by the extent to which an individual can be assisted by mechanical power. Unless the system manages to transcend individual task organization its productivity will still be limited. Even when self-correcting and self-programming machines are used by which whole fabrications can be put into the control of one individual sitting at an instrument panel, there is still a need for a complex and differentiated system to control machine service and maintenance and to link the operations of raw material acquisition, marketing, manning, and finance.

Every differentiation in the technological, economic, or social dimensions of a production system requires a corresponding integration to maintain coordination between sub-systems. Every increase in the complexity of differentiation increases the chance of breakdown through the failure of the mechanisms of communication and control. On the other hand, just as the productivity of simple systems is limited by their inflexibility, so also is their capacity for change, and hence for taking advantage of technological elaboration. Complexity, with the associated problems of regulation and communication, is a necessary condition for technological advance. As industry becomes science- rather than craft-based, it has to adapt to technological change as a permanent circumstance, and therefore to develop more sophisticated techniques for the controlled assimilation of continuous change.

The management of technological change requires a three-phase process. Each phase may be characterized by the different degrees of protection necessary to allow exploration and testing of all the dimensions of a system and their interactions with each other. By protection is meant not only security in its usual sense, but all measures designed to shield those concerned from interference. Herbst has pointed out[1] that interference with group functioning, which is experienced as stress, makes more difficult the achieving by the group of its aim. Stress gives rise to defence mechanisms that absorb energy which would otherwise be devoted to the group task. There are three types and degrees of protection:

1. Conceptual protection (complete)—required in the design stage. The premature leakage of information about technological change that may have economic or social consequences may cause so much interference, both manifest and latent, that full exploration of economic and social dimensions is inhibited. Models of a new system capable of dealing with the social and economic problems are never discovered.

2. Experimental protection (substantial)—required to allow the testing and modification of a new system under experimental conditions. Because any new system has eventually to become part of a normal industrial unit, complete protection during testing may give rise to rumours, and so set up resistance in the unit for which it is intended. Against this, too little protection may result in too early crystallization in the social and economic dimensions, because of anxiety about the disturbance of traditional patterns.

3. Operational protection (limited)—required during the transition from experimental testing to a normal industrial unit. The transition is a handing-over process, whose length varies with the deviation of the new from the traditional system. It may also vary according to the dimension in which the change is required. If little change is necessary in the social dimension, hand-over can usually be quick. Considerable social change may take longer to assimilate.

The non-automatic weaving experiment described in Part IV was designed in a development group under conditions of complete protection. The experimental loom shed itself was started under conditions of substantial protection. It was necessary to protect it from judgments on the criteria appropriate to a production unit. Nevertheless it was located in a

[1] Herbst, P. G., 'Situation Dynamics and the Theory of Behaviour Systems', *Behavioural Science*, 1956.

main gangway, and visitors were permitted and encouraged; information was given to the Union representatives; volunteers were allowed to exercise their rights of return to their former roles; regular meetings and conferences were held; permanent passes were issued to all workers; permissive and collaborative relationships were built up between management and workers. The hand-over to the weaving department took place only after the shed had been running successfully for some months, and the first extension of the experimental system into the Jubilee Mill was undertaken by those who had been in charge of the original experiment.

The introduction of research and development departments represents a recognition of the need for protection during the various stages of design, testing, and handing-over. The normal industrial research and development department, however, does not deal with other than the technological dimension. Even when personnel departments are called into consultation the attention given to the social dimension is seldom as great as to the technological. Only too frequently, the social dimension is tackled only after resistance to change has already manifested itself. Then further experiment may be difficult, even impossible.

The management of change processes is not always concerned with internal problems. Frequently it involves making and maintaining relationships with external institutions and groups—suppliers, customers, and employer and employee organizations. In the Calico Mills the introduction of three shifts and new finishing processes involved drastic changes in marketing methods; and by changing grades, titles, and wages, the new work organizations changed relationships with the recognized union. It was for these reasons that 'organization development' and 'marketing' were included from the beginning in the new Development and Research division.

It may not always be necessary to have these functions within a research and development department, but if they are not included the organization must have somewhere within itself the necessary specialist knowledge and experience in these fields capable of being brought effectively to bear at every phase during the design, experiment, and hand-over of new systems.

Effective technological performance prescribes both equipment and process, and so sets limits to the flexibility of system organization. In the Calico Mills it has been shown that within these limits there is some choice of social organization. In other words the technological dimension of a system need not determine more than the limits of the social dimension, and there may be more than one social system that will satisfy task needs. Within the limits set by technological demand the most satisfactory work organization is one providing opportunity for the adequate satisfaction of basic social and psychological needs.

The limits set both by technological demand and by social and psychological needs have to be examined for each production system and for each culture. A work organization that falls outside the limits of technological demand will lead to ineffective performance, and hence to the frustration of the satisfaction derived from membership of it. A work organization that does not satisfy the social and psychological needs of its members will inhibit the full realization of technological potential. With a given technology and a given culture, social and psychological consistency between the technological and the social system may not always be possible. The formulation of principles and criteria to assist the discovery of the existing possibilities is a basic task of social research in industry.

Every society provides cultural mechanisms, both manifest and latent, by which its members satisfy their social and psychological needs—some more effectively than others. Every society limits the kind and range of mechanisms that may be used. Apart, therefore, from the limits set by technological demand, there may also be elements within a society that place further limits on the kinds of work organization possible. Such limits may make it difficult for the members of any given production system to find satisfaction in work. The kind of reorganizations described in the automatic and non-automatic sheds in the Calico Mills, though desirable theoretically, may not be possible in another society because the creation of internally structured small work-groups and the associated methods of wage payment run counter to nationally agreed role definitions and wage structures. By contrast, the introduction of Western organizational mechanisms into the managing systems of the Calico Mills, while manifestly more closely related to the technological demands of production than the previous informal executive, may in the course of time prove to deviate so much from their cultural setting as to require modification.

Whatever limitations are imposed either by technological demand or by cultural setting, a simultaneous examination of all of the dimensions of a production system, particularly when change is occurring, is the best way to provide evidence on which more effective and satisfactory systems can be based.

CONCLUSION

In our era most societies are trying to exploit the possibilities that arise from the application of an ever improving technology to human effort. In different societies, various social, political, and economic methods may be used to initiate and sustain change. Whatever the method, most societies are concerned with increasing man's power to adapt natural resources to his own material needs.

Although there may remain parts of the world, usually idealized, where material progress is still regarded as unimportant, elsewhere the demand for improved standards of living requires that more and more products be made available to more and more people. To increase productivity presupposes the exploitation of improvements in technology, and it is the same technology and the same improvements that are being introduced and exploited everywhere. Apart from nostalgic regrets for the lost beauty of unstandardized handicrafts, and for the idealized lives of their makers, the exploitation of improvements in technology must lead to some social dislocation. The degree of dislocation and the extent to which it inhibits the realization of the potential productivity of technological advance varies, and will doubtless continue to vary, with the cultural backgrounds into which it is introduced.

One of the factors that have contributed largely to the rapid exploitation of technological advance in America has been the complexity and heterogeneity of its cultural background. Because of their widely varying origins, Americans have not cherished their past at the expense of their future. As Americans they have not been encumbered with a common tradition, but have become members of a new culture in which technological exploitation is a part of an accepted creed.

Even in America, as numerous studies show, the effects of different backgrounds have caused difficulties in the social adaptation to technological change. The older industrial civilizations of Europe in which mechanization had its first costly social impact have slowly and painfully learned to adapt their social institutions to technological change. Nevertheless the process of adaptation, while less rapid than that of America, has by now become part of the political, economic, and social fabric of their societies. In spite of industrial disputes, changes continue, but they are for the most part gradual and difficult to observe. By contrast with both America and Europe, the introduction of modern industry into underdeveloped countries requires such major and dramatic changes that their effects are not only more easily observable but more easily controllable.

It is not my purpose to argue for any particular political or economic approach to the problems of social adaptation to technological change, or even to suggest that an industrial civilization is a necessarily desirable human aim. Rather I have accepted the inevitability of technological change and considered some of the possibilities that arise when simultaneous attention is paid to all the dimensions of production systems. Further, I suggest that planned and accepted change is more easily controlled and less socially damaging than unplanned and imposed change. In the work of the Calico Mills it has been shown that, in certain parts of one industrial organization, attention both to the social and the technological dimensions can result in new structures arising in which modifications of technology are accepted and exploited with apparent satisfaction both to management and to workers. It has been demonstrated that the assumption, often unconscious, that technology must completely determine social organization need not go unchallenged.

Opportunities for carrying out work of the kind described are rare. They depend on the felt need for change among those who have the authority to initiate the investigation of change processes; on the existence of a situation sufficiently critical to warrant taking a chance on untried procedures; and on the capacity of those responsible to tolerate the uncertainties and anxieties of waiting for experimental results.

The choice of the automatic shed for the first experiment was based on the assumption that the system had already been disturbed by the introduction of automatic looms. The shed would therefore be an area of relative flexibility in an otherwise highly structured institution. The unexpectedly spontaneous acceptance of the proposed reorganization did much to encourage further experiments. It can be seen in retrospect that the chaotic start to the non-automatic experiment, although worrying at the time, provided an excellent opportunity to demonstrate that the toleration of initial chaos can do much towards establishing permissive and collaborative relationships among those concerned with experimental change. But had the response to the first experiment not been so dramatically spontaneous, the chaos in the non-automatic shed might have been harder to bear. Had the chaotic start in the non-automatic shed not been the prelude to a successful experiment, the long, arduous, and sometimes painful, reorganization of management might not have been so patiently pursued.

A start has been made. It remains to discover whether continuous and controlled adaptation to change can become so much a part of the new organizations that the hectic pace of the past three and a half years can itself become an accepted and acceptable tradition.

APPENDICES

APPENDIX 1

Tables Referred to in Part III

Table 1. TASKS AND OCCUPATIONAL ROLES OF THE AUTOMATIC LOOM SHED

Task	*Occupational Role*
Transport weft yarn from store to loom; charge batteries with full bobbins (battery-filling)	Battery-filler
Transport beams from beam store to loom; change empty beams for full beams in brackets at back of loom; tie in warp yarn, adjust healds, and thread reed (gating)	Gater
Draw and knot broken warp threads, deal with entanglements and fluff (warp-mending)	Weaver
Draw and knot broken warp threads after a smash, unweave and repair faults (smash-tenting)	Smash-hand
Remove woven cloth from looms and transport to Inspection department (cloth-carrying)	Cloth-carrier
Tune and adjust looms, repair broken parts, and carry out general maintenance work (maintaining)	Jobber Assistant jobber
Maintain automatic device for rejecting used or defective bobbins (*maintaining special*)	Feeler-motion fitter
Oil looms while running and during gating (oiling)	Oiler
Remove empty bobbins and transport to Spinning department (bobbin-carrying)	Bobbin-carrier
Clean and sweep; remove fluff from under looms during gating (*sweeping*)	Sweeper
Maintain humidification plant and check humidity of shed (humidifying)	Humidification fitter

Table 2. OCCUPATIONAL ROLES, LINES OF RESPONSIBILITY, AND AVERAGE WAGES ON ONE SHIFT OF EXPERIMENTAL AUTOMATIC LOOM SHED

Occupational Role	*Number per Shift*	*Lines of Responsibility*	*Average Wages less D.A.*
Jobber	2	Responsible to shift supervisor; responsible for work of assistant jobber; exercises authority over weavers, oilers, gaters and sweepers	153*
Feeler-motion maintenance fitter	1	Responsible to shift supervisor, informed of need for services by supervisor, jobber, or weaver	143
Weaver	8	Responsible directly to shift supervisor, and to jobber, and exercises some directive authority over smash-hands who rank as assistant weavers	88–120*
Humidification fitter	1	Responsible to shift supervisor	108
Assistant jobber	2	Responsible to jobber	68–108
Gater	2	Responsible to shift supervisor, but can be called upon by a jobber or assistant jobber	85
Battery-filler	5	Responsible to shift supervisor	45
Oiler	1	Responsible to shift supervisor but instructed to oil loom by jobber during gating	38

* Average piece-work earnings

Table 2 (continued)

Occupational Role	*Number per Shift*	*Lines of Responsibility*	*Average Wages less D.A.*
Smash-hand	3	Responsible to shift supervisor and to weaver by whom he is informed of need for services (in training as a weaver)	28
Cloth-carrier	1	Responsible to shift supervisor	28
Bobbin-carrier	2	Responsible to shift supervisor	28
Sweeper	1	Responsible to shift supervisor. Called to clean under loom by jobber during gating	28
Total	29		

Table 3. THEORETICAL NUMBER OF LOOMS PER WORKER BY SORTS AT STANDARD EFFICIENCY OF 85 PER CENT

Sort Number	*Short-Stops per Loom per Hour*	*Looms per worker engaged on*		
		Warp-Mending	*Battery-Filling*	*Gating*
1	1·4	38	28	80
2	1·4	38	33	116
3	1·2	42	50	96
4	1·4	38	66	114
5	1·4	38	66	114
6	1·6	35	69	114
7	1·6	35	69	80
8	1·6	35	69	98
9	2·0	32	84	80
10	2·0	32	84	115
11	1·6	35	110	300
12	1·8	33	110	360
13	1·8	33	120	300
14	1·8	33	120	360
15	1·8	33	138	360
16	2·0	32	138	360

Table 4. VARYING NUMBER OF WORKERS REQUIRED FOR CHANGES OF SORT ON 960 LOOMS

Sort		*Workers engaged on tasks of* *Warp-Mending*	*Battery-Filling*	*Total Warp-Mending and Battery-Filling*	*Gating*
Coarse	1	26	34	60	12
	2	26	29	55	9
Medium	3	23	19	42	10
	4	26	15	41	9
	5	26	15	41	9
	6	27	14	41	9
	7	26	14	41	12
	8	27	14	41	10
	9	30	12	42	12
	10	30	12	42	9
Fine	11	27	9	36	3
	12	29	9	38	3
	13	29	8	37	3
	14	29	8	37	3
	15	29	7	36	3
	16	30	7	37	3

Table 5. VARYING NUMBER OF WORKERS REQUIRED FOR 960 LOOMS*

Tasks	*Numbers Required for Each Main Sort*		
	Coarse	*Medium*	*Fine*
Warp-mending Battery-filling	60	42	38
Gating	12	12	3
Totals	72	54	41

* The greatest numbers in the columns 'total warp-mending and battery-filling' and 'gating' for each of the three main sorts were taken from *Table 4*.

Table 6. NUMBER OF WORKERS FOR OTHER TASKS REQUIRED FOR 960 LOOMS

Tasks	*Occupational Roles*	*Number Required For All Sorts*
Smash-tenting	Smash-hands	12
Maintaining	Jobbers	8
	Assistant jobbers	8
Maintaining (Special)	Feeler-motion mechanics	4
Oiling	Oilers	4
Sweeping	Sweepers	4
Bobbin-carrying	Bobbin-carriers	4
Cloth-carrying	Cloth-carriers	8
	Total	52

Table 7. MEAN PERCENTAGE EFFICIENCIES OF FOUR EXPERIMENTAL GROUPS COMPARED WITH SHED EFFICIENCY BEFORE REORGANIZATION

Phase	*Period*	*Number of Working Days*	*Experimental Group*				
			aI	*aII*	*bI*	*bII*	*Combined*
1	30 March–10 April	11	87·7	87·9	86·5	86·4	87·1
2	11 April–14 April	3	67·7	69·6	73·2	79·8	72·6
3	15 April–23 April	8	84·0	86·4	83·0	86·3	84·9
4	24 April–6 June	37	95·9	96·2	94·0	94·1	95·0
Shed Efficiency Before Reorganization*							
	1 March–28 March	23	(79·8)	(79·8)	(79·8)	(79·8)	79·8

* The range of individual weaver's efficiencies before reorganization was 74·4–85·0.

The experimental groups are identified by the symbols *a*I, *a*II, *b*I, and *b*II where the letters *a* and *b* refer to the loom groups and the Roman numerals I and II refer to the first and second shifts.

Table 8. STANDARD DEVIATIONS OF DISTRIBUTIONS OF PERCENTAGE EFFICIENCIES

Phase	*Period*	*Number of Working Days*	*Experimental Group*				
			aI	*aII*	*bI*	*bII*	*Combined*
1	30 March–10 April	11	2·4	4·9	1·8	4·0	3·6
2	11 April–14 April	3	2·7	3·7	·7	1·8	5·2
3	15 April–23 April	8	5·3	3·2	6·8	1·6	4·9
4	24 April–June 6	37	2·6	2·3	2·6	2·4	2·7
Standard Deviation Before Reorganization							
	1 March–28 March	23	(3·1)	(3·1)	(3·1)	(3·1)	3·1

Table 9. MEAN PERCENTAGE DAMAGE OF FOUR EXPERIMENTAL GROUPS COMPARED WITH SHED DAMAGE BEFORE REORGANIZATION

Phase	*Period*	*Number of Working Days*	*Experimental Group*		*Com-bined*
			aI & aII	*bI & bII*	
1	6 April–10 April	5	37·8	45·5	41·6
2	11 April–14 April	3	31·2	36·2	33·7
3	15 April–23 April	8	18·8	25·7	22·3
4	24 April–6 June	37	17·8	21·9	19·9
Shed Damage Before Reorganization					
	1 March–28 March	23	(31·8)	(31·8)	31·8

Table 10. STANDARD DEVIATIONS OF DISTRIBUTIONS OF DAMAGE OF FOUR EXPERIMENTAL GROUPS

Phase	*Period*	*Number of Working Days*	*Experimental Group*	
			aI & aII	*bI & bII*
1	6 April–10 April	5	3·2	4·8
2	11 April–14 April	3	7·1	3·8
3	15 April–23 April	8	3·5	4·3
4	24 April–6 June	37	3·2	3·3

The results show a significant difference between the mean percentage efficiencies of each experimental group in the fourth phase, and the shed efficiency before reorganization; and between the mean percentage efficiency of the combined groups in the fourth phase, and the shed efficiency before reorganization. Except in the second phase (three days) they show no significant difference between the mean percentage efficiencies of the experimental groups or in the fourth phase between the standard deviations of the distributions of percentage efficiencies of the experimental group. The standard deviations of the distributions of the experimental groups are less for each group in the fourth phase than that of the distribution for the whole shed before reorganization. No daily damage figures were available for the period before reorganization or for the experimental groups for the first six days of the experimental period. Because there was no night shift in the Inspection department, the damage of the experimental groups *a*I and *a*II, and *b*I and *b*II, had to be combined.

The results show a significant difference between the mean percentage damage of each of the pairs of experimental groups and that of the shed before reorganization. They also show significant differences between the means of the experimental groups in all phases. The differences between the means of experimental groups can be accounted for by difficulties with humidification during construction, which affected the sixty-four looms near the new building—the *b* groups—more than the others. The boundary of the affected area was, however, difficult to define, and other unknown factors may have affected performance.

Table 11. EFFICIENCY AND DAMAGE FIGURES FOR REST OF LOOM SHED DURING EXPERIMENTAL PERIOD

Phase	*Period*	*Number of Working Days*	*Efficiency per cent*	*Damage per cent*
1	6 April–10 April	5	71·0	42·7
2	11 April–14 April	3	66·6	40·5
3	15 April–23 April	8	68·8	26·6
4	25 April–6 June	37	81·4	23·0
Shed Damage before Reorganization	1 March–28 March	23	79·8	31·8

Table 12. GRADES OF GROUP MEMBERS COMPARED WITH EXPERIMENTAL GROUP ESTABLISHMENT, NOVEMBER 1953

			Work-Groups									*Training Groups*	
Sub-Group	*Grade*	*Experimental Group Establishment*	*aI*	*aII*	*aIII*	*bI*	*bII*	*bIII*	*cI*	*cII*	*cIII*	*dI* (48 *looms*)	*dII* (48 *looms*)
Gating and Maintenance	A	1	1	1	1	1 (acting)	1	1 (acting)	1	1	–	–	–
	B	1	–	–	–	–	–	–	1	–	1	–	–
	C	–	–	1	–	1	1	–	–	–	–	2	2
	D	1	2	–	2	1	1	1	1	1	1	–	–
	E	–	–	1	–	–	–	1	–	1	1	1	1
Weaving	B	2	2	1	2	2	2	2	2	2	–	–	–
	C	–	–	2	1	1	1	1	1	1	2	3	2
	D	2	2	–	–	1	1	–	1	–	1	–	–
	E	–	–	1	1	–	–	1	–	1	1	1	2
Totals		7	7	7	7	7	7	7	7	7	7	7	7

Table 13. VARIATIONS IN NUMBER OF WORKERS FOR 64 LOOMS FOR VARYING LOOM STOPPAGE RATES—INTERIM STANDARDS

Sub-Group	*Grade*	*Numbers of Workers at Stoppages per Loom per Hour* 0·6–0·8	0·8–1·4	1·4–2·0	2·0–2·5
Gating and	A	1	1	1	1
Maintenance	B	1	1	1	1
	D	1	1	1	1
Weaving	B	1	2	3	4
	D	2	2	2	2
Totals		6	7	8	9

In this table, the tasks taken away from the groups in the summer—sweeping, bobbin-carrying, and cloth-carrying—were left as shed services under the direct control of the shift supervisors.

Table 14. PROCESS OF RESTRUCTURING OF GROUPS, NOVEMBER 1953–JUNE 1955

Phase	*Period*	*Number of Working Days*	*Classification of Groups (Work, Production, Transition, Training, Experimental)*												*Total Number of Groups Working*
			aI	*aII*	*aIII*	*bI*	*bII*	*bIII*	*cI*	*cII*	*cIII*	*dI*	*dII*	*dIII*	
1	23 Nov.–20 Dec. 1953	24	Work	Work	Work	Work	Work	Work	Work	Work	Work	Train.	Train.	—	11
2	21 Dec.–27 Feb. 1954	60	Work	Work	Work	Work	Work	Work	Work	Work	—	Train.	Train.	—	10
3	28 Feb.–27 Mar. 1954	24	Work	Work	Work	Work	Work	—	Work	Work	—	Train./ Expt.	Train./ Expt.	—	9
4	28 Mar.–5 June 1954	60	Prod.	Trans.	Trans.	Trans.	Trans.	—	Expt.	Expt.	—	Train./ Expt.	Train./ Expt.	—	9
5	6 June–24 July 1954	42	Prod.	Prod.	Trans.	Expt.	Expt.	—	Prod.	Trans.	—	Train.	Train.	—	9
6	25 July–21 Aug. 1954	24	Prod.	Prod.	Trans.	Trans.	Prod.	—	Prod.	Prod.	—	Train.	Train.	—	9
7	22 Aug.–5 Dec. 1954	86	Expt.	Expt.	—	Expt.	Expt.	—	Prod.	Prod.	Prod.	Train.	Train.	—	9
8	6 Dec.–25 Mar. 1955	90	Expt.	Expt.	Expt.	Prod.	Prod.	Trans.	Prod.	Prod.	Prod.	Train./ Expt.	Train./ Expt.	Train./ Expt.	12
9	26 Mar.–30 June 1955	88	Prod.	Prod.	Prod.	Prod.	Prod.	Prod.	Prod.	Prod.	Prod.	Train.	Train.	Train.	12

Table 15. MEAN PERCENTAGE EFFICIENCIES OF WORKING, PRODUCTION, AND TRANSITION GROUPS,[1] NOVEMBER 1953–JUNE 1955

Phase	Period	Number of Working Days	Mean Percentage Efficiencies of Working, Production, and Transition Groups									
			aI	*aII*	*aIII*	*bI*	*bII*	*bIII*	*cI*	*cII*	*cIII*	*All Groups*
1	23 Nov.–20 Dec. 1953	24	83	87	85	83	84	85	78	79	77	82
2	21 Dec.–27 Feb. 1954	60	91	92	93	92	94	91	90	91	—	92
3	28 Feb.–27 Mar. 1954	24	91	93	93	94	93	—	90	91	—	92
4	28 Mar.–5 June 1954	60	94	96	97	92	92	—	(85)	(84)	—	94
5	6 June–24 July. 1954	42	91	91	94	(88)	(91)	—	91	93	—	92
6	25 July–21 Aug. 1954	24	93	95	94	97	98	—	93	94	—	95
7	22 Aug.–5 Dec. 1954	86	(82)	(85)	—	(85)	(86)	—	91	91	91	91
8	6 Dec.–25 Mar. 1955	90	(73)	(74)	(77)	96	96	96	96	96	97	96
9	26 Mar.–30 June 1955	88	94	95	95	94	95	95	91	92	94	94

[1] The mean percentage efficiencies of experimental groups are shown in parentheses. They are not included in the mean percentage efficiencies of all groups.

Table 16. MEAN PERCENTAGE EFFICIENCIES OF TRAINING GROUPS, NOVEMBER 1953–JUNE 1955

Phase	Period	Number of Working Days	Mean Percentage Efficiencies dI	dII	dIII
1	23 Nov.–20 Dec. 1953	24	83	83	—
2	21 Dec.–27 Feb. 1954	60	87	89	—
3	28 Feb.–27 Mar. 1954	24	89	88	—
4	28 Mar.–5 June 1954	60	86	86	—
5	6 June–24 July 1954	42	84	87	—
6	25 July–21 Aug. 1954	24	89	90	—
7	22 Aug.–5 Dec. 1954	86	92	92	—
8	6 Dec.–25 Mar. 1955	90	85	85	85
9	26 Mar.–30 June 1955	88	88	89	93

Table 17. MEAN PERCENTAGE DAMAGE OF WORKING, PRODUCTION, AND TRANSITION GROUPS,[1] NOVEMBER 1953–JUNE 1955

Phase	Period	Number of Working Days	Percentage Damage a	b	c	Weighted Average
1	23 Nov.–20 Dec. 1953	24	26	29	28	28
2	21 Dec.–27 Feb. 1954	60	24	21	24	23
3	28 Feb.–27 Mar. 1954	24	28	26	27	27
4	28 Mar.–5 June 1954	60	25	26	27	26
5	6 June–24 July 1954	42	18	23	26	23
6	25 July.–21 Aug. 1954	24	8	19	22	17
7	22 Aug.–5 Dec. 1954	86	(17)	(18)	19	19
8	6 Dec.–25 Mar. 1955	90	(18)	10	10	11
9	26 Mar.–30 June 1955	88	13	11	13	12

[1] The mean percentage damage of experimental groups is shown in parentheses. They are not included in the weighted average of all groups.

Table 18. MEAN PERCENTAGE DAMAGE FIGURES OF TRAINING GROUPS, NOVEMBER 1953–JUNE 1955

Phase	*Period*	*Number of Working Days*	*Mean Percentage Damage d*
1	23 Nov.–20 Dec. 1953	24	33
2	21 Dec.–27 Feb. 1954	60	22
3	28 Feb.–27 Mar. 1954	24	24
4	28 Mar.–5 June 1954	60	21
5	6 June–24 July 1954	42	28
6	25 July–21 Aug. 1954	24	11
7	22 Aug.–5 Dec. 1954	86	13
8	6 Dec.–25 Mar. 1955	90	20
9	26 Mar.–30 June 1955	88	18

Table 19. MEAN NUMBER OF STOPPAGES PER LOOM PER HOUR AND MEAN NUMBER OF WORKERS PER GROUP

Phase	Period	Number of Working Days	Mean Number of Stoppages and Mean Number of Workers							
			a		*b*		*c*		*Average*	
			Stoppages	*Workers*	*Stoppages*	*Workers*	*Stoppages*	*Workers*	*Stoppages*	*Workers*
4	28 Mar.–5 June 1954	60	1·8	8·5	2·1	8·0	3·2	8·8	2·4	8·4
5	6 June–24 July 1954	42	2·6	8·4	2·4	8·0	1·8	8·0	2·3	8·1
6	25 July–21 Aug. 1954	24	1·9	8·0	1·4	7·6	1·6	8·0	1·6	7·9
7	22 Aug.–5 Dec. 1954	86	E	E	E	E	(1·7)	8·0	(1·7)	8·0
8	6 Dec.–25 Mar. 1955	90	E	E	(0·9)	6·0	(0·9)	6·0	(0·9)	6·0

Table 20. VARIATIONS IN THE NUMBER OF WORKERS FOR GROUPS OF 64 LOOMS FOR VARYING LOOM STOPPAGE RATES—WITH IMPROVED BEAMS AND REWOUND WEFT

Sub-Group	*Grade*	*Number of Workers required at Stoppage Rates per loom per hour* 0·5–0·8	0·8–1·4	1·4–2·0
Gating and	A	1	1	1
Maintenance	B	1	1	1
	D	1	1	1
Weaving	B	1	2	3
	D	1	1	1
Ancillary Services	D	1	1	1
Totals		6	7	8

APPENDIX 2

Figure and Tables Referred to in Part IV

FIGURE 1 *REPRESENTATION OF A NON-AUTOMATIC LOOM SET UP FOR WEAVING*

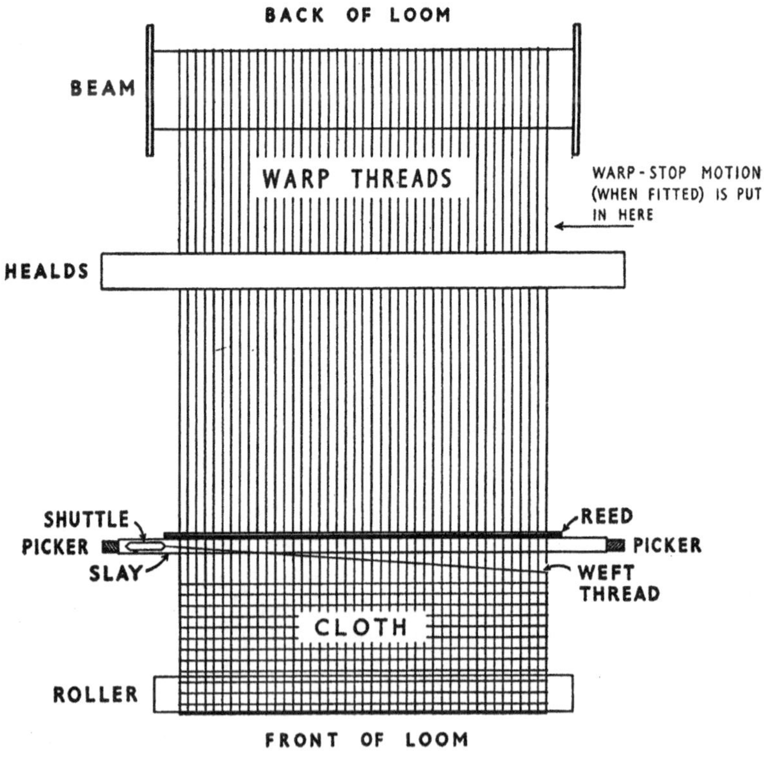

Table 1. TASKS AND OCCUPATIONAL ROLES OF NON-AUTOMATIC LOOM WEAVING

Tasks	*Occupational Role*
Transport weft from weft store to loom (weft-carrying)	Weaver
Transport assorted colour wefts from weft store to looms (weft-distributing)	Line jobber
Transport beams from preparation department to warp store and from warp store to looms (warp-carrying)	Beam-carrier
Change empty beam in loom bearings for full beam (warp-mounting)	Beam-carrier and oiler
Tie-in warp, check, tune loom, put full weft bobbin in shuttle, recheck, start loom (gating)	Line jobber
Remove empty bobbin from finished shuttle and replace with full bobbin. Remove empty shuttle and replace with full, re-start loom (shuttling)	
Observe back of loom, remove fluff, take action to prevent entanglements (fault-prevention)	Weaver
Stop loom when fault occurs, unweave and repair faults, draw and knot broken ends, restart loom (warp-mending)	
Stop loom when major fault occurs, unweave and repair (smash-tenting)	
Cut cloth at cutting marks and remove completed cloth (cloth-removing)	
Transport cloth from loom to cloth room (cloth-carrying)	
Check in cloth room and stack	
Running repairs not involving major overhaul or fitting (maintaining)	Line jobber
Cleaning and oiling (oiling [gating] and oiling [routine])	Oiler
Oiling shuttle-spindle and minor adjustments (maintaining)	Weaver

Table 2. OCCUPATIONAL ROLES, NUMBERS, TASKS, LINES OF RESPONSIBILITY, AND AVERAGE MONTHLY WAGES TO NEAREST RUPEE ON THE FIRST SHIFT —MILL A LOOM SHED

Occupational Role	*Numbers Employed*	*Line of Responsibility*	*Average Wage per month less Dearness Allowance*
Line jobber	19	Responsible to Weaving Supervisor/Head Jobber for group of weavers	139*
Weaver	380	Works on own, responsible to line jobber	66*
Beam-carrier	2	Part of gang responsible to Preparation Department Supervisor	37
Oiler	14	Works alone, except on holidays when works in gang. Responsible to Weaving Supervisor/Head Jobber	28

*Average piece-work earnings.

Table 3. WORK-LOAD STUDIES OF LOOM SHED TASKS:

a. VARIABLE WORK-LOADS

Task	*Number of Looms which could be managed by One Worker at 85 per cent Efficiency with Variable Number of Loom Stoppages per Loom per Hour of*							
	0·5–1·5	1·5–2·5	2·5–3·5	3·5–4·0	4·0–4·5	4·5–5·0	5·0–5·5	5·5–6·0
Warp-Mending	36	20	13	10	8	7	6	5
Fault-Prevention	200	100	40	30	30	30	30	30
Smash-Tenting	100	60	40	30	25	23	21	20

b. CONSTANT WORK-LOADS

Task	*Number of Looms per Worker at 85 per cent Efficiency*
Shuttling	12
Gating and Maintaining	60
Oiling (Gating)	400
Warp-Mounting*	1000
Oiling (Routine)	128
Weft-Distributing*	120
Cloth-Removing*	300

* Warp-mounting here included warp-carrying provided the warp store was close to looms and the brackets at the backs of looms were easily accessible. In the same way weft-distributing included weft-carrying from a near weft store and cloth-removing included carrying the cloth to a central point in a small loom shed.

The figures of this table were not all derived from work-load studies since not all loom stoppage rates were available for observation. They are made up of studies and interpolations after discussion with those with long weaving experience. The figures include normal allowances for fatigue and other contingencies.

Table 4. THEORETICAL NUMBER OF WORKERS FOR GROUP OF 24 LOOMS AT 4 LOOM STOPPAGES PER LOOM PER HOUR

Time Period	*Task*	*Theoretical Number of Workers*	*Totals*
	Shuttling	2·0	2·0
Short-stop	Warp-Mending	2·4	
	Fault-Prevention	0·8	3·2
	Smash-Tenting	0·8	0·8
Long-stop	Gating and Maintaining	0·4	0·4
	Oiling (Gating)	0·1	
	Warp-Mounting	0·0*	
	Oiling (Routine)	0·2	
Running	Weft-Distributing	0·2	0·6
	Cloth-Removing	0·1	
	Totals	7·0	7·0

* = 0·02.

Table 5. THEORETICAL NUMBER OF WORKERS REQUIRED FOR A GROUP OF 40 LOOMS

a. VARIABLE WORK-LOADS

Task	*Number of Workers at Variable Loom Stoppages per Loom per Hour*							
	0·5–1·5	1·5–2·5	2·5–3·5	3·5–4·0	4·0–4·5	4·5–5·0	5·0–5·5	5·5–6·0
Warp-Mending	1·1	2·0	3·1	4·0	5·0	5·7	6·7	8·0
Fault-Prevention	0·2	0·4	1·0	1·3	1·3	1·3	1·3	1·3
Smash-Tenting	0·4	0·7	1·0	1·3	1·6	1·7	1·9	2·0
Totals	1·7	3·1	5·1	6·6	7·9	8·7	9·9	11·3

b. CONSTANT WORK-LOADS

Task	*Number of Workers*	*Totals*
Shuttling	3·33	3·33
Gating and Maintaining	0·67	0·67
Oiling (Gating)	0·10	
Warp-Mounting	0·04	
Oiling (Routine)	0·31	
Weft-Distributing	0·33	
Cloth-Removing	0·13	0·91
Totals	4·91	4·91

Table 6. NUMBER OF WORKERS FOR GROUPS OF 40 LOOMS WITH VARIABLE LOOM STOPPAGES PER LOOM PER HOUR

Equivalent Number of Workers in Existing Sheds	*Tasks*	*Number of Workers required for Variable Number of Loom Stoppages per Loom per Hour*							
		0·5–1·5	1·5–2·5	2·5–3·5	3·5–4·0	4·0–4·5	4·5–5·0	5·0–5·5	5·5–6·0
20*	Warp-Mending Shuttling Fault-Prevention Smash-Tenting	5	7	9	10	11	12	13	15
1	Gating and Maintaining	1	1	1	1	1	1	1	1
1	Oiling (gating) Warp-Mounting Oiling (routine) Weft-Distributing Cloth-Removing	1	1	1	1	1	1	1	1
22	Totals	7	9	11	12	13†	14†	15†	17†

* Includes part of tasks of weft-distributing and cloth-carrying.

† At these stoppage rates the numbers of looms in the loom group would be reduced to allow a smaller work-group to manage them.

Table 7. MEAN PERCENTAGE EFFICIENCIES OF EXPERIMENTAL GROUPS

Phase	*Period*	*No. of Working Days*	*Percentage Efficiency of Experimental Group*					
			CI	*CII*	*CIII*	*AI*	*AII*	*AIII*
1	15 Jan.–29 Jan.	14	37	36				
2	30 Jan.–20 Feb.	19	58	58				
3	21 Feb.–24 Mar.	27	62	63		60	62	
4	25 Mar.–13 Apr.	17	74	74		64	67	
5	14 Apr.–3 May	17	79	79		70	68	
6	4 May–14 May	10	75	76	62	68	71	52
7	15 May–11 June	24	68	69	62	64	66	55
8	12 June–10 July	25	80	80	76	74	75	66
9	11 July–13 Nov.	104	86	86	84	80	82	75

Table 8. MEAN NUMBER OF DAMAGES PER 1,000 YARDS OF CLOTH WOVEN

Phase	*Period*	*No. of Working Days*	*Number of Damages for Experimental Group*					
			CI	*CII*	*CIII*	*AI*	*AII*	*AIII*
1	15 Jan.–29 Jan.	14	21·1	20·4				
2	30 Jan.–20 Feb.	19	9·1	9·3				
3	21 Feb.–24 Mar.	27	5·7	5·2				
4	25 Mar.–13 Apr.	17	4·9	4·3		7·9	7·6	
5	14 Apr.–3 May	17	2·7	3·1		6·1	7·0	
6	4 May–14 May	10	4·0	5·7	7·9	8·1	7·5	15·9
7	15 May–11 June	24	7·8	10·5	15·9	15·0	15·9	28·6
8	12 June–10 July	25	5·4	5·3	9·3	11·4	8·4	15·0
9	11 July–13 Nov.	104	2·8	2·9	3·7	6·6	6·8	7·9

Table 9. SAMPLED MEAN LOOM STOPPAGES PER LOOM PER HOUR OF EXPERIMENTAL GROUPS

Phase	*C Groups*	*A Groups*
1	9·9	
2		
3	4·4	
4		2·8
5	2·8	3·1
6	2·9	3·6
7	3·7	3·9
8	3·3	3·9
9	2·9	3·5

Table 10. COMPARISON OF EARNINGS OF EXPERIMENTAL SHED AND OTHER LOOM SHEDS WEAVING IDENTICAL CLOTHS

	Experimental Shed				*Other Sheds*			
Grade	*Basic Wage Rs.*	*Average Bonus Rs.*	*Dearness Allowance Rs.*	*Total*	*Equivalent Occupational Role*	*Average Earnings Rs.*	*Dearness Allowances Rs.*	*Total Rs.*
A	145	41	62	248	Line-jobber	139	62	201
B+	125	35	62	222				
B	115	32	62	209	Weaver	66	62	128
C	90	25	62	177				
D	55	15	62	132	Oiler	28	62	90

Table 11. NUMBERS TRANSFERRED TO EXPERIMENTAL SHED AND RETURNING TO PREVIOUS DEPARTMENT

Phase	*Period*	*No. of Working Days*	*Transferred to Experimental Shed*	*Returned to Previous Department*	*Rate of Returning as Number Returned per 100 Days*
1	15 Jan.–29 Jan.	14	20	2	14
2	30 Jan.–20 Feb.	19	21	1	5
3	21 Feb.–24 Mar.	27	5	2	4
4	25 Mar.–13 Apr.	17	7	1	6
5	14 Apr.–3 May	17	25	2	12
6	4 May–14 May	10	30	15	150
7	15 May–11 June	24	13	8	33
8	12 June–10 July	25	18	14	56
9	11 July–13 Nov.	104	10	14	13

APPENDIX 3

Table Referred to in Part V

Table 1. ALLOCATION OF DUTIES BETWEEN THE TWO MANAGERS

A (Production and Sales)	*B (Purchasing and Finance)*
Production and Discipline	*Production and Discipline*
Mechanical and Electrical Engineering	Chemical Division
Spinning	
Weaving	
Bleaching	
Dyeing and Printing	
Sewing thread	
Mosquito netting	
Cloth Department	
Civil Engineering	*Civil Engineering*
General supervision and efficiency	Contracts for Civil Engineering work
Departmental routine work	Passing of all bills
Letting of Quarters	
Cotton	*Cotton*
Storing of cotton	Cotton purchases
Consumption of cotton	
Stores	*Stores*
Consumption of Stores	Purchases of stores and all materials, machinery, etc..
	Annual contracts
	Storage
	Maintenance of stock
	Passing of bills
	Checking and reporting on consumption

Table 1 (continued)

A (Production and Sales)	*B (Purchasing and Finance)*
Coal	*Coal*
Consumption of coal	Annual contracts
	Maintenance of stock
Sales	*Sales*
Local sales of cloth	All chemical products
Upcountry cloth exports	Sales of waste and waste products
Retail sales	Sales of old machinery of the Textile and Chemical Divisions
Sewing threads	
Mosquito netting	
Agencies	
Publicity and Exhibition	
Shops and showcases	
Brokers' office	
Artists' office	
Purchase of New Machinery	*Purchase of New Machinery*
All specifications for machinery for Textile division, fixing specifications, checking material on arrival	Preliminary inquiries
	Placing of orders
	Application for import licence
	Confirmation of Draft
	Payment of advance, if any
	Arrangement for shipping and insurance
	Fixing of foreign exchange
	Clearance and transport
Miscellaneous Departments	*Office Departments*
Gate-Keeper's office	Finance office
Time-Keeper's office	Share department
Watch and Ward	Board of Directors' and Shareholders' meetings
Statistics	
Laboratory and Mills Library	Pay department
Maternity Benefits	Typists and General office
Hospital	Credit Cooperative Societies
Crèche	Records
Grain shop	
Workers' restaurants and dining places	

Table 1 (continued)

A (Production and Sales)	*B (Purchasing and Finance)*
Employment and Labour Relations	*Taxes and Legal Work*
Employment of Workers	All matters relating to municipal taxes
Employment of Jobbers	All matters relating to Income-tax and other State taxes
Employment of Technical Supervisors	Legal work other than the work relating to labour matters and matters referred to the Industrial Court
Contact with Labour Union	Documents
Contact with Millowners' Association	
Labour disputes	
Waste	*Insurance*
Control of waste produced	All matters relating to annual and periodical insurance
Storing of waste produced	
Internal Audit	*Welfare Work*
Checking of departmental productions	Credit Cooperative Societies
Checking of canteen accounts	Primary school for workers' children
Checking of grain shop accounts	Primary school for children of other staff
	Library
Costing	*Expansion and Planning*
Cloth and yarn costings	All matters relating to expansion and planning of the Textile and Chemical divisions
Excise	
All matters pertaining to Excise, including duty	
Motor Transport	
All matters pertaining to motor transport	

BIBLIOGRAPHY

ADAMS, S. 'Status Congruency as a Variable in Small Group Performance', *Social Forces*, Vol. 32, 16–22, 1953.

ADAMS, S. 'Social Climate and Productivity in Small Military Groups', *American Sociological Review*, Vol. 19, 421–425, 1954.

ARENSBURG, C., and MACGREGOR, D. 'Determination of Morale in an Industrial Company', *Applied Anthropology*, Vol. 1, No. 2, 1942.

ARGYRIS, C. *Executive Leadership an Appraisal of a Manager in Action:* New Haven, Yale Labor and Management Center, 1953.

ARGYRIS, C. 'The Fusion of an Individual with the Organization', *Sociological Review*, Vol. 19, 267–272, 1954.

ARGYRIS, C. *The Behavioral Sciences and Organization:* New Haven, Yale University Press, 1956.

BAKKE, E. W. *Team Work in Industry*, New Haven, Yale Labor and Management Center, 1948.

BAKKE, E. W. *Bonds of Organization*, New York, Harper & Bros., 1950.

BAKKE, E. W. *The Fusion Process*, New Haven, Yale Labor and Management Center, 1953.

BARNARD, C. L. *The Functions of an Executive*, Cambridge, Harvard University Press, 1948.

BAVELAS, A. 'Communication Patterns in Task-Oriented Groups', *The Policy Sciences*, Lerneer, O. and Lasswell, H. (eds.), Stanford University Press, 1951.

BENEDICT, R. *Patterns of Culture*, London, Routledge and Kegan Paul, 1949.

BERTALANFFY, LUDWIG VON. 'The Theory of Open Systems in Physics and Biology', *Science*, Vol. III, 1950.

BION, W. R. 'Experiences in Groups, I, II, III, IV, V and VI', *Human Relations*, Vols. I, II and III, 1948, 1949, 1950.

BION, W. R. 'Group Dynamics: A Re-view' in *New Directions in Psycho-Analysis*, London, Tavistock Publications, 1955.

BOWLBY, J., JAQUES, E., KELNAR, J., MENZIES, I. E. P., MORRIS, B. S., SUTHERLAND, J., and WILSON, A. T. M., 'Social Therapy', *The Journal of Social Issues*, Jaques, E. (Ed.), Vol. III, No. 2, 1947.

BROWN, J. F. *Psychology and the Social Order*, New York, McGraw-Hill, 1936.

BROWN, W. B. D., and RAPHAEL, W. *Managers, Men and Morale*, London, Macdonald and Evans, 1948.

CAMERON, D. E., and ROSS, H. G. (Eds.), *Human Behaviour and its Relation to Industry*, Montreal, McGill University, 1944.

CARLSON, J. *Executive Behaviour*, Stockholm, Strömbergs, 1950.

CARTWRIGHT, D., 'Achieving Change in People: Applications of Group Dynamics Theory', *Human Relations*, Vol. 4, No. 4, 1951.

CARTWRIGHT, D., and ZANDER, A, (Ed.), *Group Dynamics*, London, Tavistock Publications, 1953.

CENTRAL INSTITUTE OF TECHNICAL INFORMATION, Ministry of Coal Mining Industry, U.S.S.R. 'Coal Mining Industry of the U.S.S.R.' *Colliery Guardian*, Vol. 193, No. 4981, 1956.

COCH, L., and FRENCH, J. R. P. 'Overcoming Resistance to Change', *Human Relations*, Vol. 1, No. 4, 1948.

COOK, P. H., and WYNDHAM, A. J. 'Patterns of Eating Behaviour', *Human Relations*, Vol. VI, No. 2, 1953.

COOK, P. H. 'Methods of Field Research', *Australian Journal of Psychology*, Vo. III, No. 2, 1951.

CURLE, A, 'Incentives to Work: An Anthropological Appraisal', *Human Relations*, Vol. II, No. 1, 1949.

CURLE, A. 'A Theoretical Approach to Action Research', *Human Relations*, Vol. II, No. 3, 1949.

DIEBOLD, John. *Automation—the Advent of the Automatic Factory*, New York, D. Van Nostrand Company, 1952.

DRUCKER, P. F. *The Practice of Management*, London, Heinemann, 1955.

DURKHEIM, E. *Le Division du Travail Social*, Paris, 1893.

FESTINGER, L., and KATZ, D. *Research Methods in the Behavioral Sciences*, New York, Dryden Press, 1953.

FESTINGER, L., and KATZ, D. *Social Pressures in Informal Groups*, New York, Harper & Bros, 1950.

FOLLET, M. P. 'Dynamic Administration', *Collected Papers* Metcalf, H. C., and Urwick, L. (Eds.), New York, Harper, 1942.

FRENCH, J. R. P. 'Changing Group Productivity', *Experiments in Social Process*, Miller, (Ed.), New York, McGraw-Hill, 1950.

FRIEDMANN, G. *Où va le Travail Humain?* Paris, Librairies Gallimard, 1950.

FRIEDMANN, G. *Industrial Society: The Emergence of the Human Problems of Automation*, Glencoe, Free Press, 1955.

FRIEDMANN, G. 'Outline for a Psycho-Sociology of Assembly Line Work', *Human Organization*, Vol. 12, No. 4, 1954.

GANDHI, MOHANDAS KARAMCHAND. *The Story of My Experiments with Truth*, Ahmedabad, Navjivan Publishing House, 1940.

GANGRADE, K. D. 'Employee Morale', *Indian Journal of Social Work*, Vol. 15, No. 3, 1954.

GARTNER, B., and WHYTE, W. F. 'Methods for the Study of Human Relations in Industry', *American Sociological Review*, Vol. II, 506–512, 1946.

GEDDES, A. 'The Social and Psychological Significance of Variability in Population Change', *Human Relations*, Vol. 1, No. 2, 1947.

GILLESPIE, J. J. *Dynamic Motion and Time Study*, London, Elek, 1947.

GILLESPIE, J. J. *Principles of Rational Industrial Management*, London, Pitman, 1938.

GORDON, T. 'Group-Centered Leadership and Administration', *Client Centered Therapy*, Boston, Houghton-Mifflin, 1951.

GROSS, E. 'Some Functional Consequences of Primary Controls in Formal Work Organizations', *American Sociological Review*, Vol. 181, 368–373, 1953.

HERBST, P. G. 'Situation Dynamics and the Theory of Behaviour Systems', *Behavioural Science:* Vol. 2, No. 1, 1957.

HERBST, P. G. 'Measurement of Behaviour Structures by means of Input-Output Data', *Human Relations* Vol. X, No. 4, 1957.

HERTZ, D. B., and LIVINGSTONE, R. T. 'Contemporary Organizational Theory', *Human Relations* Vol. 3, No. 4, 1950.

HILL, J. M. M. 'A Consideration of Labour Turnover as the Resultant of a Quasi-Stationary Process', *Human Relations,* Vol. IV, No. 3, 1951.

HILL, J. M. M., and TRIST, E. L. 'A Consideration of Industrial Accidents as a means of Withdrawal from the Work Situation', *Human Relations,* Vol. VI, No. 4, 1953.

HILL, J. M. M., and TRIST, E. L. 'Changes in Accidents and other Absences with Length of Service', *Human Relations*, Vol. VIII, No. 2, 1955.

HOMANS, G. C. 'Group Factors in Worker Productivity', *Readings in Social Psychology*, Newcomb and Hartley (Eds.), New York, Holt, 1947.

HOMANS, G. C. 'The Cash Posters: A Study of a Group of Working Girls', *American Sociological Review*, Vol. 191, No. 6, 1954.

HOMANS, G. C. *The Human Group*, London, Routledge and Kegan Paul, 1951.

JACOBSON, E., *et al.* (Ed.). 'Human Relations Research in Large Organizations', *Journal of Social Issues*, Vol, 7, No. 3, 1951.

JAQUES, E. *The Changing Culture of a Factory*, London, Tavistock Publications, 1951.

JAQUES, E. 'On the Dynamics of Social Structure', *Human Relations,* Vol. VI, No. 1, 1953.

JAQUES, E. *Measurement of Responsibility*. London, Tavistock Publications, 1956.

KAHN, R. L. 'An Analysis of Supervisory Practices and Components of Morale', *Groups, Leadership and Men,* Carnegie Press, 1951.

KING, P. H. M. 'Task Perception and Interpersonal Relations in Industrial Training, I & II', *Human Relations,* Vol. 1, Nos. 1 and 3, 1947.

KATZ, D., and HYMAN, H. 'Morale in War Industries', *Readings in Social Psychology*, Newcomb, T. M., and Hartley, E. L. (Eds.), New York, Henry Holt and Company, 1947.

KATZ, D., and KAHN, R. L. 'Human Organization and Worker Motivation', *Industrial Productivity*, L. R. Tripp (Ed.), Industrial Research Association, 1951.

KATZ, D., and KAHN, R. L. *Productivity, Supervision and Morale among Railroad Workers*, Ann Arbor, Survey Research Center, University of Michigan, 1951.

KATZ, D., and KAHN, R. L. *Productivity, Supervision and Morale in an Office Situation*, Ann Arbor, Survey Research Center, University of Michigan, 1950.

LEITER, R. D. *The Foreman in Industrial Relations,* New York, Columbia University Press, 1948.

LEWIN, K. 'Frontiers in Group Dynamics', *Human Relations,* Vol. I, No. 1, 1947.

LEWIN, K. *Field Theory in Social Science,* Cartwright, D. (Ed.), London, Tavistock Publications, 1952.

LEWIN, K. *Resolving Social Conflicts,* New York, Harper & Brothers, 1948.

LEWIN, K., LIPPITT, R., and WHITE, R. K. 'Patterns of Aggressive Behaviour in Experimentally Created Social Climates', *Journal of Social Psychology,* No. 10, 1939.

LIKERT, R. 'Developing Patterns in Management', *Personnel Management,* Vol. XXXVIII, No. 337, 1956.

LIPPITT, R. *Training in Community Relations,* New York, Harper and Brothers, 1949.

MAIER, N. R. F. *Psychology in Industry,* Boston, Houghton-Mifflin, 1946.

MANN, F. C. 'Changing Superior-Subordinate Relationships', *Journal of Social Issues,* Vol. 7, No. 3, 1951.

MAYO, E. *The Human Problems of an Industrial Civilization,* New York, Macmillan, 1933.

MAYO, E. *The Social Problems of an Industrial Civilization,* Cambridge, Harvard University Press, 1945.

MAYO, E., and LOMBARD, G. F. F. *Teamwork and Labour Turnover in the Aircraft Industry of Southern California,* Cambridge, Harvard University Press, 1953.

MILLER, D. C., and FORM, W. H. *Industrial Sociology, an introduction to the sociology of work relations.* New York, Harper, 1951.

MONEY-KYRLE, R. *Psycho-Analysis and Politics,* London, Duckworth, 1949.

MOORE, W. E. *Industrial Relations and the Social Order* New York, Macmillan, 1951.

MOORE, W. E. 'Social Consequences of Technological Change from the Sociological Standpoint', *International Social Science Bulletin,* Vol. 4, 1952.

MORENO, J. L. *Who Shall Survive?* Washington, Beacon House, 1934.

MURPHY, G. *In the Minds of Men,* New York, Basic Books, 1953.

NATIONAL INSTITUTE OF INDUSTRIAL PSYCHOLOGY, *The Foreman, A Study of Supervision in British Industry,* London, Staples, 1951.

NEWCOMB, T. M. *Social Psychology,* London, Tavistock Publications, 1950.

NEWCOMB, T. M., and HARTLEY, E. L. (Ed.) *Readings in Social Psychology,* New York, Holt, 1947.

OSTVOLD, O., and KING, D. 'Case Study in Modern Factory Development', *The Manufacturing Clothier,* Vol. 21, 420–423, 1956.

PARSONS, T. *The Social System,* London, Tavistock Publications, 1952.

RANJAN, K. S. 'Seasonality in the incidence of strikes in the Bombay Textile Industry', *Sankhyan,* Vol. 13, 1954.

RANJAN, K. S. 'Statistical Studies of Labour Problems—A Review', *Indian Journal of Social Work,* Vol. 15, No. 2, 1954.

REAVELEY, C., and WINNINGTON, J. *Industry and Democracy,* London, Chatto and Windus, 1947.

RICE, A. K. 'The Experimental Reorganization of Non-Automatic Weaving in an Indian Mill', *Human Relations,* Vol. VIII, No. 3, 1955.

RICE, A. K. 'Productivity and Social Organization I and II', *Human Relations,* Vol, VI, No. 3, and Vol. VIII, No. 4, 1955.

RICE, A. K. 'The Role of the Specialist in the Community', *Human Relations,* Vol. II. No. 2, 1949.

RICE, A. K. 'The Use of Unrecognized Cultural Mechanism in an Expanding Machine-Shop', *Human Relations*, Vol. IV, No. 2, 1951.

RICE, A. K., HILL, J. M. M., and TRIST, E. L. 'The Representation of Labour Turnover as a Social Process', *Human Relations*, Vol. III, No. 4, 1950.

RICE, A. K., and TRIST, E. L. 'Institutional and Sub-Institutional Determinants of Change in Labour Turnover', *Human Relations*, Vol. V, No. 4, 1952.

RICHARDSON, F. L. W., and WALKER, C. R. 'Work Flow and Human Relations'. *Harvard Business Review*, Vol. 27, No. 1, 1949.

ROETHLISBERGER, F. J. *Management and Morale*, Cambridge, Harvard University Press, 1941.

ROETHLISBERGER, F. J., and DICKSON, W. J. *Management and the Worker*, Cambridge, Harvard University Press, 1939.

RONKEN, O. H., and LAWRENCE, P. R., *Administrating Changes*, Cambridge, Graduate School of Business Administration, Harvard University, 1952.

SCHRÖDER, M. 'Bedrijfsgroothe en Moreel' (The Relationship of Groups Size and Morale), *Mens Onder*, Vol. 9, No. 5, 1955.

SCOTT, J., and LYNTON, R. P. *Three Studies in Management*, London, Routledge & Kegan Paul, 1952.

SCOTT, W. H. *Joint Consultation in a Liverpool Manufacturing Firm, a Case Study in Human Relations in Industry*. Liverpool, University Press of Liverpool, 1950.

SCOTT, W. H. *Industrial Leadership and Joint Consultation: a Study of Human Relations in Three Merseyside Firms*. Liverpool, University Press of Liverpool, 1952.

SHARTLE, C. L. 'Organizational Structure', *Current Trends in Industrial Psychology*. Dennis, V. (Ed.) Pittsburgh Press, 1949.

SIMON, H. A. *Administrative Behaviour*, New York, Macmillan, 1947.

SIMON, H. A. 'Comments on the Theory of Organization', *American Political Science Review*, Vol. XLVI, No. 4, 1952.

SOFER, C. 'Reactions to Administrative Change', *Human Relations*, Vol. VIII, No. 3, 1955.

SMITH, E. D., and NYMAN, R. C. *Technology and Labour*, New Haven, Yale University Press, 1939.

STOGDILL, R. M. 'Leadership, Membership and Organization', *Psychological Bulletin*, Vol. 47, No. 1, 1950.

STOGDILL, R. M. *Aspects of Leadership and Organization*. Ohio State University Research Foundation, Columbus, 1953.

STONE, R. C. 'Conflicting Approaches to the Study of Worker-Manager Relations', *Social Forces*, Vol. 31, No. 2, 1952.

STRAUSS, G. 'The Set-up Man: A Case Study of Organizational Change', *Human Organization*, Vol. 13, No. 2, 1954.

SURVEY RESEARCH CENTER, *Productivity, Supervision and Employee Morale*, Ann Arbor, University of Michigan, 1948.

SURVEY RESEARCH CENTER, *Productivity, Supervision and Morale in an Office Situation*, Ann Arbor, University of Michigan, 1950.

TAYLOR, F. W. *Scientific Management*, New York, Harper and Brothers, 1911.

TENDULKAR, D. G. *'Mahatma'—The Life of Mohandas Karamchand Gandhi*, Vol. 5, Bombay, Published Privately, 1951.

TRIST, E. L., and BAMFORTH, K. W. 'Some Social and Psychological Consequences of the Longwall Method of Coal-Getting', *Human Relations*, Vol. IV, No. 1, 1951.

URWICK, L. G. *The Elements of Administration*, New York, Harper, 1943.

WALKER, C. R. 'Adjustment, Individual and Social to Technological Change', *Industrial Productivity*, Industrial Relations Research Association, 1951.

WALKER, C. R., and GUEST, R. H. *The Man on the Assembly Line*, Cambridge, Harvard University Press, 1952.

WALKER, C. R., GUEST, R. H., and TURNER, A. N. *The Foreman on the Assembly Line*, Cambridge, Harvard University Press, Mass., 1956.

WARNER, W. L., and LOW, J. O. *The Social System of a Modern Factory* (Yankee City Series, 4) New Haven, Yale University Press, 1947.

WARNER, W. L., and LUNT, P. S. *The Social Life of a Modern Community* (Yankee City Series, 1), New Haven, Yale University Press, 1948.

WARNER, W. L., and LUNT, P. S. *The Status System of a Modern Community* (Yankee City Series, 2), New Haven, Yale University Press, 1948.

WARNER, W. L., and SROLE, L. *Social Systems of American Ethnic Groups* (Yankee City Series, 3), New Haven, Yale University Press, 1947.

WESCHLER, I. R. 'Job Satisfaction, Productivity and Morale', *Occupational Psychology*, Vol. 26, No. 1, 1952.

WESTERLUND, G. *Group Leadership, A Field Experiment*, Stockholm, Nordisk Rotogravyr, 1952.

WHITEHEAD, T. N. *The Industrial Worker, a statistical study of human relations in a group of manual workers*, 2 vols. London, Oxford Univ. Press, 1938.

WHYTE, W. F. 'Small Groups and Large Organizations', *Social Psychology at the Cross-Roads*, Rohser, J. G., and Sherif, M. (Eds.), New York, Harper Bros., 1951.

WHYTE, W. F. *Patterns for Industrial Peace*. New York, Harper, 1951.

WHYTE, W. F. *Leadership and Group Participation*, S.S.I.L.R. Cornell University, 1953.

WHYTE, W. F. *Money and Motivation*. New York, Harper, 1955.

WILSON, A. T. M. 'Some Aspects of Social Process', *The Journal of Social Issues*, Kurt Lewin Memorial Award Issue, 1951.

WILSON, A. T. M. 'A Note on the Social Sanctions of Social Research', *The Sociological Review*, Vol. III, No. 1, 1955.

WILSON, A. T. M., DOYLE, M., and KELNAR, J. 'Group Techniques in a Transitional Community', *The Lancet*, 1947.

WORTHING, I. O. 'Organizational Structure and Employee Morale', *American Sociological Review*, Vol. 15, 169–179, 1950.

INDEX